Freedom's Currency

Freedom's Currency

Slavery, Capitalism, and Self-Purchase in the United States

Julia Wallace Bernier

PENN

UNIVERSITY OF PENNSYLVANIA PRESS

PHILADELPHIA

Published by
University of Pennsylvania Press
Philadelphia, Pennsylvania 19104-4112
www.upenn.edu/pennpress

Printed in the United States of America on acid-free paper
10 9 8 7 6 5 4 3 2 1

A Cataloging-in-Publication record is available
from the Library of Congress.

Hardback ISBN 9781512826470
eBook ISBN 9781512826487

To my parents and for all those forced to buy their freedom

The being of slavery, its soul and body, lives and moves in the chattel principle, the property principle, the bill of sale principle . . .

—James W. C. Pennington, *The Fugitive Blacksmith*

Some might call freedom the dearest currency of all.

—Colson Whitehead, *The Underground Railroad*

CONTENTS

Introduction

When Denmark Vesey declared to a meeting of coconspirators who gathered in his house in Charleston, South Carolina, that they should "unite together," as the people of Haiti had, to rebel against slavery, he had already been free for about twenty years. In November 1799, Vesey won $1,500 in the city's East Bay lottery. It was the lottery's top prize, and he spent some of the money to buy what most enslaved people could only dream about. Just weeks later, Vesey purchased his freedom from his enslavers, Mary Clodner and Joseph Vesey, who accepted $600 to free him "for ever" from the "yoke of servitude."[1] While this was an incredible stroke of luck, Vesey would come to find that his freedom alone was not enough. He wanted something more.

By the time Vesey held that 1822 meeting at his house, his self-purchased freedom was crucial to his role as leader of the attempted uprising for which he is widely known. To "conquer the whites," Vesey supposedly called for fires to be set across the city, weapons to be at the ready to kill the white people who would rise against them, and "money from the Banks" and "goods from the stores" to be secured. From there, the liberated revolutionaries would converge on Charleston harbor and sail for Haiti. Just weeks before it went into action, the plan was betrayed. Vesey was never able to experience the better kind of freedom that he imagined was awaiting him in the Black nation that had revolted against slavery and won.[2]

Although Vesey wanted more than the freedom South Carolina offered, for himself and others, the court appointed to try the rebels claimed that the "qualifications and advantages" stemming from his freedom were "absolutely necessary for the Chief in a Conspiracy." The court said that as a free man he could go where he pleased, on his own time, and "without interruption." The "obstacles" to such activity, so necessary for planning an insurrection, would have been great if Vesey were still enslaved. The members of the court probably could not imagine why he would want anything more than the limited legal freedom he had purchased.[3] Instead of being satisfied, however, Vesey made use of his freedom's advantages to challenge the entire system of slavery through outright insurrection. It was a gamble that cost him his life. Vesey and thirty-five others who had supposedly participated in planning the rebellion were executed by the state.

Self-purchase was critical to building the world of Black freedom that Vesey dreamed about. This world was clearly one that he believed should be secured by any means necessary, whether by spending money on it or seizing it with force. Nor was Vesey alone in understanding the many uses of self-purchase and the legal freedom it provided. Enslaved people in the United States bought themselves and their loved ones out of slavery for as long as the institution existed. In Charleston, Vesey joined more than seventeen others who paid something for their freedom in 1799. The sums paid ranged from nominal amounts as small as five shillings to six hundred dollars.[4]

This book examines the stories of enslaved people like Vesey, along with their friends, families, and activists, who set out to buy freedom from slavery in the United States from the nation's founding period to the Civil War. It examines their hopes and dreams, plans and labor, and success and disappointment on their way toward freedom. Through their experiences, it considers how the enslaved navigated freedom's currency across the difficult process of self-purchase and why they chose to do so.

The interventions in this book revolve around five main themes: how enslaved people shaped self-purchase as a process, how they cultivated and depended on community networks and market practices to do so successfully, and what buying freedom can tell us not only about the complex nature of the relationship between slavery and capitalism but also, and, more important, how the enslaved made sense of this relationship. And, because this economy was rooted in the law, and vice versa, I show how the enslaved navigated both as they bought freedom. I argue that to buy freedom enslaved people had to master not just an economic market but also their political and social worlds.

I use the concept of freedom's currency to reflect the complicated relation-ships among money, value, and freedom in a nation in which almost anything could be had for a price, including human beings and liberty. Enslaved people lived at the nexus of an economic market that determined those prices and a legal regime that decided what could be had for them.[5] I am interested, there-fore, in the ways that the enslaved who purchased their freedom made meaning out of their place in a market that not only turned them into commodities but transformed freedom into something they could buy. As Vesey's life shows, self-purchase illustrates the meanings, possibilities, and limits of that freedom in the nineteenth-century United States.

Rather than being a base resignation to the economy of slavery, this path to freedom had a practical utility that was used as part of a grammar of resistance through which African Americans secured and protected freedom for themselves and their loved ones.[6] Buying oneself was not easy in a political economy that was dependent on slave labor and a property regime rooted in white supremacy and hostile to Black freedom. It meant amassing capital and credit, securing legal acts of manumission, and negotiating the practical and theoretical boundaries that equated Blackness with unfreedom in the United States. Enslaved people challenged slavery on multiple registers by rupturing the sanctity of both white property and freedom as the property of whites as they bought freedom and a kind of legal personhood while being considered chattel.[7] They also forced enslavers to contend with their differing ideas about value.

Given the circumstances, it is difficult to think about self-purchase outside of the diverse efforts of the enslaved to contest slavery, its law, and its economy. I therefore argue that resistance is one of the contexts for understanding their actions. While self-purchase is representative of how enslaved people challenged slavery and tried to live freely, I am also interested in it because it was a part of their social and economic lives. Outside of the context of resistance, this reading alone gives self-purchase historical meaning and makes it worthy of deeper study than it has so far been given.[8]

Everyone knew that enslaved people were so much more than the eco-nomic determinations made by the men and women who owned them and the state that sanctified that ownership. So how the enslaved made sense of these determinations and tried to escape them by loving and valuing themselves, each other, and freedom is at the center of this book. These are the ways they gave freedom meaning and laid the foundations for seeking liberation.[9] Racial slavery's inheritance regime meant that questions of gender, kinship, and familial formation were at the heart of buying freedom. So, too, was a relentless commitment to freedom, community, and value beyond enslavement. Those who bought their freedom depended on friends, family, their neighbors, and a whole range of connections that helped them secure manumission. Like Vesey, many also thought about freedom as something that you used to help others. Although self-purchase often led to the freedom of a single individual, this masks its function as a communal undertaking. This is also, then, a story about the social lives of the enslaved.[10]

The chapters that follow are organized both thematically and chronologically. We begin in the North. Chapter 1 focuses on the role that compensation, in a variety of forms, played in the gradual abolition regimes that shaped the end of slavery in the region. It concentrates on Pennsylvania, the first state to enact gradual emancipation. Chapter 2 examines self-purchase in the mid-nineteenth-century South. It follows how enslaved people created economic, social, and legal opportunities for buying freedom amid a changing landscape of American slavery, including the rise of the domestic slave trade and slavery's expansion. The third chapter lays out abolitionist debate over buying freedom during second-wave abolition. It concentrates on how African Americans who bought their freedom, or hoped to do so, worked to contextualize issues of compensation and complicity within the movement and how they centered practical techniques such as self-purchase. While most of this chapter takes place in the northern United States, like those seeking freedom, it moves back and forth through the North and South and even across the Atlantic. The last chapter takes a national approach, studying self-purchase after the passage of the Fugitive Slave Act of 1850. It examines the role of buying freedom in debates about slavery, emancipation, and sectional tensions in the decade preceding the Civil War and during the war.

Slavery's Capitalism and Capitalism's Freedom

Central to conversations about self-purchase is the intertwinement of slavery, capitalism, and freedom in the antebellum United States. Enslaved people were held captive to and their lives were embodied in the relationship between slavery and capitalism. As those with the most to fear, and to lose, from this economy they understood the way these systems were intertwined better than anyone else. In recent years, historians have built on what the enslaved, such as J. W. C. Pennington, the abolitionist and reverend whose freedom was purchased in 1851, had long formulated, that slavery was based in the "property principle" and that its very being was bodies and souls like his.[11] As Pennington stated in 1849, the "soul" of slavery was the "chattel principle, the property principle, the bill of sale principle. . . ."[12] Because slavery's economy and law rested in this principle, the study of self-purchase can better illustrate how enslaved people understood and lived at the intersection of these systems and sought to escape them. Studying their actions and intellectual thought around buying freedom can help us return to the enslaved as the original theorizers of what it meant for slavery and capitalism to be so intimately related and how that intimacy shaped the world we inherited from them.[13]

Scholars in this field have elaborated on the ways that slavery's "bill of sale principle" undergirded the American economy and ensured its growth. In the nineteenth century, this economy depended on the capacity of enslavers to sell, trade, and mortgage enslaved people. Their forced labor produced the goods and crops on which the economies of the global North depended.[14] After decades of debate, historians have come to acknowledge what Seth Rockman and Sven Beckert have described as "slavery's capitalism." As they describe, this term represents the ways that slavery, and the slave trade in particular, "became central to and perhaps even constitutive of a particular moment in the history of capitalism" and "helped constitute capitalist modernity."[15] In this vein, I am most interested in how the enslaved understood the "technologies of capitalism," like the "practices of quantification and abstraction" that led to their commodification, and how that commodification shaped the meaning of almost everything in the world around them, including freedom.[16]

The slavery that "helped constitute capitalist modernity" in the United States was rooted in commodification that arose from both chattel status and race. The legal concept of *partus sequitur ventrem*, enshrined in seventeenth-century Virginia, meant that the property or free status of the child followed that of the mother. Racial slavery, then, as Jennifer Morgan has succinctly described, "rested upon a notion of heritability" and "relied on a reproductive logic that was inseparable from the explanatory power of race."[17] Given the racial nature of slavery and freedom, the context for self-purchase is not just the relationship between slavery and capitalism, but what Black studies scholars understand as racial capitalism. In their recent collection of essays on the subject, Destin Jenkins and Justin Leroy describe racial capitalism as the "process by which key dynamics of capitalism . . . become articulated through race." Just as it is rooted historically, as Cedric Robinson so brilliantly laid out, racial capitalism as a concept also "captures the way slavery epitomized a racialized system of valuation and extraction that continues to this day." These continuities are what Saidiya Hartman describes as "slavery's afterlife."[18]

The ways that this "racialized system of valuation and extraction" continues to inform our present has revealed to scholars, and to those who live it, that the end of slavery did not mark the end of racial capitalism. While the limits of freedom under this system have been made apparent by studies of the postemancipation United States, the enslaved who purchased their freedom would have felt this at the micro level much earlier. Black abolitionists who had been forced to buy their liberation critiqued this kind of freedom, tinged as it was with slavery's market. They used their experience to shape abolitionist critique of slavery more broadly.[19] For them, self-purchase's necessity spoke to the ways that racial slavery shaped not only the political economy of the world but also the very meaning of what it meant to be alive and human in it.[20] Something more than slavery held sway over their lives. The framework of racial capitalism helps us to better situate their existential discomfort with buying something as precious as freedom in ways that neither slavery itself, nor capitalism alone, could fully account for.

It is no mistake that Cedric Robinson linked his history of racial capitalism with that of the Black radical tradition. For Robinson, this tradition was informed by the collective struggle of people of African descent to imagine a different way of being in the world.[21] His work on this tradition offers us a way to understand the confines in which people of African descent lived across the history of the Atlantic world, but also the ways they came together to make new worlds outside of slavery.[22] Enslaved and free African Americans who bought freedom were part of this longer tradition that critiqued racial capitalism. They did so in the ways they used self-purchase to protect themselves and each other from slavery's market, as well as in the ways they condemned its necessity.

Enslaved people's economic activity and their centrality to the marketplace of slavery might suggest that self-purchase occurred with much greater frequency than it did, yet successful self-purchase was not just a question of cash. The enslaved had to navigate much more than the market in their persons. Their efforts to buy freedom depended on their ability to negotiate not only as economic actors but as social and political ones too. The enslaved understood themselves as bound and unbound by all these systems, often simultaneously. To survive under slavery, enslaved people had to be extremely interested in the ways their value as slaves was determined by those who enslaved them. The value of freedom in these cases was often decided by their value as property, and they negotiated accordingly. Yet to buy freedom was to buy something that they knew their enslavers had never rightfully owned. Slaveholders, however, still had the legal and economic power to require payment for it. To outwit them at their own game took opportunity, knowledge, tenacity, and the vision that something else was possible.

This book shows how African Americans, rather than being simply complicit with slavery's market or capitalism, carefully and skillfully crafted their own ideas about value, exchange, systems of negotiation, and capital accumulation, and how they used these ideas as economic praxis to free themselves from bondage. Enslaved people working to buy freedom reimagined the meaning of their labor, expanded its possibilities, and set out to use the world around them as it already existed to escape slavery. They participated in this market for freedom because they had to, but also because they intimately understood the value of freedom. Its meaning was something beyond what any market could account for. It was invaluable in ways beyond our ideas about capital or anything material. In fact, the language of the market is imperfect for describing both the actions of the enslaved as they liberated themselves and each other and the violence of the system in which they were forced to pay for freedom.

Self-purchase was a route to freedom based in the economy of slavery. Enslaved people were economic actors, and their independent economic activity was tied up with that of the society in which they lived. Sometimes that economic activity could lead to freedom, but this is not an argument for the liberatory powers of capitalism. Nor is a concentration on the ingenious ways that enslaved people made self-purchase happen meant to elide the violence of being forced to invest in slavery by paying enslavers to become free. Enslaved people did not get their freedom through capitalist enterprise but despite it.[23]

Those who purchased their freedom undermined the ownership of enslavers because they understood their worth in relation to liberation and each other. These were value relations that existed outside of their enslavement. As they lived under the "bill of sale principle," enslaved people nurtured an alternative system of value described as "soul value" by the historian Daina Ramey Berry. For Berry, soul value is part of a "multilayered" set of values that applied to the enslaved. These overlapping values came from the "self-worth" of the enslaved, their appraisal value (based on their potential as capital), and their market or sale value. She argues that this system helps us to "consider enslaved people as human beings and tradable goods without divorcing one from the other."[24] In cases of self-purchase, these differing values were especially linked, and the enslaved navigated both all the time.

Despite the ways that self-purchase existed within slavery's market in human commodities, soul value was created in the ways that African Americans understood their own self-worth, their right to be free, and their bonds with each other. For the enslaved, as Robinson claimed, "slavery altered the conditions of their being, but it could not negate their being."[25] Soul value, as Berry conceives it, represents the more intimate and intrinsic side of enslaved people's ideas about value. The importance of this value, however, partly derived from and clashed against the commodifying forces of slavery. The enslaved had to constantly negotiate and inhabit a place between the two. In cases of self-purchase, they could concede to engaging with their market value and price and the ways these were structured through racial capitalism without necessarily compromising on the integrity of their soul value.

While enslavers may have determined the value (or price) of freedom according to the appraisal and sale value of the enslaved, the enslaved moved according to both their own value and this price. As they were forced to, I use value and price as interlocking but distinct phenomena. Enslaved people had to consider each of these simultaneously as they planned for freedom. We may imagine that enslavers had all the power in such a precarious market-based process, yet the value that the enslaved placed on themselves and their freedom guided their actions in entering that market. Their negotiations for the price of freedom were based in both their soul value as human beings and in their value as capital investments of their enslavers.[26] As we will see, they used their position as valuable property to create opportunities for entering markets, making and saving their own money, and building connections they could use to secure credit and legal support, and to negotiate for the opportunity to buy freedom. At the same time, enslaved people often used their soul value to call on familiarity and common humanity to do each of these things. Both aspects of their value were present throughout the process of buying freedom.

Freedom was many things to those who did not have it. Indeed, we can hardly understand it as a concept at all without their unfreedom. This text presents freedom as a process that did not always have a linear progression. In cases of self-purchase this process was at once economic and legal. But I also do not want to lose sight of freedom's deeper meaning. It was so much more than the exchange of funds or a simple legal transaction. Freedom was also a dream, and the enslaved dreamed about freedom and all it could be.[27] For some it meant being paid for their labor and buying things with their own money or going wherever they pleased. For others it meant being reunited with family members, living together in safety, and never having to fear separation. One witness at Denmark Vesey's trial in Charleston suggested that his desire to free his children and perhaps even his inability to buy his family might have been the source of his plans for rebellion.[28] By using self-purchase, enslaved people took practical steps to give their dreams shape. Still, freedom's meaning was also contested in their own communities and across the divide between enslaver and enslaved. Like market forces, the law played an important part in defining the meaning of freedom and how one could try to make it turn from a dream into a reality. The state intervened in these contests to determine the boundaries between slave and free, if and how one could access freedom, and what rights attended liberation for African Americans.

Self-Purchase and the Law of Slavery

Self-purchase took place within larger struggles over slavery, race, and freedom in the early United States. Black communities across the nation insisted on negotiating over freedom while living in a society that associated liberty, legal personhood, and citizenship with whiteness.[29] Under the logic of slave law, to become free was to become a legal person, if one with curtailed rights because of race.[30] That position held power both socially and legally, and free African Americans threatened the racial order of individual states and the nation.[31] Access to manumission, or the legal act of releasing a person from slavery, was therefore a key but contested component of being able to buy oneself.

From their litigation in freedom suits to self-purchase, African Americans shaped a Black legal culture around manumission in ways that challenged their limited access to formal freedom and the restrictions placed on that freedom.[32] In this sense, the state, through laws at both the state and federal level, must be understood as another kind of actor in stories about self-purchase. States attempted to outlaw the mobility and market activity of free and enslaved African Americans and limited access to cash and the economic and social networks necessary to raise the money needed to buy freedom. Some states made manumission itself nearly impossible. Forcing free people out of state and attempting to control the relationships between free and enslaved African Americans could also sever kinship ties and leave families even more vulnerable to separation. While most African Americans lived in the space between the law and its actual practice, the power of the possible enforcement of the law remained a threat.[33] Despite its limitations, technical freedom under the law, which only manumission could secure, was of the utmost importance.[34]

Before one could get to the point of negotiating with their enslaver to pay for freedom, they needed to either have the cash to pay for themselves or know how they could get it. Buying freedom often depended on access not only to cash but also credit. As was true for everyone who relied on credit, social connections could help. Southern states made these opportunities more difficult by regulating the economic and social activity of African Americans, free and enslaved alike. Nonetheless, some enslaved people still amassed and maintained small, and sometimes shockingly large, amounts of property.[35]

Dating back to Roman times, the custom of *peculium*, under which the enslaved were allowed to hold, if not fully possess, property with the permission of their enslavers, was more common practice than law. That ancient idea translated into customary rights for the enslaved in other slaveholding societies like the American South. In 1825, for example, Louisiana law not only recognized contracts for freedom, the only kind of contract the enslaved could formally enter, but also the slave's peculium.[36] Louisiana was an outlier in the region. The abolitionist Henry Bibb, enslaved in Kentucky, reflected on the more common experience when he complained that as a slave he could "possess nothing, nor acquire anything" that did not belong to his "keeper."[37]

Making money, let alone keeping it, was no small feat. Southern states controlled what enslaved people could sell and how they could do it. Access to money quite obviously mattered to self-purchase, but so too did the connections made through trade and hiring. Self-hire, for instance, provided some independence and access to cash which the enslaved saved to buy freedom. Slaves who were hired out sometimes made their own living arrangements and could claim their wages after paying a portion to their enslaver. Although hiring was illegal in many states, enslaved people were often able to sidestep these laws because southern white people took advantage of lax enforcement as they benefited from these arrangements too.[38]

To successfully negotiate buying freedom, enslaved people had to make contracts, even if they did so informally. As southern courts argued, an enslaved person was considered property and therefore did not have the capacity to freely make any contract independently of their enslavers.[39] Because their contracts did not have legal standing in most states throughout the nineteenth century, enslaved people were liable to failure at any point during the process of self-purchase. They could still be sold, have their savings claimed, or be affected by changes in manumission law, market increases in their value, and just plain trickery.

From the turn of the century to the Civil War, southern states further limited access to manumission because they feared free African Americans and the ways their claims to freedom posed a threat to the state. This threat was imagined in the way they claimed rights, undermined slavery by simply undoing the racial binary that divided enslaved and free people, or by becoming a nuisance or burden to the state and their communities if they could not care for themselves. States attempted to deal with these issues by restricting access to manumission. By controlling manumission, state governments limited slaveholders' property rights in the interest of the greater common good. Manumission was thus thought of as a private act with public ramifications.[40] In some southern states manumissions had to be granted by state legislatures, while other states restricted the reasons for which enslavers could manumit, some restricted the age range for enslaved people to be freed, and still others required additional bonds to be posted to ensure that the newly free would not become a burden on the overseers of the poor.[41] These laws continued apace across the antebellum era. For instance, in 1860, only a year before the start of the Civil War, Maryland ended manumission and debated forcing all free Black people to leave the state or be subject to reenslavement.[42]

Nor did legal freedom end the trouble. States throughout the South tried to stem the tide of Black population growth by banning the entry of free African Americans and sometimes attempting to expel those already there.[43] Beginning in the 1830s, most of the ten states enacting removal legislation for free African Americans did so on a timeline of anywhere from thirty days to a year from manumission. Tennessee's requirement was immediate removal. These laws had drastic effects on manumission rates in some locales.[44] Restrictive laws left people in slavery or in informal freedom arrangements who would otherwise have been legally free. Some lived as free people but never achieved formal freedom. Many of these situations led to guardianship and familial enslavement, a predicament created when kin could buy each other but not complete the process of official manumission.[45] Those who purchased family members to emancipate them had to think deeply about how to protect their loved ones against any number of threats in which they would be treated as legal property, such as in being seized and sold for debts.

Given these restrictions, those who undertook self-purchase did so at an extreme disadvantage under a legal system in which their enslavers held almost all the power. Scholars of slavery in the Atlantic world rightfully caution against the creation of clear and fast distinctions between the legal and social experiences of enslaved people in the United States and other slave societies in the Americas. However, the differences around self-purchase show just how extreme the legal disadvantages were for African Americans who wanted to buy their freedom. While on-the-ground differences for enslaved people across Atlantic slave regimes do not appear to be as drastic as the law might suggest, laws regulating self-purchase, such as the Spanish system of *coartación*, did not exist in the United States. Despite its limitations, the coartación system did help enslaved people achieve manumission.

Although far from foolproof, coartación was meant to legally regulate the contracts through which enslaved people could hold property and purchase themselves. This system formalized price and how the payments were to be made over time and protected the enslaved from the whims of enslavers and changes in value. The purchase price and the protected status of an enslaved person engaged in coartación, known as a *coartado*, were secured through the courts via an independent appraisal process. This status protected their contracts for freedom, even if they were sold to another slaveholder. In some instances, the enslaved could also request a transference of ownership to secure their status.[46]

How important this legal support could be has been shown by historians studying manumission across the administrations that ruled Louisiana Territory, which was colonized by France and Spain before becoming part of the United States. In the final years of Spanish rule from 1798 to 1803, over half of all manumissions involved purchase agreements. In 1806 the United States administration tried to restrict any of the legal vestiges of coartación by declaring that no enslaver could be forced to emancipate their slaves. After coartación ended, enslaved people there paid what Shawn Cole has described as a 19 percent "manumission premium." Without the protections of coartación, the price they paid for freedom was more than their market value. While overall manumissions declined sharply, rates in Louisiana remained higher than in other states. This was likely due to the residual social and legal effects of Spanish rule. Although it no longer was law, the enslaved ensured that the custom remained. Indeed, their insistence on self-purchase despite what the law allowed is one of the key findings for thinking about self-purchase across slave regimes.[47]

Rather than mark a stark divide in experience between those who had access to coartación and those who did not, the study of self-purchase across these systems can tell us more about how enslaved people navigated the laws regulating slavery and freedom. Historians of self-purchase have shown that even with coartación in place, access to freedom was still difficult for the enslaved in other slave societies. Many of the difficulties they experienced would have been familiar to African Americans. Buying freedom depended on the enslaved navigating many of the same dangers and support networks as those in the United States.[48] The enslaved everywhere were dedicated to freedom and self-purchase and shared a determination to overcome what was a mix of the legal system's equivocation and hostility toward Black freedom.

Note on Method

It is worth beginning here by mentioning numbers. It is beyond the purpose of this project to answer definitively how many enslaved people bought their freedom. A generation of economic scholars have gathered data about manumission and explored various equations for how manumission rates were affected by things like commodity prices, societal events, skin color, age, and gender. While I draw on that kind of information, I am more interested in the ways that the enslaved negotiated these contexts, and so I hope to add additional qualitative analysis to the quantitative work that has already been done.[49]

Where it is possible, I give a sense of scale. These numbers suggest that in many places and across time, self-purchase was fairly widespread. It was likely more common than most people think. In this sense, numbers are important. They are not, however, the main kind of information I set out to find about self-purchase. They also present a deeper archival issue. As someone who has spent a decade looking for stories of self-purchase in all kinds of places, I am unsure how accurate any accounting could be.

While many deeds of manumission include information about what precipitated the liberation, including money, many do not. What information was deemed pertinent by the official or enslaver who recorded the manumission, what blank spaces there were on a preprinted form, and what capacity the enslaved had to shape the legal record of this defining moment in their lives all determine what kind of accounting historians can do now. There are likely recorded manumissions that involved compensation that leave no trace of that exchange. There is no telling how many of these legal records elide the stories of how the enslaved made freedom and whether they paid for it or not. Nor do numbers tell us the ways enslaved people thought about self-purchase nor how they were able to make it happen, nor how the numbers of people who were able to do so influenced the ways others dreamed about getting free. For everyone whose manumission record we have, many more would have hoped or tried to get there themselves. As with most stories about slavery, one can only wonder what the enslaved would have told us if they could.[50]

This book takes an abolitionist worldview in more ways than one. First, in response to archival problems, the book relies heavily on close readings of abolitionist materials. Stories of self-purchase are found everywhere in abolitionist print culture and organizing. Their appearance there, in some senses, makes them exceptional. Yet networks were critical to buying freedom, and abolitionists were part of that network, if farther afield for most enslaved people. Some African American abolitionists lectured and published narratives to raise money to buy their freedom or that of loved ones. One might assume that being able to connect with abolitionists would mean certain success, but they also witnessed cases of heartbreaking failure. The examples we find in abolitionist print culture still mirror those that never made it so far into the historical record.

Slave narratives, although usually written from the other side of slavery, provide much needed information to understand those whose personal stories of self-purchase are not detailed otherwise. Abolitionist authors reveal difficult and twisted paths to freedom and so, in some ways, we can read them as representative.

I have also come to see self-purchase as a distinctive trope in the genre. Many of these scenes play within a particular abolitionist politics. Buying freedom showed African Americans as the quintessential American who was smart, independent, responsible, entrepreneurial, and economic. This played directly into abolitionist calls for the end of slavery and full equality, which required African Americans to prove that they could succeed as free citizens. However, when read against the grain, many of these narratives also undermine any strict divide between slavery and freedom and other political tropes we have come to know in the genre. This was especially true for fugitives who were forced to buy their freedom after escaping slavery. Fugitive abolitionists such as J. W. C. Pennington, Frederick Douglass, William Wells Brown, and Harriet Jacobs used their experience to critique not only slavery but the very essence of freedom in a nation whose spirit was so deeply chained to it. Abolitionists could challenge slavery in a variety of ways only because the enslaved did, and I argue that those who purchased their freedom were in a special position to push the movement toward a more radical critique of slavery and the ways it shaped the nation.

Discussions of self-purchase in abolitionist print culture are also central to this history because they function as the main outlet for Black intellectual thought about self-purchase and its relation to freedom and how their ideas entered American public discourse not only as a practice but as a problem of political thought for the movement and the broader nation. I follow how these discussions changed over time based on their national significance in sectional debates over slavery. I also center them as an important part of the movement's history.[51] From the first-wave abolition of the Revolutionary age to the more radical second-wave abolition of the 1830s and beyond, African Americans and enslaved people demanded that abolitionists deal with self-purchase. This history also tells us something about the positional politics of the movement. I want to follow these discussions as a historical phenomenon as much as I do that of self-purchase itself. In some ways a more accurate subtitle for the book might be "Slavery, Abolition, and Self-Purchase in the United States." Just as we can learn about self-purchase through the abolition movement, we can learn something more about abolition through self-purchase in ways that have not been fully discussed by historians of the movement.

The book is also about abolition in a deeper sense, in that I believe the ways that Black abolitionists theorized self-purchase help us understand something more about the connections between slavery, racial capitalism, and their continuities in the present. Buying freedom is not solely a historical phenomenon.[52] What it meant to buy freedom still haunts the capacity of freedom in slavery's afterlife. Abolitionists today similarly critique systems like cash bail that require people who cannot pay for their freedom to be held captive in jails across the country while they await trial. Freedom is still something that can be traded for money, and activists continue to debate issues of complicity, necessity, and how to reduce immediate harm for incarcerated people. Thus there are lessons to be learned from the enslaved people and abolitionists whose stories this book tells.[53]

While abolitionists often described buying freedom as *redemption* or *ransom*, wrangling with the theoretical impossibility of purchasing someone whom they believed could not be held as property, I mostly use more current terms for buying freedom such as *self-purchase* and *compensated manumission*. While I use both somewhat interchangeably, there are distinctions marked in how historical actors experienced the process. To buy oneself was different than to have someone buy your freedom for you, and I try to respect that difference in my language. The complications of this distinction will be discussed further throughout the book. Given the importance of networks, all language of kinship used here is meant to reflect the multifaceted communal relationships built and valued within Black communities.

*   *   *

In 1834, the antislavery newspaper *Genius of Emancipation* published correspondence between the abolitionists Theodore Weld and Lewis Tappan about the African American families Weld had recently met in Cincinnati, Ohio. Weld described men, women, and children who worked day and night to raise money to buy themselves and their loved ones out of slavery. He told Tappan about the "sheer heart-ache and agony" he experienced while visiting some thirty families in the city, more than half of whom were working to purchase family members who were still enslaved. Weld recalled one woman who had bought her husband by taking in washing and working late into the night after her day's labor was completed.[54] Their reunion in freedom was probably worth every penny, and maybe more, yet that does not mean we should underestimate the sheer excess of what was required to buy someone you love, nor the role that the process played in her life or his or their life together.

Weld's letter highlights the nature of this investment in freedom that Black communities made across the nation. This investment was made not only in dollars but also in time, emotion, and labor. Surely the vast sums spent on freedom could have aided many in a world in which Black life was so precarious. Buying freedom was far from a perfect solution; hardly anyone would have argued such. But, as this book will show, for so many it meant the difference between slavery and freedom. That difference meant the world. The work of buying freedom was done by thousands of African Americans who labored to buy themselves and their loved ones out of enslavement and, as I argue, it was central to the daily lives of Black communities across the country throughout the antebellum era.

CHAPTER I

"In Hand Paid"

Compensation and Gradual Emancipation in the North

Just after the New Year ushered in 1795, Marie Rose Louis manumitted a fifteen-year-old girl named Fanny in the city of Philadelphia "from motives of humanity and benevolence." These reasons suggest that Louis, who was "late from the French West Indies," had taken to heart the spirit of revolution that surrounded her in the French and Anglo-Atlantic worlds in which she and Fanny traveled. Surely the politics of the new American republic, the spirit of abolition in Pennsylvania, and the ongoing revolutions in France and Haiti had influenced Louis's decision. Fanny's manumission was recorded some fifteen years after the Pennsylvania General Assembly passed an "Act for the Gradual Abolition of Slavery" and only one year, nearly to the day, since the National Convention of France decreed the abolition of slavery in the nation's colonies on February 3, 1794.[1] Louis was influenced by the age of revolutions, although not exactly in the way we might hope for the teenager she enslaved.

Louis and Fanny joined the thousands of people who left Haiti and other French colonies during the 1790s in response to the Haitian Revolution and imperial abolition and arrived in Pennsylvania. Some eight hundred of the émigrés from Haiti were Black. When French colonial emigrants left the turmoil of the West Indies for Pennsylvania to protect their human property, many tried to maneuver around gradual emancipation. Although the 1780 gradual abolition act included a sojourner clause that protected the status of the enslaved as property, the Pennsylvania state legislature had amended the act in 1788. The law required immediate freedom for those who had been brought into the state by enslavers who intended to remain there as residents. If Louis and Fanny had arrived in Philadelphia after February 3, 1794, Fanny would have had double cause to fight for her freedom according to both French and Pennsylvania law.[2] Perhaps Louis intended to return home after the violence of war had subsided in the Caribbean. Even faced with the legal ramifications of gradual emancipation, she may have figured she could better command Fanny from the United States. Regardless, enslavers held fast to those they enslaved after gradual abolition began. Enslaved people fought these efforts, but many found themselves entrapped by indentures and other types of term slavery and servitude for years to come.[3]

While Fanny likely followed the news around her with excitement about what it meant for her life and legal status, Louis took advantage of her new home's gradual abolition act to maintain her control over Fanny by both manumitting and indenturing her for an additional thirteen years in one fell swoop. Fanny's indenture would expire when she was twenty-eight years old. This was the legal limit for maintaining the services of people of African descent who were under the age of twenty-one, according to section 9 of the gradual abolition law. Fanny would be free on January 4, 1808.[4] Louis ensured she would benefit from Fanny's labor for as long as she possibly could. While Fanny was no longer a slave, she was not yet quite at liberty to act on it.

Fanny was just one of thousands of enslaved people caught up in the slow demise of slavery in the northern United States during a period most associated with the revolutionary ideals that set her life into uncertain motion. Her manumission is representative not only of the entanglement of freedom and unfreedom that defined the lives of African Americans across the region for decades, but also of the particular slowness of emancipation for women and girls.[5] Although her manumission did not include any exchange of funds per se, Fanny paid for her freedom with her life and continued service. Many in the North in the early republic would have been familiar with at least this part of her experience.

Paying for liberty, life, and the pursuit of happiness was an integral part of emancipation in the region during the revolutionary age, and the enslaved did so in a variety of ways. Their efforts turned ambivalence and outright hostility over emancipation into Black freedom. Studying these efforts helps us to better understand how emancipation happened in the early republic. Enslaved people, free African Americans, and Black and white abolitionists contested the boundaries of slavery and freedom through a combination of techniques that pushed emancipation forward despite the best efforts of enslavers like Louis. The study of buying freedom illuminates the moral, legal, and financial compromises that would come to mark the structures of slavery and emancipation in the North.

While Black Pennsylvanians' experiences tell a particular kind of story about buying freedom, they have much to say about the general practice during the period. As Fanny's manumission indenture exhibits, Pennsylvania was home to many people of African descent from as far away as the Caribbean with complicated legal statuses ranging from enslaved to free and encompassing everything in between. After 1780, Pennsylvania's experimentation with abolition meant that it was also the original border state, delineating a blurry sectional line between slavery and freedom.[6] Despite gradual abolition's limitations, many still believed their chances would be better there than from where they came. Even as men, women, and children of African descent faced the complications of gradual emancipation, African Americans continued to move to Pennsylvania because of its status as a free state. Together they would shape ideas about buying freedom in the North and the nation.

Marie Rose Louis learned something from Pennsylvania's gradual abolition act. Like her motives for Fanny's manumission, the law opened with promise. The legislators, recalling the recent "Tyranny of Great Britain," described it as not only their "duty" but a pleasure to "extend a Portion of that freedom" that the nation would soon wrest from their oppressors to others. Yet, like Louis's action, the act's function was less magnanimous than its revolutionary rhetoric might suggest.

The act was the first of its kind in the nation, but other northern states like New York, Connecticut, Rhode Island, and New Jersey would follow in Pennsylvania's footsteps. While no one born before March 1, 1780, would be freed, every child born after that date was to be free at the age of twenty-eight. Despite its limitations, the act was not without meaning to enslaved people because it technically ended lifetime inheritable slavery across the state. The law required

the registration of all enslaved people, and those who were not properly registered before the deadline would be free. As previously mentioned, the sojourner
comity clause allowed travelers to bring enslaved people into the state for a
period of six months without losing their property. However, the enslaved could
sue for their freedom if they were held beyond these terms. With freedom at
stake, enslavers and the enslaved fought over these stipulations. That the act
passed by only thirteen votes suggests the divisive nature of the battles to come.[7]

As historians have claimed, gradual emancipation was "philanthropy at bargain prices."[8] That framing, however, understates the actions of African Americans to shape the process. Recent scholarship has shown the central role that
African Americans played in making revolutionary age emancipation happen.[9]
Seizing on the age's politics of freedom, enslaved and free African Americans
put into action the words like those of the founders and the Pennsylvania legislature.[10] Buying freedom helped them to do so against the recalcitrance of enslavers. Like gradual emancipation itself, buying freedom could act as a compromise
between the property rights of slaveholders and the rights of the enslaved to
freedom. It was a freedom technique that could satisfy appeals to both economic
interest and liberty.

Given the rates of self-purchase in the states surrounding Pennsylvania, we
can read it as a regional technique situated in two contexts. The first was the
founding period, in which economies and ideas about slavery underwent significant change. The second was gradual abolition, debated in many states although
only passed by those in the North. At the nexus of these two contexts was Pennsylvania. Those subject to gradual emancipation and those who sought to escape
slavery by moving to the state merged their understandings of buying freedom to
challenge slavery on both practical and political grounds.

Unfree people in Pennsylvania who worked to buy themselves out of
slavery after gradual emancipation began had much in common with those
in neighboring states during the period. This is true even in states where only
opportunities for individual manumissions existed.[11] According to Ira Berlin, it
is likely that a greater percentage of enslaved people pursued self-purchase in the
founding period than at any other point before slavery was abolished in 1865.[12]
Although general manumission and self-purchase remained more prevalent in

the North, Upper South, and urban areas, these techniques helped to expand Black communities across the nation. Eva Sheppard Wolf's work on manumission in Virginia has shown that payment was the cause of around 8 percent of the state's deeds of manumission from 1782 to 1806 and 12 percent for the period 1794 to 1806. These numbers are higher when considering African American manumitters, suggesting their important role in buying the freedom of friends and loved ones. Men completed 25 percent of these manumissions.[13] Delayed manumission and term slavery agreements also acted as payment for freedom and were common not only in northern states but also in places like Virginia and Maryland.[14]

In states north of Pennsylvania, enslaved and unfree people used self-purchase as one technique among many to contend with the slowness of gradual abolition. According to Michael Groth, in New York even enslaved people outside the city in places like Dutchess County were able to buy their freedom despite enslavers' dedication to maintaining the institution after the state's gradual emancipation act of 1799.[15] As James Gigantino's work has shown, things were much more difficult for unfree people in New Jersey, especially those in the eastern portion of the state. Although New Jersey enacted gradual abolition in 1804, it maintained age restrictions on private manumission that limited the usefulness of gradual emancipation for the enslaved.[16] Slavery's economic importance to the state in the aftermath of the Revolution also meant that enslavers were unwilling to negotiate for freedom because proslavery sentiment remained strong and slavery maintained economic viability.[17] Although individual manumissions did help to undo slavery in western counties, in the eastern portion of the state the enslaved population grew by 20–30 percent.[18]

Without the economic, political, or social pressure experienced in other northern states, enslavers in New Jersey simply did not need to negotiate. Given the arduousness of these circumstances, enslaved people had a difficult time finding the independence they needed to raise money to buy freedom. Although purchasing freedom did still occur, trading time for freedom was far more common than buying it. Enslaved people in New Jersey used all of the same techniques they would use elsewhere to try to obtain their freedom, even if their enslavers were especially recalcitrant.[19]

In August 1805, about one and a half years after New Jersey enacted gradual abolition, a woman named Dorcus Tonkins purchased her daughter, Temperance, for fifty dollars "in hand paid" from Howard Bilderbach. Bilderbach and Temperance lived in Pilesgrove, New Jersey, around thirty-four miles southwest of Philadelphia, where Dorcus Tonkins lived. Temperance was to serve a term of four years under her mother, after which she would be manumitted. While the document does not record an age for Temperance, only calling her a "certain negro girl," this stipulation was likely meant to skirt the laws of New Jersey which, as of 1798, only allowed for manumissions of people aged twenty-one to forty.[20] Tonkins did not appear to wait long to take advantage of gradual emancipation to free her daughter. However Tonkins had escaped slavery herself, living in Philadelphia likely helped her make the money she needed to reunite with her daughter and protect her from term slavery.

Cities like Philadelphia, New York, and Baltimore offered more opportunity for the conditions of self-purchase. These cities drew African Americans like Tonkins because they offered larger Black populations that free, enslaved, and fugitive individuals took advantage of to find work and community.[21] Work opportunities and extended networks of support were key to making self-purchase successful. In 1849, a census conducted by the Pennsylvania Abolition Society (PAS) found that some 194 out of 604, or roughly 32 percent, of manumitted African Americans in the city who they interviewed had bought their freedom.[22] Stephen Whitman found that 25 percent of manumissions in Baltimore were completed through an exchange of funds.[23] In New York City, records of self-purchase, delayed manumission, and indentures abound in city registers and the papers of the New York Manumission Society (NYMS). Some records represent a combination of possible avenues for freedom. In 1793, for instance, Hetty Franklin was sold to a man who would become a member of the NYMS. She was bound to him for a term of twenty-six years. By 1806, after the state enacted gradual emancipation, he decided that she would only have to serve for two more years and that, if her husband returned (from an undisclosed location) and wished to purchase her remaining time, he could do so for "reasonable compensation."[24]

The PAS report showed that African Americans in Philadelphia had spent some $45,000 on freedom. Market prices in the surrounding region meant that it cost well over a year's wages to buy an adult's freedom with no other costs.[25] As the mention of Hetty Franklin's husband in her term sale shows, many in these cities were also working to procure the liberty of family members, with some doing this after they had already purchased themselves.[26] We can hardly speculate about the rates of these occurrences, for only those who were successful would be recorded in the archive, and success was extremely difficult. Freedom was expensive. It was even more so if one tried to buy multiple members of their family. Life was already challenging and uncertain enough for most African Americans.

Compensated emancipation, freedom paid for with either money or time, consumed the lives that African Americans attempted to make for themselves in more ways than one. Some scholars have argued that self-purchase was an "ideal strategy for masters seeking to extract the most" they could from the people they enslaved.[27] Given the tenacity with which enslavers held on to slavery despite gradual abolition, many enslaved people would likely have felt as though they had no choice but to pay. From the enslavers' point of view, all forms of delayed manumission were beneficial and representative of the power they had over those who wished to be free. However, if these arrangements were a "form of insurance" for enslavers to maintain power, then freedom was the ultimate form of insurance for the enslaved and they took great risks to make paying for it a reality.[28]

For Philadelphia's underclass, especially African Americans, money was not necessarily easy to come by. The 1782 manumission agreement of a man named James who was enslaved by Thomas Irwin in Philadelphia gives some indication of the kind of labor needed to purchase oneself. The terms, recorded by the PAS, included payment of £90 Pennsylvania currency to be paid within six months' time or at the rate of two Spanish dollars per week until James had paid £100. If James failed to meet the demands of either payment plan, then the agreement would be voided and, under the terms of the gradual emancipation law enacted two years earlier, he would remain enslaved. While the math does not clearly add up, notes at the bottom of the page give some clues as to how James made the money he needed to complete the terms of his manumission. James appears to have gone on at least three voyages, the longest of which was for six months on the ship *Congress*. Irwin, James's enslaver, was a merchant and shipowner.

Whether or not James had been forced to man Irwin's ships as an enslaved man, he now tried to use these voyages to facilitate his freedom. He was paid eight to eleven dollars per month for his labor. Sailors made up a large portion of the city's poorer class, and life at sea offered difficult work that was relatively easy to get. By the early nineteenth century over 20 percent of sailors leaving Philadelphia were African American.[29]

Life at sea was not easy, as James would have known well. To be enslaved by Irwin meant that James would have been familiar with the more dangerous side of seafaring. Irwin and the *Congress* itself were involved in privateering during the American Revolution. Writing to President George Washington in hopes of gaining an appointment due to financial hardship, Irwin claimed that "Fortune" had "proved unkind" to him during the war; he had over a dozen ships captured by "the enemy." After the war, another ship owned by Irwin and his brother, the *Dauphin*, was captured off the coast of Portugal, and those on board were taken captive in Algiers. Writing to Thomas Jefferson in 1785, the captain of the *Dauphin* said they had "become Slaves." The captives remained there for years while the federal government tried to negotiate their release and ransom.[30] These were no pleasure cruises, and James likely knew what he risked. He would also have been familiar with the fear the captives of the *Dauphin* must have experienced while they waited for their release, although he knew much better than they did what it really meant to be a slave. There were no calm seas for enslaved people.

The spirit of revolution may have influenced the agreement between James and Irwin. For James, the war and gradual abolition that surrounded him could have pushed him to negotiate for his freedom. If he had already worked for his enslaver on Philadelphia's docks or ships, he may have gotten a taste of that freedom through conversations with free sailors, including other Black men like himself, or with those from other countries. Maybe he also enjoyed having time away from his enslaver's direct supervision while at sea. Any or all these experiences could have led James to want to escape slavery. Irwin, on the other hand, might have been forced to acquiesce because of the way the war affected his finances. Irwin's economic misfortune could have been James's boon. Whatever the circumstances, this was an opportunity he might not have otherwise had since he was born before March 1, 1780.[31]

James's success might have influenced other people that Irwin enslaved. He shows up again in 1784 making a deal with his "late slave" Ned and his "present slave Dina and her son Cato." Ned and Dina were to pay £100 over three yearly September payments, after which Dina and Cato would be free. If the payments were not made by 1787, Dina and Cato were to "remain slaves." Ned and Dina must have had trouble keeping up. In October 1792, Irwin manumitted Dina(h), who was twenty-eight years old, for the nominal sum of five shillings paid by Ned and "other good causes thereunto moving." Then, in October 1795, Cato, described as "Son of Ned and Dinah," indentured himself "with the consent of his father" to Irwin for a term of seventeen years. Instead of being fully free in 1787, Cato would now have to remain in the service of Irwin until 1809.[32] At twenty-eight, Dina may have been less valuable to Irwin, which meant that he was more willing to let her go. Certainly, this was good for her family as she would no longer have children whose first twenty-eight years of life would be commanded by Irwin. Cato's position, indicative of his remaining value, was a reminder of this danger. Despite their best efforts, Ned and Dina were not able to free their son or maintain his care. Still, they were able to shift his status from term slavery to indenture, which might have been a comfort.[33] From this family and James, Irwin received not only money but also years of additional labor.

The opportunities presented by cities like Philadelphia, although still hard won, caution us from telling this story from only their point of view. As recent historical work shows, scholarly concentration on cities like Philadelphia and New York has skewed our understanding of the success of gradual abolition. Outside the city, varying kinds of unfreedom lasted much longer. Gradual abolition did not work evenly across the state. Slavery was not just a regional institution on a national level but also within the states themselves. This is true of New York State and eastern New Jersey as well as rural Pennsylvania. In some senses, then, people in these areas paid more for everyone's freedom.[34] In Pennsylvania, enslavement remained strongest in the state's southern counties, where politics and geography aligned with the slave states they bordered. Slave labor was important to the economic development of the region, especially in the early period when sources of labor were scarce.[35]

While enslavers everywhere tried to game the system, those outside of Philadelphia were especially adept at it. The capacity of groups like the PAS to support the enslaved, though wide, was not enough to always be vigilant across the entire state.[36] Enslavers held people past their terms and maintained the services of people to whom they had no claim according to the law. Enslaved people from states like Virginia were also purchased at low rates and registered with conditional manumissions. Thus enslavers in Pennsylvania could take advantage of the slave market that grew unabated in the Upper South despite gradual abolition. James Gigantino has shown the extensive participation of New Jersey enslavers in the domestic slave trade.[37]

Enslaved and unfree people in these areas of Pennsylvania had less access to the networks and economic opportunities that they needed to make money to buy themselves out of slavery. Outright self-purchase was, therefore, rarer in rural areas.[38] This would remain true everywhere across the United States until the abolition of slavery. Still, enslaved people across Pennsylvania were paying dearly for freedom with cash, credit, and time. In lieu of money, which was often even harder to come by outside of urban centers, the enslaved sometimes traded what they had. For many, that meant further years of service.

According to the law anyone born before March 1, 1780, was going to be a slave for life unless, like James, they managed to find their way out of it. Although permanent inheritable enslavement was no longer law, gradual emancipation, as the historian Cory Young explains, "retained the logic of matrilineal inheritance that allowed enslavers to treat Black women's children as their property."[39] Not just racial slavery, but gradual abolition as well, created a "social [and legal] condition forged in African women's wombs," as Jennifer Morgan has argued.[40] In Pennsylvania, enslaved women's children were not born into freedom but instead into a kind of term slavery. For the next twenty-eight years of their lives they would bear the brunt of the gradualness of emancipation. Across the state these unfree laborers were "practically indistinguishable" from the enslaved in "treatment and status."[41] Poor treatment, questionable rights, and the threat of being separated from family and friends by geography or legal status meant that those subject to term slavery looked for routes out of it, too.[42]

The hereditary nature of gradual abolition wreaked havoc on enslaved people's families, just as slavery did.[43] For mothers, term slavery meant that, although enslavers might no longer have owned their children for life, they certainly still owned their children's time. Slaveholders continued to enslave mothers since they benefited from any children born as term slaves. Because of this, women faced sexual violence and the inability to protect their children against all manner of abuses and from separation. To protect their families, women tried to negotiate for their own freedom and that of their children in ways they would have already been familiar with under slavery.[44] From the term slavery produced by gradual abolition to compensated or conditional manumissions and indentures, African American women across Pennsylvania traded time for their freedom and that of their children. The sooner unfree women could escape their owners, the better it would be for themselves, their children, and their chances at experiencing the security of generational freedom.

Christopher Osborne estimates that in western Pennsylvania during the first few decades of gradual emancipation, some one thousand children were born into gradual abolition's term slavery.[45] Women in Pittsburgh, like their Philadelphia counterparts, used techniques to speed up the end of slavery or to protect their children, although they would have had a more difficult time. Scattered in deed books belonging to the Allegheny County Recorder of Deeds are a small collection of manumission and indenture records that show the complicated nature of freedom in the state's westernmost outpost and the many forms of compensation enslavers wrested from those whose labor they controlled.

These records include relatively straightforward cases of self-purchase, although many of those concerning women and girls are, as might be expected, more complicated. In 1790, Peter Cosco, for example, purchased his freedom for £100 from John McKee. McKee's family ran the McKeesport ferry south of the city. He himself was one of the largest landowners in the area. According to the census that year, McKee owned two slaves.[46] The deed gives some clues as to the circumstances of Cosco's manumission. McKee records that the £100 was paid through "sundrey obligations," suggesting that Cosco paid in small and/or irregular amounts over time. He also hinted at what led him to agree to Cosco's self-purchase when he claimed that Cosco had "always behaved himself as an honest trusty servant." Within a few years of Cosco's manumission, McKee ran into serious financial trouble, but Cosco, at least, was safe from being affected by his former enslaver's debts.[47]

Having lost Cosco and much of his land, McKee enters these records again in 1793. This time, he was indenturing a young girl. Kut was indentured to McKee by her mother, Suck, for a term of twelve and a half years. Suck was enslaved by James Torrons, also of Allegheny County. According to the terms of the indenture, Kut was to serve McKee "faithfully" and obey "cheerfully." She was not allowed to marry or "commit fornication nor frequent taverns, cards, dice nor any unlawful games." McKee was to provide food, washing, and lodging as well as teach Kut to learn to read the "holy scriptures." Her freedom dues were two sets of clothing, one of which had to be new. While this indenture was handwritten, preprinted forms used in the state contain many of the same standard stipulations.[48]

Under the terms of gradual emancipation, Torrons would have technically maintained control over Kut until she was twenty-eight years old. It is of note, then, that Suck was the one to indenture her daughter. While her reasons for doing so are not described, Suck's actions show she had possibly achieved some control over her daughter's life. While the connection to McKee probably came through Torrons, Suck might have wanted her daughter to work for someone who was known to have emancipated at least one of his enslaved people.[49] Perhaps she thought this was a good omen for how he would treat her daughter, or that, with continued negotiation, she would be able to get McKee to release Kut early. Although we do not know how old Kut was, this indenture might already have taken years off her daughter's service that was due to Torrons. Perhaps learning to read and leaving with two new sets of clothing after twelve and a half years was the least bad option Suck had to protect her daughter. The indication that Suck was "not free by her Master" suggests that while her daughter moved from term slavery to indenture, nothing was to be done about Suck. She, like so many others, would be separated from her family across the line between enslaved and, in this case, quasi-free.

Familial complexities were markers of both slavery and gradual emancipation. As with buying freedom more broadly, familial reunion and protection were often at the heart of challenges to gradual abolition. Community and kinship made people desire freedom but also helped them make it a reality. From free friends and family to activists and community leaders, Black communities were the first line of defense for those looking to buy freedom and escape slavery.[50] This is partly why people in Philadelphia and New York were able to secure their freedom more readily. Better access to those with experience buying freedom who could share their knowledge and provide social and financial support was also crucial.

In Philadelphia, two of the city's most prominent Black leaders, Richard Allen and Absalom Jones, purchased their freedom and later settled in the city to build a Black community whose size and power was unrivaled in the period. Allen and Jones put their freedom to good use. Together, they formed the Free African Society in 1787, and they would go on to form the nation's first independent Black churches. They stood at the center of Black politics in the city, state, and the nation. They were also early examples of how African Americans used self-purchase to shape national discussions over slavery, freedom, and Black belonging.

As influential men and community leaders, their examples mattered. Their stories shaped beliefs about the practical and political benefits of self-purchase. The determination and economic responsibility needed to purchase one's freedom worked well to challenge racist stereotypes about Black people's place in the new nation. Gradual emancipation was not just about compensation; it was also meant to train African Americans to be free citizens. According to John McKee, Peter Cosco was not only free but also well-behaved, honest, and trustworthy. While paternal in tone given the context, these attributes were not without meaning. Buying freedom showed self-sufficiency, economy, industry, and self-making, which were all key to being part of a virtuous citizenry defined by white men. Through their individual stories and community organizing, Allen and Jones expanded their race's capacity to seize the rights they knew to be theirs.[51] Allen and Jones discussed their paths to freedom in autobiographical writing,

and both men connected the political rhetoric of buying freedom to republican ideas of ownership of property in oneself and one's labor. These kinds of
arguments would inflect later narrative uses of self-purchase in the nineteenth-
century slave narrative genre.[52]

Published in 1833, Richard Allen's *The Life, Experience, and Gospel Labors
of the Right Reverend Richard Allen* revealed how Allen and his brother purchased themselves while enslaved in Delaware. Demonstrating the capacity of
buying freedom to address economic demand and philanthropic desire, Allen
recalled how his enslaver, Stokeley Sturgis, proposed the plan to the men when
he became dissatisfied with slaveholding because of a religious awakening. Sturgis could not square his newfound spiritualism with owning people. However,
he was not so unsatisfied that he would manumit the brothers outright. Agreeing
to purchase his freedom, Allen hired his time and paid in yearly installments.
After about three and a half years, he had paid a total of £60 and received his
freedom in 1783.[53]

Allen spent very little time on this part of his life in the narrative. Instead,
he reveals the story in a matter-of-fact way that we might read as a something
of a reflection on the common occurrence of self-purchase in the mid-Atlantic
revolutionary age. It also indicates that Allen wished to concentrate on what he
considered to be the more important parts of his narrative. Shortly after relating
how he freed himself, Allen declared that he had "reason to bless my dear Lord"
that the opportunity arose for him to buy his "time, and enjoy [his] liberty."[54] It
was through God and a more divine labor that Allen understood the blessing he
received in buying himself.

Like Allen, Absalom Jones was born enslaved in Delaware in 1746. In an
autobiographical sketch, Jones described his early relationship to money and his
"careful" savings, as well as his efforts to educate himself by using the money he
had to buy primers and spelling books. When he was sixteen years old, Jones's
mother and six siblings were separated and sold. Jones was then taken to Philadelphia, where he worked and continued his education so that he could commu-
nicate with his family. In 1770, Jones married a woman named Mary and asked
to purchase her freedom. Mary's enslaver agreed to take £40 for her liberation.
Jones called on friends and allies in the city for donations and arranged to borrow

money so that he could save his wife and protect their future together. With the help of his father-in-law, Jones raised £30, which his wife's enslaver accepted for her freedom. He worked long hours to pay back the money he borrowed to buy Mary's freedom.[55]

This was an act of love and the ultimate romantic gesture. Having been separated from his own family, Jones well understood that slavery posed a danger to kinship and that his wife would have produced children her enslavers would consider their property. Freedom was the best foundation for a family. Next, Jones tried to purchase his own freedom, but his owner denied the request. Although he was still enslaved, Jones became a landholder, which increased his concern over his legal status. As long as he was enslaved, his house and land were at risk of being seized as the property of his enslaver, which would leave his wife and family with nothing. Jones finally purchased his own freedom in 1784.[56] Sharing experiences like these could have influenced others to pursue a similar course.

Absalom Jones assisted others by using his connections and securing financial support for those trying to follow his example. Thirteen years after his own emancipation, Jones wrote to the businessman Henry Banks to request his assistance in arranging to buy the freedom of a man named Richmond Bryan. Bryan was enslaved by the Shewel family in Virginia, where Banks lived. In his letter, Jones requested that Banks contact Bryan's enslavers to see if they would agree to let Bryan purchase his freedom. Banks could be of service because, as Jones claimed, he had better connections in Virginia. Jones was willing to pay up to $120 for Bryan's manumission and "properly authenticated" free papers.

Jones told Banks he was inclined to help Bryan because he was a "poor Black man" who appeared to be "orderly" and "well disposed." Jones's letter implied that these characteristics made Bryan worthy of his support and, more important, Banks's assistance. Opportunities for self-purchase and assistance were sometimes directly linked to respectability. No matter what they thought about the necessity of respectable connections, Jones's experience and his assistance to Bryan attest to the fact that African Americans relied on them.[57]

Both Allen and Jones understood the importance of legal freedom and had interracial and interclass connections that they used to their advantage in their personal and public lives. Their free status and societal standing put them in a special position to lead the city's Black community and support African Americans looking for freedom. Both were important connectors between the city's Black community and white abolitionists.[58] Because of people like Jones and Allen, Philadelphia's free African Americans were highly organized with strong independent institutions that worked to define and protect Black freedom across the United States. Reflecting on the transformative power of Pennsylvania's African American communities, W. E. B. Du Bois noted in his groundbreaking work *The Philadelphia Negro* that it was the perfect place for the "continuous study" of African Americans.[59]

Given the size and organizational strength of Black Philadelphia, it should be no surprise that antislavery activism also flourished in the city in the eighteenth and nineteenth centuries. The nation's most important antislavery organization during the period was the Pennsylvania Society for Promoting the Abolition of Slavery and for the Relief of Free Negroes Unlawfully held in Bondage, and for Improving the Condition of the African Race, which was first founded in 1775 and reconstituted after the American Revolution in 1784.[60] Quaker abolitionists such as Anthony Benezet and Isaac Hopper as well as national leaders like Benjamin Franklin and Benjamin Rush were among the organization's leadership. The African American leader and activist Robert Purvis was the PAS's only Black member.[61] Purvis would later go on to become a founding member of the interracial American Anti-Slavery Society.

The PAS's activism centered around legislative and legal tactics.[62] Despite these limitations and the group's overwhelming whiteness, which also shapes the society's archive, it is possible to reconstruct how this work was done in conjunction with Black activists and the enslaved and free African Americans who came to the society for help.[63] The circumstances of gradual abolition and fugitivity guided the activism of white abolitionists along with that of their Black counterparts. The legal work of groups like the PAS mattered on the ground in many ways, including by making gradual abolition mean something and by helping African Americans escape slavery through legal means. Individualized legal and illegal support offered important practical assistance to those African Americans at the crossroads of enslavement and freedom. At the same time, their lobbying and petitioning of state and federal governments on issues related to slavery and gradual emancipation worked to draw the borders of slavery more clearly.[64]

The importance of this antislavery network to self-purchase is apparent in the connections made between African Americans trying to buy freedom across the state and PAS members. Beyond Pennsylvania, the PAS had a regional influence, which meant that enslaved people and fugitives from the surrounding slave states also accessed its help.[65] These early relationships would blossom into the interracial abolition movement of the 1830s. Even as the movement radicalized, Black and white abolitionists would continue to express concern over legal freedom. Buying it would remain central to abolitionist organizing throughout the nineteenth century, as will be shown in Chapter 3.

Given the importance of being able to prove one's freedom to maintain it under both gradual abolition and the Fugitive Slave Act, one of the most common and everyday functions of the PAS was to record manumissions and indentures for African Americans in Philadelphia and its neighboring region. These records were meant to ensure the safety of free African Americans from kidnapping by recording proof of their free status, to protect against unlawful enslavement or the extension of term slavery and indentures, and to maintain copies of the manumission documents of free African Americans who moved to the state. Stories of compensated manumission in these records provide clues to how African Americans negotiated for freedom with the help of the PAS in a variety of circumstances.

One of the very first cases taken on by the PAS culminated in the purchase and liberation of Dinah Nevill and her three children in 1781. Nevill, who was Native American, claimed to be a free woman when her New Jersey enslaver sold her to Virginia. She was sold via Philadelphia, which allowed PAS members Thomas Harrison and Israel Pemberton to hear about her situation and take legal action to establish her freedom. Despite their efforts, the court ruled against Nevill. After several appeals and delays, Harrison, who was the PAS's secretary, bought Nevill and her children to free them.[66]

While Nevill's story shows that buying freedom was sometimes resorted to when other options had been exhausted, Harrison was involved in other kinds of situations that reveal the many uses of compensation.[67] Ten years later, an enslaver named Susanna Budd agreed to manumit a man named Pero for £120. Budd's clarification that she was taking the money as "compensation" for his "*bringing up*" suggests that if she was going to lose her claim on his life's labor, then she wanted to recoup what she imagined to be her sunk costs. This phrasing is particularly interesting in the context of gradual abolition, as enslavers and legislators tried to determine who would pay the costs of emancipation and how much they would owe for it. Budd certainly thought Pero should reimburse her and provided an idea of what she thought she was owed for her loss.[68] For Pero, this meant paying not just for his future freedom but also his past enslavement.

The PAS was engaged to track Pero's payments and to receive his wages. As Budd stipulated, the "monies earned" were "not to be paid to him." Harrison, as a member of the acting committee, was to save £4 a month from Pero's wages, which he would send to Budd on the first Monday of every month until the sum was paid in full. It is impossible to know from this document the role that Pero played in this plan. It is unclear whether he had been the one to request the intermediary role of the PAS and how he felt about having the PAS act as his bank. These manumission records often leave unanswered important questions about their full circumstances. Lengthy negotiations between multiple parties boil down to a few handwritten lines that are just enough to mark the outlines of an enslaved person's path to freedom. These stipulations can be read as a breach of Pero's independence and the active role he took in buying his own freedom.

Yet this arrangement, however it was decided on, also added a layer of protection for Pero by creating a third-party witness to the process of his emancipation. Having the PAS record the agreement, as well as safeguard his payments, meant they could help Pero hold Budd accountable if anything were to go wrong.[69] As Pero's arrangement shows, emancipation could be a long process that was financial and social. At £4 a month, it would have taken Pero two and a half years to save enough money for his manumission. A note from 1792 stating that Pero could have one dollar out of every three in his account and, after that, five pence out of every twenty, with the remainder going to Budd, may reveal something of the financial difficulty of self-purchase. Pero faced having to pay for his freedom and his living expenses over an extended period. Emancipation was not a onetime legal event, although most manumission deeds make it appear to be such. Being lengthy meant that this process was almost constantly liable to failure. Black and white activists did not only depend on aboveground and legal tactics of the PAS to answer slavery's staying power.

Despite the gradual abolition act explicitly stating that Pennsylvania would not offer any "Relief or Shelter to any absconding or Runaway Negroe or Mulatto Slave or Servant" who had "absented" themselves from their owners, enslaved people from near and far tried to escape slavery by moving across state lines.[70] Some nine thousand enslaved people escaped into Pennsylvania from surrounding slave states before 1860. In Philadelphia, especially, they could blend in with the city's Black community and seek the support of their neighbors, friends, and activists to skirt the law or face it to buy the freedom they had already taken for themselves. Given the integration of fugitives into this community, their experiences and the risks they faced, while different, blended with the lives of those trapped in varying degrees of slavery. They learned from each other how to use compensation to their advantage. Even in an antislavery stronghold like Philadelphia, the risk of recapture was difficult to bear as runaways built new lives for themselves. This danger only increased after a fateful change to federal law.[71]

In 1793, the federal government created the legislative apparatus for the Constitution's Fugitive Slave Clause. This constitutional clause was meant to be an act of interstate comity to secure the status of fugitives across state lines and to ensure their return. The Fugitive Slave Act of 1793 formalized the extradition of persons "held to labor" who were claimed in free states and territories. Any enslaver, or their agent, could reclaim a fugitive and bring them before a judge to prove ownership through testimony or affidavit from their home state. Harboring, assisting, or attempting to rescue fugitives could result in fines of up to $500 and threatened imprisonment for up to one year. The act affected ideas about self-purchase by turning people determined to be runaways at the state level into fugitives according to federal law. Further, the law nationalized ideas about the surveillance of Blackness and legal status. Many resisted these ideologies just as surely as they did the law itself.[72]

In Pennsylvania, Black and white abolitionists fought anti-Black immigration bills and tried to get the state to speed up emancipation. They also risked breaking federal law to help enslaved people escape. While unable to get immediate emancipation on the books, activists and antislavery legislators in Pennsylvania were successful in passing protective personal liberty laws that made the 1793 Fugitive Slave Act more difficult to enforce.[73] Through both their legislative and on-the-ground work, Pennsylvania activists influenced antislavery activism across the nation.

Vigilance committees, formed to support fugitives and guard against kidnapping, became an important part of abolitionist activism across the North in the 1830s. Robert Purvis, the only Black member of the PAS, helped form Philadelphia's Vigilant Association in 1837. In cities like Philadelphia, New York, and Boston, these organizations were led by Black activists and provided mutual aid for runaways and kidnapped African Americans. These groups were not so much concerned with techniques, like moral suasion, that abolitionists used to convince white Americans that slavery was wrong. Instead, their work centered on practical abolitionist tactics that varied from sharing information about the arrival of suspected traders and enslavers, self-defense, and litigation, to monetary support and providing passage on the Underground Railroad. These groups also helped to arrange for the purchase of fugitives when escape failed. In Philadelphia, the Vigilant Association received some one hundred requests for help yearly.[74]

Examining self-purchase helps reveal how a clandestine network of antislavery allies, often associated more closely with second-wave abolitionism and the Underground Railroad, established itself in the early republic. As would be true later, the experiences of fugitives shaped the movement's understanding of the politics of buying freedom. Isaac T. Hopper was a white Quaker abolitionist from New Jersey who was known for doing this kind of work. While he was a long-standing member of the PAS, his activism spanned both first- and second-wave abolition. Hopper was legendary for his assistance to fugitives and his legal machinations to secure their freedom. He was an expert in leveraging his legal skills and partnering with African Americans to protect Black freedom, even when those he helped had little legal claim to it. Hopper's adept handling of the legal issues facing African Americans led William Still, a leading Black abolitionist and central figure in the operation of Philadelphia's Underground Railroad, to claim that no one was better equipped to deal with the "intricacies of law questions" related to slavery. Still said that Hopper had hope of "victory" when a case "seemed hopeless to other minds."[75]

Stories of Hopper's escapades made the rounds of abolitionist print culture, which probably played no small part in his legend and in helping abolitionist audiences think about buying freedom. From 1840 to 1842, the *National Anti-slavery Standard* (*NASS*) printed "Tales of Oppression," a series in which Hopper recalled many of the rescue attempts that involved his know-how. These stories were printed at the request of Lydia Maria Child, who was then editor of the paper. In 1853 Child published *Isaac T. Hopper: A True Life*, which retold many of the stories in "Tales of Oppression" to honor Hopper after his death in 1852. Of the eighty-six stories shared by Hopper in this series, around thirty cases, or 35 percent, involved compensation in some fashion.[76]

These stories make clear that enslaved and free African Americans networked with men like Hopper and Thomas Harrison because of their legal, social, and political connections.[77] Members of the PAS were well known not only to African Americans but to slaveholders as well, and both parties sought them out for assistance. For enslavers, PAS members represented a path to open communication with those they enslaved but no longer had access to.[78] For the enslaved, these negotiations could lead to legal freedom if handled correctly. One thing that most African Americans had in common, no matter their legal status, was economic precarity. With Hopper's help, they could create favorable conditions to secure freedom at prices they could afford. He often created those conditions through a mix of law and subterfuge.

Mary Holliday escaped from Maryland when she was twenty-four years old. When her former enslaver, Mrs. Sears, tried to reclaim Holliday in Pennsylvania, Holliday worked with Hopper to secure her freedom. Hopper began by putting as many legal obstructions in Sears's way as possible. When Sears first attempted to claim Holliday, Holliday's current employer offered to buy her freedom, but Sears refused the offer. After this failed attempt, Hopper worked his standard magic on the legal proceedings. Lydia Maria Child claimed that no one was better at multiplying "difficulties" for enslavers. First, Hopper served a writ of *homine replegiando* to free Holliday from unlawful detention. Hopper did this to ensure that Holliday's case would be tested outside of the city's mayor's office as it was well known that he was unfriendly to both African Americans and abolitionists. Hopper's "difficulties" kept Holliday's case pending in the state's higher courts for several years. The long and slow-going tactic eventually worked when Sears finally became "exceedingly weary" of the legal trials and costs.[79]

Worn down in this manner by Hopper, Sears directed her lawyer to work out a compromise. Hopper offered to pay $250 for Holliday's freedom, if Sears would pay the costs of the extended legal battle. Sears agreed, and Holliday's employer, Isaac W. Morris, paid the money. After Holliday was emancipated, she paid back the cost of her freedom and some of the remaining trial expenses through day labor and collecting money from friends. Eventually she was able to pay Morris about $300 in small payments.

It remains unclear if Hopper took risks with the permission of the enslaved. The tales, told from his perspective, often leave unclear the extent to which he acted of his own accord and how closely he consulted with those for whom he negotiated. While Holliday's story is focused on the legal genius of Hopper, we get very little information about Holliday's journey as her case lingered in court. Although Hopper's tactics depended on the participation of local African Americans and mirrored their own, that did not mean that those he helped were not nervous about his games. Given the limitations of the archive, we can only guess that these years must have been marked by extreme uncertainty for Holliday and fear of having to give up her quasi-free life in Pennsylvania.

Even after her grueling legal battles, Holliday remained quietly indebted to her employer and labored to pay back the cost of her freedom. As Erica Dunbar has described, emancipation in Philadelphia was a gendered experience. Freedom provided little economic opportunity, and it took women more time to get free.[80] Staying on with her employer likely offered Holliday some security, even if she remained only to pay off her debts. Still, we might gain a window into the trust she had for Hopper, her employer, and the legal process because she chose to remain in Philadelphia rather than moving farther out of Sears's reach. It is possible she felt she had no other choice.[81]

Ben Jackson also relied on the assistance of his interracial community to protect his freedom. Jackson escaped slavery in Virginia when he was twenty-five years old and landed in Philadelphia. Jackson created the life he had dreamed about in the city. He secured a variety of jobs and joined the city's free African American community. Like James and many other African Americans, Jackson worked aboard ships for the first few years of his life in the North. It is possible that he did this because being out to sea offered him protection from being recaptured, or because the job was accessible for someone like him, or both. Jackson wished to settle down, however, because within five years he had married a free African American woman and worked as a coachman for Benjamin Rush, one of the most famous members of the PAS. Through working for someone with the notoriety of Rush and getting him to certify his freedom, Jackson was able to gain some protections, even if they were based on false information. Jackson would come to rely on each of these connections when he was arrested in 1799.

When Jackson was taken before the magistrate after his arrest as a fugitive, he produced the letter from Rush that certified his freedom and good character. While this document could have been given to him when he left his job in Rush's household to help him seek new employment opportunities, Jackson now produced it as a legal document that was proof of his freedom. Given Rush's status, he was not wrong to assume it would carry weight in court, even if the evidence it was supposed to provide was based on false claims. He also requested that Isaac Hopper represent him. Jackson was released by the court when his enslaver failed to show up.

When advised to leave the city, Jackson thought he might return to his life as a sailor to protect himself. His life was different now, though, and his wife did not want him to leave. She would soon have to face her nightmare of losing him for good when Jackson's enslaver and a constable came to their home to arrest him. This time, not willing to take further risks, Jackson sailed on a voyage to the East Indies while Hopper negotiated the terms for Jackson to buy his freedom for $150. Jackson could hardly be recaptured while at sea, which may have made his enslaver more willing to negotiate with Hopper.

Despite Jackson's wife being free herself, by creating a partnership with a man who had escaped slavery, she was still subject to the threat slavery posed to kinship. Even in Philadelphia, Jackson's family life was influenced by his enslavement. In addition to living in constant fear that her husband would be arrested, she also had to spend months alone while he was at sea. Many a sailor's wife would have related to her putting her foot down when Jackson wanted to leave. Yet not all sailor's wives were married to enslaved men. "Fear and anxiety" wore away at her health as she worried about possible separation from the man she loved and with whom she had made a life.[82] The emotional journey of Jackson's wife reveals both the strain of fugitive living on family and community life and the promise of buying freedom to remain together. While she probably was reluctant to see him go, his wife helped with his escape. And, although it goes unmentioned, it is likely that she also assisted Hopper with the negotiations for her husband's freedom so that they could live together without the fear and anxiety that plagued their home.

Enslaved African Americans in Philadelphia, such as Mary Holliday, not only undertook extended legal battles but, like Jackson, also worked to secure opportunities to buy their freedom by using fugitive techniques to outwit slave catchers. Using these techniques, many were finally able to buy their freedom at reduced prices. Sometimes freedom could be had for a "sum so small, that it was merely nominal."[83] By escaping slavery, the men and women who fled to cities like Philadelphia had already made their status as human property unstable.[84] Abolitionists multiplied that instability by making the Pennsylvania border birthed through gradual abolition into one that they could use to their advantage.

Enslavers and slave catchers hedged their bets on capturing fugitives. The possibility of making up costs for someone they were unlikely to recapture forced many into negotiating for freedom with the likes of people who were their legal property and with abolitionists like Isaac Hopper. As we have seen, Hopper used several tactics to control prices during freedom negotiations. These purchase arrangements were not ideal for enslavers, but they were a relatively easy way for them to recoup something from their investment in human beings. Allowing runaways to buy their freedom could lower their costs and the trouble they would have to go through to recapture them. Enslavers and slave catchers had a captive audience with whom to broker a settlement as the enslaved were faced with the choice of paying or being returned to slavery. Still, enslaver power over these purchases was already constrained by the actions of the self-emancipated, and they came up against formidable and nimble negotiators.[85]

Lydia Maria Child claimed that it was common for speculators and slave traders to buy fugitives at a reduced cost to try to get them back. According to Child, this was known in the "language of the trade" as "buying them running." This traffic in escapees reflects slavery's market in which risk management and profit went hand in hand with "contextualized" geographical value. The value of enslaved people increased the farther south they were sold by traders.[86] For those who moved northward, different calculations had to be made. Slave traders speculated that they could successfully find those they purchased and that it was worth the bargain. Whether they just hoped to take advantage of enslaved people's desire for freedom, or sought a cheaper entry point into slave trading, these traders undoubtedly knew what they were doing. In fact, there was a clear geography to the market for those bought running. Slave traders who had bought the rights to runaways in the South made the journey North to cities like Philadelphia to search out their property. For some, their first stop was to call on men like Isaac Hopper to inquire after fugitives and offer to negotiate the terms under which the enslaved could buy their freedom.

In 1806, a Delaware slave trader named Daniel Godwin bought an enslaved man named Ezekiel. This sale was sight unseen because Ezekiel was no longer in Delaware. Like other slave traders, Godwin was speculating on Ezekiel, but not in quite the same way as most. Godwin was known for buying runaways like Ezekiel, betting on his ability to recoup his investment. After his purchase, Godwin supposedly traveled directly to Philadelphia and visited Isaac Hopper to gather any information he could about Ezekiel's whereabouts. Godwin suggested that if Hopper could get word to his new slave, that he would be happy to let him to buy his freedom on "moderate terms." While Godwin talked with Hopper, a Black man came into the shop and asked Godwin if he recognized him. When Godwin failed to do so, the man introduced himself as Ezekiel's brother. He said that Godwin had made a poor "speculation" because Ezekiel would never be worth the investment. The brother implied that freedom had ruined Ezekiel and he had gotten into "bad company" during his time in Philadelphia. According to his brother, he would never be "one cent's worth of good."

Not deterred by this description, Godwin asked the man if he wanted to buy his brother and offered a low price. Godwin said he would take $150. With the man's continued remonstrances about Ezekiel's worthlessness, Godwin finally offered to sell him for $60.[87] As a slave trader, Godwin was likely an expert negotiator, but Ezekiel's brother made clear that Godwin was not the only one who knew how to wield slavery's conventions of valuation. Suggesting his brother's worthlessness and rebellious nature worked because enslavers were wary of purchasing people with a reputation for trouble.

Ezekiel's brother left Hopper's shop and quickly returned with the money. Hopper supposedly drafted a deed of manumission directly after the money was exchanged, although it would need to be certified. Ezekiel's brother requested that Hopper complete the manumission papers with his new name, Samuel Johnson. Like many other fugitives, Ezekiel had taken on a new identity to protect his freedom and to establish a new life for himself. After making sure that the transaction was complete, Samuel Johnson made a bow and exclaimed to Godwin, "I am happy to see you, sir. I am Zeke!"[88]

Godwin had been outsmarted and was infuriated at being shown up by the person he had come to Philadelphia to claim. He grabbed and threatened Johnson. According to Child's rendition, Johnson declared that he was now a "free citizen of these United States" and refused to be physically assaulted in this manner. Trying to deescalate the situation, Hopper interjected that Johnson and Godwin could bring the manumission before a court to ensure its legality. As Hopper likely suspected would happen, the magistrate declared that Johnson was indeed a legally free man. Taking full advantage of his newfound freedom, Johnson requested that the judge take out a warrant against Godwin for assault. Once again, Hopper intervened and suggested that Johnson be satisfied with his freedom and leave Godwin to go on his way. While Johnson agreed, his attempt to bring charges against Godwin shows that Johnson directly associated his newfound freedom with the full rights of citizenship and protections against harassment and physical assault.[89] These were the kinds of rights for which African Americans and abolitionists fought. Clearly those discussions had influenced Johnson.

Child does not make clear what might have transpired between Hopper and Johnson before Godwin came to the abolitionist. Whatever Hopper knew or did not know in the moment, Johnson knew that he would be of assistance in completing his ruse. Given his preferred mode of business in buying fugitives, Johnson also knew that Godwin would be unable to recognize him. Johnson likely entered Hopper's shop with at least that advantage. This is information that he could have gathered from other members of his community, like those who tracked the arrivals of enslavers and warned each other about them. Johnson knew Godwin was in town, that he was Godwin's property, and how to outwit him. Godwin was knowable and malleable while Johnson was not.[90] Samuel Johnson employed ingenuity, trickery, and the performance of valuing (or devaluing). His mastery of the market for enslaved people allowed him to buy his freedom at a sum that he already had readily available to him.

Hopper's stories, while useful for understanding how enslaved runaways created opportunities to buy their freedom, are heavily focused on men. The recollection of Samuel Johnson's almost immediate claims on citizenship reflect, in part, the political work of Hopper's tales. Claims on the state and a fitness for freedom were often gendered as the terrain of masculinity. Only eight of the cases involved women like Holliday. Yet African American women were at the center of Black life in Philadelphia and at the forefront of the abolition movement. Certainly Black women, like Ben Jackson's wife, were present and active in the communities that supported men like Johnson, even if they remain in the shadows in Hopper's recollections.[91]

For all their desire to live free, without legal manumission many African Americans who called Philadelphia home lived in a state of liminal freedom. Reflecting and responding to African American legal culture in this period, activists like Hopper worked to push the boundaries of the law to be more inclusive of who could claim its protections. African Americans and white abolitionists blurred the lines between legal and extralegal activism to support the liberation of the enslaved who sought refuge in the North.[92] This occurred when they challenged the legal system on its own terms by seeking protection from the laws related to slavery and Black belonging. It also happened through the collaborative maneuverings described in Hopper's recollections. They used illegal techniques to make slave property less secure, thereby causing enslavers to negotiate terms for compensated manumission.

Their actions wore down both state officials and enslavers who were otherwise reluctant to relinquish their power and property. By making enslavers realize that it was sometimes best to cut their losses and sell their property into free people, Black Philadelphians and white antislavery activists worked to expand the boundaries of freedom. This work was particularly important in Pennsylvania since it was a "vital borderland" between slavery and freedom where national conflicts were borne out in the daily lives of so many.[93]

While the American Revolution and the founding of the nation spurred a new politics of freedom, gradual abolition succeeded insofar as African Americans born into it, and those influenced by it to move to the North, made it work.[94] Given the complications of gradual emancipation, African Americans in Pennsylvania well understood the ways that slavery could continue to influence the freedom of others like them across the nation. Individual experiences of buying freedom like those of James, Pero, and Mary Holliday show that paying for freedom was expensive and laborious but that enslaved people thought it was worth the effort. These stories of self-purchase are singular. That is partly why gradual emancipation took so long.

However, African Americans in the midst of these regimes would have understood the collective nature of compensation. Someone had to pay for the end of slavery, and while most African Americans living in states with gradual plans enjoyed their freedom, others were left behind to pay the costs of compromise.[95] In Pennsylvania, African Americans also tried to use compensation to secure the final release of their friends and family across the state.

At numerous points after 1780, the Pennsylvania state legislature debated other emancipation plans to free those who were still enslaved. By February 1800, a full twenty years after gradual abolition began, African Americans had grown tired of waiting for the end of slavery and offered to share the costs. State legislators proposed a compensated emancipation plan that would shift the costs of emancipation to free Black taxpayers.[96] Calculations suggested that it would only cost each taxpaying African American citizen a few dollars. For many this probably seemed a small price to pay for the end of slavery and the institution's hold over their loved ones who remained subject to gradual abolition. The special tax would compensate the state's remaining enslavers after an assessment process that would determine how much each individual enslaver was owed. The proposed act also included an additional fee to be levied against free African Americans who entered the state. Even as they agreed on how to end slavery, Pennsylvania legislators still tried to stem the tide of African American population growth. A month later, the legislature passed the act. The state senate failed to take up the bill, and compensated emancipation remained unlegislated by this and future sessions.[97]

While this plan was debated by politicians, the PAS, like their later abolitionist counterparts, continued to lobby for immediate and uncompensated abolition instead. The PAS worried that the legislation set a bad precedent. They argued that the state's willingness to tax only African Americans could lead to future discrimination. Echoing the ideas expressed by second-wave abolitionist groups like the American Anti-Slavery Society, the PAS further believed that to pay for emancipation was to admit the validity of slavery and thus undermine the principle of equality, which they believed in and was assumed by the state constitution.[98] Clearly, so was slavery and the remaining forms of unfreedom in the state, but that matter was left for another session. Although the PAS actively assisted individual African Americans in gaining their freedom by paying for it, the society could not support a broad plan for compensated emancipation. This differentiation between individual cases of compensation and rewarding slaveholders as a class would remain an issue for the abolition movement.

Taking into consideration their own and their communities' experiences with buying freedom, Pennsylvania's free African Americans offered to make that same sacrifice by paying for the freedom of others. Despite the bill's failure, this was a collective effort on the part of Black Pennsylvanians to buy the state out of the business of slavery once and for all. The state's African Americans worked to negotiate a practical and lasting freedom at any cost. In doing so, they also stood in opposition to the PAS's lobbying plan.[99]

Despite gradual emancipation laws, African Americans in the North in the early republic paid a steep price for freedom.[100] They did so with time and money. Their stories show the complicated history of manumission in the North and the importance of compensation in accelerating the process of emancipation. They depended on a layered web of community support to successfully escape slavery.

As slavery faced slow destruction in the North, slave states like those surrounding Pennsylvania became ever more entangled with the institution as enslavers and their political allies expanded slavery's power and geography with the territorial growth of the United States. For the enslaved in the South, there was no end of slavery in sight. The centrality of the institution to the region's economy shaped access to manumission and the means of compensation. Enslaved people in the South faced conditions that were much different than in states where African Americans took hold of gradual abolition. For those in the Upper South, the domestic slave trade would come to define the economics of both slavery and buying freedom. The trade meant that enslaved people virtually guaranteed value for their enslavers. Despite changing uses of slavery in the Upper South, the domestic slave trade ensured that the institution remained profitable. The growth of free African American communities in the region during the first decades of the United States, although slower than in states like Pennsylvania, also worried enslavers and white people there. In response, state legislatures looked for ways to restrict this growth and the rights of those who were already free. One of the ways they did this was by making manumission more difficult. Still, opportunities to buy freedom remained possible in the border states across most of the remainder of the nineteenth century. African Americans were determined to make use of self-purchase no matter how constricted their opportunities were. In the Deep South, on the other hand, opportunities for moneymaking were difficult to come by, and manumission would become near impossible to achieve.

Even with the greater difficulty, African Americans in the North would have recognized many of the dangers their counterparts in the South faced when trying to buy their freedom. Indeed, some of them, like Ben Jackson's wife, would have experienced these difficulties along with their friends and loved ones who escaped slavery. While interracial networks were crucial to securing viable terms for self-purchase in the North, enslaved people in the South also depended on the extensive social and economic networks that they built with free African Americans, southern whites, and sometimes even abolitionists to successfully buy their freedom. In the South, many of these networks would mirror the larger markets on which slavery depended in the forms of cash, credit, and social capital. The enslaved transformed these market relations into opportunities for liberation because, as enslaved people everywhere knew, their very lives depended on it.

CHAPTER 2

"Plans for Money-Making"

Financing Freedom in the South

According to his narrative, Lunsford Lane was just ten or eleven years old when he was put to work by Sherwood Haywood in Raleigh, North Carolina. As he began to labor for Haywood, Lane was introduced to the full weight of slavery. Indeed, work was how many enslaved children were introduced to their status. Prompted by their parents, Haywood's children now gave him orders. They learned to read while literacy remained one of the gravest offenses for the enslaved. Lane, a child himself, spent his time laboring and living in fear of being sold away from his family. Instead of learning the alphabet, the education Lane received taught him that he faced the sprawling and repeating terror of being "entirely under the control" of the Haywood family.

Lane, like most other enslaved people, worried about being "sold away" to the "far South" and described it as the "worst of all calamities." This fact of life weighed heavily on him. Although he had little hope of escape, he contemplated constantly how he might get free. One day, while he was in this "state of mind," Lane described how his father gave him a basket of peaches that he sold for thirty cents. This was the first money that ever came into Lane's possession. According to Lane's biographer, Craig Friend, Lane's father, Ned, was a skilled gardener who landscaped and tended the gardens where he was enslaved.[1] Despite belonging to his enslaver, Ned may have cultivated the peaches himself and taken them as a sweet reward for his son. In doing so he taught his son a vital lesson about freedom, one that was not just economic. As he collected other small sums in a variety of ways, Lane began to hope that he would eventually be able to purchase his freedom. This hope made him "long for money; and plans for money-making took the principal possession" of his thoughts.[2]

Like many enslaved people who purchased their freedom in the mid-nineteenth-century South, Lane made money through a variety of methods. In the early stages, he cut wood for twenty-five cents a load and did other tasks in the "dead of night" after he had completed his work for the day. He did this independent night work at the risk of punishment by his enslaver in the morning light. In these ways, Lane made his first hundred dollars, which was a long way from thirty cents, especially for an enslaved person. Lane would move on to selling tobacco with the help of his father.[3] Eventually he was allowed to hire his time and sold the tobacco to whoever would buy it, including members of the state legislature.[4] Yet, just as Lane harbored his dreams of being free, he kept the money he saved a secret and worried about what might happen to it. Like Lane himself, it technically belonged to his enslaver. In 1829, Lane entered an agreement with Eleanor Haywood, the widow who was now his enslaver, to pay her $1,000 for his freedom. It took him six years to save the money. By 1842, Lane had also purchased the freedom of his wife, Patsy, and their seven children: Laura, Edward, William, Lunsford, Maria, Ellick, and Lucy. He paid some $3,000 dollars and risked his life, which we will return to later, to do so.[5]

Lane was not alone in longing for money in nineteenth-century America, nor was he alone in thinking it could bring him some kind of freedom. Many American pockets were lined with money made by enslaved people's labor and lives. As workers, the enslaved produced the goods that made the southern economy function. They were not only its main source of labor but, as property, were also bought and sold as chattel and used to secure credit.[6] In southern markets, white Americans turned African Americans into slaves as they made their own fortunes and the social order in which they ruled, as Walter Johnson has argued.[7]

While enslaved and unfree people in the North took advantage of gradual abolition to buy their way out of slavery, their counterparts in the South would have to do so as the institution became still more profitable and powerful in the region. Slavery was not going anywhere quietly or easily, as members of the founding generation may have hoped. Some worried about this commercialization, or what J. W. C. Pennington had called the "bill of sale principle," and what it meant for the "paternal obligations" of enslavers and their power over the enslaved and markets. No one who had been through the process of self-purchase would have been confused about the paternalism of those who made them pay for freedom.[8]

Slavery's capitalism was built so that enslavers controlled the lives, time, and labor of the enslaved. Enslavers' interest in increasing the profitability and efficiency of slavery also led them to make use of the economic interest of their slaves. As Justene Hill Edwards has shown, the market participation of enslaved people "became an aspect of the capitalist economy of slavery." By the mid-1830s, as Hill Edwards claims, this was happening "more directly than in previous generations."[9] This was not the only way enslavers tried to make slavery work for them in this period.

Sales of enslaved people in the domestic slave trade, which moved them from the Upper South to the newly incorporated lands in the Southeast, increased after the official close of the transatlantic slave trade in 1808. This affected the terms of the commodification of the enslaved and the role of slavery in regional and national economies.[10] The threat of sale was how Lane's commodification presented itself in his daily life. Yet it was under these precise conditions in which his labor, and therefore his freedom, had commercial value. It was something he could buy because it was something his enslaver would sell because they could make money from it, just as they could through the slave trade. As people who held financial value as property, the enslaved understood themselves to be at the whim of these markets. The slave market often determined the price for which they could have their freedom.

Using research into market values from the late eighteenth century to the Civil War, Daina Ramey Berry found that enslaved people had average values at sale ranging from $236 for an enslaved girl under ten to $792 for an older adult man. These prices depended on time, place, market demands, age, skill, gender, and health. Enslaved people were often worth very much more.[11] At these prices, the enslaved were often one of their enslaver's most valuable assets. As their lives depended on their enslavers' financial health, many enslaved people had an idea of what they were worth, and they saved and negotiated the cost of their freedom accordingly. Lane, for instance, assumed while saving money to buy himself that his enslaver would take $1,000 for his freedom. He was right.

When Lane said he feared being sold "far South," he reflected his immediate fear of being taken away from his family but also commented on the role that the domestic slave trade and the commodification of the enslaved played in their everyday lives. It has been estimated that one million enslaved people were sold across state lines in the forty years between 1820 and 1860. Enslaved people who lived in the Upper South were particularly vulnerable to sale in the mid-nineteenth century, but the trade shaped everyone's lives and the process of buying freedom.[12] If one was lucky enough not to be sold, one always had to fear it. If you were unlucky enough to be sold, you were faced with the unknown and forced to rebuild your life somewhere new. The slave trade was a constant companion to enslaved people's lives. It marked them as property and as people who were at the whim of others. It made them want to escape slavery any way they could.

Since the economy that shaped their lives depended on their subordination as property, the enslaved were, in theory, excluded from the markets that determined their status. This was certainly the case for the slave market. While the slave trade was a large-scale and regional, if not national, threat to enslaved people, like so many other parts of the economy it often worked at the individual level. As many sales were done through "private bargaining," the enslaved could make use of the smaller-scale aspects of the slave trade to influence negotiations, just as enslavers did with their neighbors, friends, and debtors.[13] Their knowledge of people, market price, value, and their simultaneous refusal to understand their value as only that which defined their price, to return to Berry's idea of "soul value," could sometimes help the enslaved turn a market for their lives into a market for freedom.[14] This was no easy transition. Slaves, after all, were not meant to be free. They were the antithesis to freedom.

Thus, in working to buy freedom, African Americans not only faced economic and legal challenges to compensated manumission, but they countered slavery's very political economy as they made use of its market to free themselves. They attempted, in whatever ways possible, to realign the systems of capital that threatened Black freedom and family in favor of their liberation. Self-purchase worked to repudiate the market of slavery as the enslaved could buy themselves into legal personhood, if not full citizenship, through emancipation.[15]

The enslaved were independent economic actors. Like others, they started businesses that answered the needs of their community, hired themselves out, and worked independently in addition to the labor they were required to perform for their enslavers.[16] As with the men and women who traded them, enslaved people's participation in local markets gave them access to consumer goods, cash, and credit. Their market participation also allowed them to build connections and network with others in their community, and so African Americans entered networks of trust, credit, and exchange that would have been familiar to many in the period.[17]

As American trade expanded across the continent, the nation's economy increasingly depended on finance and credit that linked faraway regions together. Credit depended on trust and ways of knowing both the quality of the product and the reliability of fellow traders. Trust and credit were linked in early American business through slave-produced commodities and the value of enslaved people. This happened as national banking and standard monetary values continued to work themselves out behind quickly expanding markets dependent on the institution. As Calvin Schermerhorn has noted, "American capitalism hinged on an economy of knowledge." Slavery's economy thus depended not only on money and goods, but on social capital and networks.[18] Freedom's economy did too. As Schermerhorn also describes, the "enslaved were networkers as well as workers."[19] Sometimes the enslaved could still leverage economic opportunity into freedom.

What Lane would come to realize is that while money may have ruled the confines of his life, for the enslaved it was not enough to secure freedom. Thus, while enslaved people across a wide spectrum of experiences throughout the South amassed property, even if their legal claim to that property was tenuous, it remained rarer for self-purchase to occur. No matter what access enslaved people had to money and markets, they had to work toward mastery of their political and social worlds. The threat of separation, sale, or remaining enslaved lay at the intersection of these worlds. The enslaved had to groom social connections to support them when opportunities for self-purchase arose or went amiss. This was as true for gradual abolition in the North as it would become for the enslaved in the South who could not anticipate the end of slavery.

Although most enslaved people in the South would have been able to make some spending money to purchase something nice or necessary for themselves or a loved one, buying freedom meant making and saving money on a scale few could easily afford. Freedom was expensive and a serious investment. It was the most important investment unfree people could make. As far as making money is concerned, Lane's story is exemplary, although by no means simple. There are a few common characteristics of those who were the most successful at buying freedom. First, many had a special skill or product to sell. Second, they were able to hire themselves out and make money from their labor.[20] Those with access to urban markets also had an easier time. For a variety of economic, legal, and social reasons, these conditions would remain easier to achieve in the Upper South. As was true in the rural North, where slavery remained stronger and self-purchase rarer, however, the enslaved in the Deep South and rural outposts still made their own opportunities to buy freedom.

Slave hiring, through which Lane and so many others made money for their freedom, was another mechanism to ensure the profitability of slavery that the enslaved could sometimes use to make money and connections. Across the South, hiring allowed enslavers to recoup their investment in people. These arrangements were convenient because during the rental term, enslavers did not have to care for the enslaved. Paying for their housing, food, and clothing was left to the person who rented them, or to the enslaved if they had hired themselves out. The benefits to the enslaver of hiring arrangements were twofold: it cut costs and brought in cash payments for the labor of the enslaved. While in many states hiring was illegal because it provided the enslaved with some independence, its economic rewards made many turn a blind eye. Because it offered them something akin to wages, and thus more money than they could get through almost any other venture, enslaved people made frequent use of hiring to make the money they needed to buy freedom.

Hiring arrangements were no utopian solution to slavery for either enslavers or the enslaved. Most often these arrangements were made to the distinct disadvantage of the enslaved. In many instances of self-hire, a large portion of the money made by the enslaved would go to their owner. Some people also faced harsh conditions as renters of human beings did not necessarily have concern for their long-term well-being.[21] Even under the best of circumstances, these arrangements also caused many to balk at the oppression of slavery that forced them to turn over their earnings to someone who was unjustly entitled to their labor.[22]

Enslavers worried about the independence and dissatisfaction that hiring could produce in the enslaved. Some claimed that hiring gave enslaved people too much independence. They believed that hiring was a threat to slavery and the racial order of their communities. In Kentucky one author complained that both free African Americans and enslaved people hiring their time "need[ed] weeding very much." This complaint collapsed freedom with the practice of self-hire, and both needed to be done away with. The *Jackson Mississippian* reported that there was no "greater evil" than allowing the enslaved to hire their own time. According to the paper, it was an "unlawful privilege" that the enslaved used as a "license for all manner of rascality." Recognizing the independence that self-hiring could produce, the paper claimed that those who hired themselves were a bad influence and poor "companion of the slave." When self-hire led to freedom, it is not difficult to see why some enslavers were worried.[23]

Like self-purchase itself, hiring and self-hiring agreements were most common in urban areas and among skilled workers. In addition to money, hiring out and access to urban work and living enhanced opportunities for enslaved people to build relationships with free African Americans and white people besides their enslavers. Self-hiring could thus allow enslaved people to amass capital, both social and economic. These conditions were especially common in the Upper South but not exclusive to the region. Urban living also influenced trends in self-purchase, as many enslaved workers in cities or who were hired out did not live with family members.[24] Buying freedom could bring families back together under these circumstances.

Lott Cary was born enslaved in Charles City County, Virginia. Beginning in 1804, Cary was hired out by his enslaver and worked as a laborer at a tobacco warehouse in Richmond's Shockoe Bottom. Cary joined other enslaved people who packed and shipped tobacco grown by others like them outside the city. After learning to read and write and proving his usefulness, Cary began to supervise shipments. As a trusted worker, he was given opportunities to make extra money here and there, some of which he made by selling discarded pieces of tobacco.[25]

By 1813, Cary had saved $850, which he used to purchase his freedom and that of his two young children. His wife had died before he was able to buy her. In 1820, Cary made $800 a year as a free worker in a supervisory role. Enslaved people made much less when hired and had to give their enslaver some, if not all, of their salaries. Lunsford Lane, for instance, paid Eleanor Haywood $100–120 a year for the privilege of hiring himself.[26] We can imagine how hard Cary had to work during the ten years he was hired at the warehouse to save that much money.

Cary's success was not only about money. Through his skill and reliability, Cary positioned himself to be useful to his employer. While he was enslaved, he was rewarded with special opportunities including those that helped him raise extra money to buy his family's freedom. When he decided to leave Richmond as a free man, his employer even offered to raise his pay by $200 more a year to get him to stay. By 1821, Cary had found another calling as a Baptist minister and missionary. That year he joined a group of Virginia settlers who sailed for the American Colonization Society's colony of Liberia on the west coast of Africa to found the town of Monrovia.[27]

Not everyone was as successful as Cary in turning hiring into legal freedom. Like Cary, Caroline Taylor hired her time in Norfolk, another Virginia city. During the mid-1840s, Taylor hired herself out for $75 a year. Taylor also had two children. To protect her eleven-year-old daughter, Taylor hired her for $24 a year. This meant that Taylor paid her enslaver for access to her own daughter, who would have been hired out to labor for a stranger otherwise. Taylor's other child was not old enough to be hired out and so Taylor was able to keep the child with her in return for paying for all their expenses. For her enslaver, this meant that Taylor, as both hired and hirer, paid for the entire family's expenses. From her perspective, this was probably a small price to pay to maintain control over her children. Like Dorcus Tonkins, who purchased and indentured her daughter, Temperance, from a New Jersey enslaver, Taylor tried to keep her daughter close and to give her something like freedom for as long as she could. Unlike

Temperance, however, Taylor's daughter was not paid for. She was, in effect, only renting her daughter's freedom.

It probably helped that the Taylor family was enslaved by an absentee owner from New York. Peter March appeared to be content to let them stay together if he did not have to give their care any concern. As a bonus, he made some money from what Taylor paid him. That uncertain freedom that she paid for dearly did not last. What Lane had feared most, Taylor was soon to experience when March made an appearance in Norfolk to arrange for her sale. The asking price was $2,000. Taylor was described as "refined" and "intelligent" and biracial. Her children were "almost fair enough to pass for white." Taylor was certainly valuable, but the high price in combination with these descriptions might tell us something about what she feared would happen to her or her daughter: being sold for sex and all manner of gendered violence in what was known as the fancy-girl trade.[28] Given her parental responsibilities and the cost of keeping her family together, this was probably too high a price for her freedom, if she had ever considered paying for it. Instead, Taylor stole it. She escaped with her children from the port city by boat. When she arrived in Philadelphia, she told her story to the abolitionist William Still.[29]

Henry Wright, enslaved on a plantation outside of Atlanta, Georgia, remembered that his enslaver, Phil House, encouraged skilled trades among the people he enslaved because it would increase their value and thus add to his investment. According to Wright, House hired out the enslaved to white craftsmen to learn trades like masonry and carpentry. Wright described how the enslaved trained in this way were allowed to hire themselves out and, after House had "taken his share," could use their earnings to buy their freedom. Thus the hiring arrangements and the trades that benefited House could be used by the enslaved who sought liberation. These skills, however, would have added to their value and thus the price of their emancipation, just as it would have raised their sale price in the slave market, as House banked on.[30]

While hiring was relatively common for people who purchased their freedom, enslaved people would have more commonly made their own money through other means. Most made it by growing their own crops, trading other goods, and laboring for themselves when possible.[31] Those enslaved across the

South found ways to participate in their local economies to raise money to buy freedom. They did so even though much of that economic activity was considered illegal. There were many ways they made money. They were paid for overwork, or laboring beyond the tasks required by an enslaver. They could sometimes receive incentive pay, in which they were paid for work done well, quickly, or beyond what was required of them. While these opportunities to make money depended on their enslavers and what their community needed or allowed, different labor systems also mattered. Task systems, common in the Deep South and in the production of cash crops, allowed the enslaved to build out daily or weekly time for independent work, although they could only do so after grueling labor. Under this system, each enslaved person was assigned a task that they had to complete. Once they had done so they were free to use their time for their own purposes. Task systems were essential to the accumulation of property by the enslaved.[32]

From 1936 to 1938, workers at the Federal Writers' Project, part of the Works Progress Administration's larger New Deal programming, collected some two thousand oral histories from formerly enslaved people across the South.[33] In many of these stories, formerly enslaved people recalled how those around them made money. Some linked those practices to buying freedom. Taken down, as they were, during the Great Depression, these narratives certainly reflect the contemporary economic needs and desires of those who had lived through slavery. Their historical context informs the ways that the interviewees remembered how enslaved people could make money and what that money could do. Still they provide clues as to the varied ways enslaved people made money.

Amanda Jackson, who was born on a plantation outside of Davisboro, Georgia, was asked directly about opportunities for self-purchase. She recalled that the only people she knew to "go free" were those whose enslavers "willed" them enough money to do so. As might be imagined, Jackson claimed that there were "mighty few" who were successful.[34] This would have been something like winning the lottery, which, of course, did happen at least once, to Denmark Vesey. William Porter, interviewed in Arkansas, recalled that his father was working to buy his freedom when the Civil War ended. Porter's father worked at "night for himself" by splitting rails and raising watermelons to sell.[35] In Louisiana, Gus Clark remembered that his father said that the enslaved were given every other

Saturday to themselves. Those on his plantation would cut wood to make extra money. They were paid one dollar a cord. The men would cut two cords a day and the women one. Sometimes the men would be able to buy themselves from their enslaver. He claimed that they could save the money because they did not have to pay for anything else since their enslaver paid for their care.[36] Not all enslaved people would agree.

Describing his enslavement in Virginia in the years before the Civil War, Duncan Gaines recalled that enslaved people on his plantation were also allowed to work for themselves on their own time. Like Lane, they did so at night "by the light of a torch." They grew food and cared for animals they could sell. Gaines described how those he knew earned enough money for "small luxuries." Here, unlike Gus Clark's claim, the money the enslaved made went to all varieties of goods. These were often things that their enslaver, who benefited from their unfree and unrequited daily labor, did not furnish. These were items purchased for pleasure and subsistence. Gaines also made it a point, however, to state that while the most "ambitious" among them could sometimes save enough money to buy their freedom, this practice was "not encouraged very much."[37] Freedom was not meant to be a luxury of the enslaved.

Jonathan Thomas's story of saving money to buy his freedom by overwork fills out these WPA narratives and shows just how long and uncertain a process saving enough money for freedom could be. Thomas was from Kentucky and entered into an agreement with his enslaver, Henry Beale, to purchase his freedom for $1,000 in the mid-1840s. Thomas, who was a millwright by trade, planned to pay Beale in installments with money he made through his extra labor. When the *NASS* described Thomas's payment plan, the paper claimed that he would not have paid off his freedom until he was fifty-two years old. With the addition of interest, the paper calculated that Thomas would have had to pay an extra $930. The cost for his freedom would have amounted to $1,930. This was above market value for a man his age.[38]

Thomas had paid almost $400 toward his freedom when he faced another difficulty, this time a legal one. Beale's son had taken over his father's estate and refused to recognize the agreement his father had with Thomas. While Thomas could have tried to petition the courts for recognition, the enslaved had no guaranteed legal standing. Instead, Thomas, like Caroline Taylor, decided to take his freedom. In fleeing to Canada, he was forced to forfeit his investment of $400 and left it behind to enhance the wealth of the Beale family. Still, he had stolen something worth much more to his enslaver—himself. From Thomas's perspective, his freedom was priceless.

We can only guess at the kind of risk-versus-reward calculus that Thomas made in deciding to escape. Although he may have trusted Beale, he had taken a risk in entering into this agreement in which he could lose his investment and freedom due to forces just like the ones he would experience. When his new enslaver took Thomas's money, he also took his own kind of risk in not holding up the agreement. Perhaps he miscalculated that someone who wanted to buy their freedom would not run away. He would keep the money and the slave. Thomas's decision, on the other hand, was surely based, at least partly, in recognizing his freedom's value beyond the price he had already agreed to pay. Anger at the injustice of his situation was probably another part of his accounting. No matter how Thomas determined to run, in this instance, his risk paid off. He made it to Canada, where his family later joined him.[39] While many who tried to purchase their freedom did so because they preferred the security of legal freedom, some, like Thomas, were prepared to get it no matter what it cost.

The enslaved also financed freedom by using special skills to fulfill the needs of their communities. In *Incidents in the Life of a Slave Girl*, Harriet Jacobs's famous slave narrative published in 1861, she describes the roles that skill, talent, and labor played in her family's quest for freedom. Living in Edenton, North Carolina, Jacobs's family was industrious. Her father was a particularly talented carpenter who traveled great distances when called on to lead construction projects. He hired himself out for $200 a year. Her grandmother was a skilled baker who made crackers "so famous in the neighborhood" that she received permission to bake at night when her work was done. In exchange, she had to clothe her family with the money she made.[40] Both Jacobs's father and grandmother valued their talents because they offered an avenue to seek freedom for their loved ones and to secure familial bonds.

Just like Lunsford Lane did with tobacco, Jacobs's grandmother Molly Horniblow created a market for her business through talent, social networks, and economic savvy. She, too, tried to use it for freedom. When Horniblow's enslaver died, her youngest son was sold so that each white child inherited an equal share of the estate. The rest of Horniblow's children were "divided" evenly. The sale was a "terrible blow" for Jacobs's family, but her grandmother set out to work with "renewed energy" to purchase her remaining children to protect them from exactly this kind of sale and separation.[41]

Eventually, Jacobs's grandmother saved $300, which her enslaver then requested as a loan. Horniblow turned her savings over to her enslaver, trusting their honor to repay the money she had worked so hard to raise to buy her family. Jacobs's grandmother never saw the money again. Horniblow's savings were used to purchase a silver candelabra. When her enslaver died, she requested repayment for her loan from the executor of the estate. She was told that because the estate was insolvent, she could not get her money back. Jacobs noted that a "slave, being property can hold no property" and that no promise is "legally binding." There was little she could do to recoup so great a loss.

The estate did not sell the candelabra to settle any debts. In fact, Jacobs recalled, the candelabra would be "handed down in the family, from generation to generation." Thus, like her children, the money raised by Jacobs's grandmother to ensure generational freedom within her own family was instead transformed into part of the white family's inheritance. The parallels between Jacobs's family and the silver candelabra, both helping to maintain a legacy of white wealth, contrast vividly with the ways Jacobs describes the economic activities within her family and their attempts to secure the ultimate legacy of freedom.[42] The history of Jacobs's family shows that obstacles to familial freedom were great.[43] It also stands as witness to an intergenerational interest in buying freedom. Jacobs weaves the hope that money engenders in her family, as well as its perils, into her narrative. Access to money and its possibilities for freedom became a part of her familial legacy.[44]

As Jacobs showed, African American families and communities had their own patterns of property accumulation and inheritance. These traditions were essential to the ways that African Americans understood their enslavement and their social, economic, and kinship positions in southern society at large.

Certainly how property was won, maintained, and passed down through generations, and across family groups, helped to define relationships in enslaved and local communities. This was quite literally true in the case of buying freedom. Within families who labored to buy each other out of slavery, the relations between property and kinship were represented by the freedom of mothers, grandmothers, fathers, friends, sons, sisters, daughters, and brothers.[45]

Jacobs also described how these patterns could be interrupted by the institution of slavery and the property and inheritance patterns of white people.[46] Familial life under slavery was shaped first by the confines of *partus sequitur ventrem*, which made slave status inheritable through the lineage of the mother. When enslaved people made decisions about buying freedom, they asked practical questions about gender, property, and status. These categories also influenced how the labor of making and saving money would be done within kin groups. For many kinds of people, including the enslaved, the family unit or household was how they understood economic activity.[47] As is true with many of the cases described here, the economic and social position of enslaved people affected their ability to succeed, and they had to work toward freedom together.

At times, self-purchase was necessary to even enter familial relationships. Joseph Leonidas Star from Knoxville, Tennessee, described how his father worked to buy his freedom for "just a little of somethin'" to marry a free woman. Star claimed that a slave could not "marry a free'd person."[48] While enslaved people did indeed marry free people across the South, although no slave marriage was recognized by law, we see in Star's comments how an interest in freedom affected Black marital relationships and what kind of familial legacy self-purchase could provide.

If both parents were free, they could better care for and protect their families from separation and ensure their children would be free too. Ellen Craft, who was enslaved in Georgia, was separated from her mother when she was a child. This experience meant that the possibility of motherhood under slavery filled Craft's "very soul with horror." Her husband, William Craft, accepted this "important view of her condition." They planned to escape slavery before they got married. After an escape that will be described later, the Crafts refused to purchase their freedom when faced with recapture. Instead they left for England, where they had five children. The family would not return to the United States until after the Civil War, when they became legally free through general emancipation.[49]

Elizabeth Keckley thought about enslaved motherhood similarly to Ellen Craft. Rather than run away, Keckley made buying freedom a condition of her marital vows because she refused to bring another enslaved child into the world. She would not add "one single recruit to the millions bound to hopeless servitude." Once she had secured an arrangement with her enslaver, Hugh Garland, Elizabeth's marriage to James Keckley took place in Garland's parlor in St. Louis, Missouri. We can only imagine what Keckley, a talented but overworked seamstress who supported the entire Garland family with her creations, might have worn that day.

Soon after her wedding, Keckley discovered that even if she was going to purchase herself and son, her family would not be completely free from slavery. She found out that her husband was still a slave, despite having passed himself off as a free man. Not only was he enslaved, Keckley also found him to be so "dissipated" that he was incapable of being the "helpmate" Keckley had imagined when she married him. As someone whose labor already supported her enslaver's family, Keckley likely imagined married life to be about shared responsibilities and care. While Keckley refused to speak ill of her husband, this must have been a blow to her dreams of living in freedom as a family.[50]

Despite the disappointment she found in marriage, Keckley continued to work for years as a seamstress, slowly saving money for freedom. Looking back, she complained how the years seemed to pass by, each one finding her still enslaved. Her dressmaking business brought her into close contact with customers who proposed numerous schemes to raise the money she needed more quickly, including traveling to New York. When that plan fell through, one such customer offered to raise the money among her "friends in St. Louis." On November 13, 1855, Keckley and her son George were at last "free by the laws of man and the smile of God."[51]

Keckley facilitated her emancipation with the connections she made through her successful seamstress business. Despite the assistance of her "lady patrons," Keckley took the money as a loan. Like Mary Holliday, she worked to pay them back. The loan of $1,200 was no small debt, and although she claimed to pay it off quickly, "too close occupation" with her sewing contributed to her poor health and exhaustion.[52] Freedom was labor.

In 1860, Keckley left her husband and moved to Washington, DC. In the city she continued to design dresses and became a sought-after dressmaker for DC elites, including the wife of Jefferson Davis, who would soon become president of the Confederacy. Later, she worked for the First Lady of the United States, Mary Todd Lincoln. Keckley never commented fully on what it felt like to discover that her husband was enslaved as she labored to be legally free. Yet, once free, she left him behind to start a new life for herself and son. If Keckley ever thought of buying his freedom too, she did not mention it in her narrative. The familial complications of slavery and freedom were many.

As in earlier periods, buying one's entire family could be an incredibly daunting and complex process. Growing families added to the cost of freedom, and being separated by sale could mean permanent disunion. Sale could also mean the involvement of new enslavers, which could complicate matters even further. Given the confines in which enslaved people acted, buying a family member did not always lead to manumission and legal freedom. Instead, it sometimes led to what can be understood as a kind of familial slavery. When he wrote his will in 1818, Lewis Turner, a free Black farmer from Sussex County, Virginia, hoped to emancipate his wife, Aggai. Turner had purchased his wife and continued to hold her enslaved. Turner owned his wife because, in 1806, Virginia law required that anyone emancipated in the state leave within twelve months or face reenslavement.[53]

While these laws were not always enforced, Turner's will shows that he was still cautious about how his death would affect his wife and her freedom. He was also aware of changes in state manumission laws. Turner directed the executor of his estate to petition the legislature to allow Aggai to remain in Virginia after her emancipation according to law. If that petition was refused, Turner directed that Aggai be turned over to his nephew, a free person of color. Even if she remained enslaved, Turner ensured via a trust that she would have the continued and full use of his property. Aggai was also to have the continued service of a "black boy" named James Wright who was under the "controul" of Turner until he was twenty-one. Upon Turner's death, Wright was left fifteen acres of land. Given the description of his sizable estate, Wright may have been indentured to Turner by his parents or possibly placed in Turner's care by relatives. As with many other African American families, Turner's household served as a home for people of varied status. The extended Turner family would continue to live with this experience. In December 1818, Turner's estate petitioned the state legislature for Aggai to remain. The petition was rejected and the bill withdrawn.[54]

Other state laws tried to address connections made in mixed-status families like the Turners. These laws affected how they went about ensuring freedom. Starting in 1832, free African Americans like Turner could only purchase enslaved people if they were in their immediate family. In North Carolina, it was unlawful after 1830 for the enslaved to marry or cohabitate with free African Americans. Those couples already doing so were allowed to remain together. In 1826, the state outlawed trade between free African Americans and the enslaved. These laws attempted to sever the social and economic ties that people made across legal status and helped them buy freedom.[55]

For those in the Deep South, who faced even more difficulty and restrictive laws, these familial and community connections were key. In Alabama, where manumissions were severely restricted and required special acts of the legislature as well as bond payments until 1834, the enslaved still managed to buy freedom with help. Around two hundred and twenty-six manumissions are listed in the legislative records from 1818 to 1832. Forty-one, or around 18 percent, of the emancipations reveal evidence of familial purchase and emancipation. Most of these examples come from Mobile, Tuscaloosa, and Madison Counties and show a free person of color as the emancipator. Some record the familial relationships between the emancipator and emancipated, showing that these were cases in which free African Americans purchased loved ones for manumission. Daniel Reed, a free African American man in Washington County, located just north of Mobile, was able to secure the freedom of his wife and at least three children between 1818 and 1830.[56]

Within nuclear family groups the first person to be freed through purchase was often the father figure. This was one of the most important forms of paternal care a father could provide for his enslaved family.[57] Once free, the man, in theory, would be able to get more work and make more money to free the rest of his family. A family might want to secure the freedom of the mother next so that she would no longer be at risk of bearing children who were enslaved, thus adding to the time and money it would take to save their entire family. Women and girls were at risk of sexual abuse and assault and of bearing children who would be born enslaved, as Elizbeth Keckley and Ellen Craft worried. Black families understood the gendered economies that they lived under and that, as Amrita Chakrabarti Myers has written, "slavery and freedom were transmitted through black women's bodies."[58] While the enslaved made strategic decisions, sometimes they had to make decisions based on money and exigency. Sometimes that meant they had to buy whichever family member whose enslaver would allow it or to purchase the freedom of someone who was at particular risk of poor treatment or sale. At other times decisions were based on price and how much money was available. Young children, for instance, might be had for less.[59]

The role of enslaved men in freeing their families partly reflects the precariousness of enslaved women's access to economic opportunity. In discussing mobility for enslaved people, the historian Stephanie Camp has shown how slavery's "geography of containment was somewhat more elastic for men." This allowed men more opportunity for economic activity, which, in turn, led to social connections and business opportunities. In addition, the labor enslaved women had to perform during their off hours was a "more consistent burden."[60] Although women certainly raised money to purchase their freedom, these gendered experiences limited their ability to do so in much of the South, even as it may have been more important to protect the freedom of their families.

Some scholars have also suggested that there was a gendered difference to networking and that people who had a harder time raising the cash they needed "sought and exchanged human resources instead." This meant that women were more dependent on networking and that they used interpersonal relationships and emotion to win access to freedom.[61] While women's enactment of freedom was complex, cash and sentiment were intricately intertwined for both men and women. All African Americans who created alliances in the interest of buying freedom relied on emotion, not just women or those without access to the cash needed to influence the decisions of enslavers. Indeed, it has been well-documented that Black women were also at the forefront of using the law to expand freedom's boundaries.[62]

The manipulation of emotion and the forging of human connection and relationships, no matter how limited, feigned, or regulated by slavery, were central to networking and liberation. Both African American men and women understood this and worked to ensure that they secured networks of freedom in addition to financial means. While women faced different challenges, these strategies were used across gendered lines during negotiations over compensated manumission. Acting in contentious and threatening landscapes, these networks and the relationships made by enslaved people became a lifeline to liberty.

Historians have found that Black women were manumitted more frequently than men and that in many communities they outnumbered free men. They controlled much of the property owned by African Americans in the South in the antebellum era. It has been suggested that women were more frequently manumitted because of their intimate relationships with white men. Given the large representation of women in free Black populations across the South and their extensive property holding, it is likely that their personal relationships, either forced or those they cultivated for security, were far from the only way that they secured manumission.[63]

That African American women were able to free each other suggests this as well. In 1836, the District of Columbia Free Negro Register records that Sabra Wise freed her sixteen-year-old daughter, Sarah Ann Wise, in consideration of one dollar paid by Sarah. Wise had purchased her daughter a month earlier. Some twenty years later, Elizabeth Duncan manumitted her eighteen-year-old daughter, Emily, whom she had previously purchased for fifty dollars. The ages of Sarah Ann Wise and Emily Duncan suggest that their mothers had perhaps worked to emancipate them to shelter their daughters from the gendered threats that young enslaved women faced.[64]

Studying manumission in Washington, DC, in the 1850s, Mary Beth Corrigan's work shows that teenage women were three times more likely to be emancipated, suggesting that enslavers in urban areas did not want to take on the added burden of caring for enslaved children. Despite their future value, some enslavers imagined enslaved children as a drain on their resources because they would only become fully productive later in life. This is probably why Caroline Taylor's enslaver let her keep her children if she paid for them. In addition, due to the local urban labor market and high demand for domestic service, Black women in the district had more access to work than those in other areas of the South. In the antebellum period, women in the district could make fifty to seventy-five cents a day by taking in washing, or eight to ten dollars a month as domestic servants.[65] Although Wise freed her daughter almost two decades before Duncan, they both certainly may have taken advantage of these local economic conditions to free their daughters.

As each of these stories suggests, buying freedom was a precarious business, and more people were unsuccessful than successful. That proportion is one we can never know. Every story of success remains something of a marvel. It was incredibly hard to make money let alone use it for freedom. The enslaved were at risk of failure from numerous avenues, only the most common of which were theft, trickery, sale, and legal barriers to manumission, moneymaking, and contracting for freedom. These dangers were always present. Thomas Jones and his wife, Mary Moore, enslaved in North Carolina, would bury the box in which they kept their freedom savings when they expected visits from the patrollers. Slave patrols were not the only "enemy" they feared. Jones recalled that hearing the "loud ring" of coins being dropped into the box and hitting other coins was enough to cause him "sudden and terrible alarm." He feared any "prowling enemy" who might have heard the sound outside their cabin and steal their "hoarded treasure." While for most people hearing money sound against money would bring a sense of accomplishment and pride or make one greedier for more, for Jones it induced the terror of losing it and thus his family's chance for freedom. Jones had good reason to fear losing this opportunity as he had already lost his first family when his wife's enslaver moved to Alabama.[66]

Enslavers also took advantage of their power. Many enslaved people would have imagined them as the "prowling enemy" Jones feared. Those who wished to buy their freedom were a captive market for the prowling of the people who owned them.[67] The enslaved knew this and always acted accordingly. The control their enslavers had over their lives was precisely why they tried to buy their freedom. The danger of this liminal position would have been just as familiar to Jones and Moore as it was to those who bought themselves out of gradual abolition a generation earlier. Self-purchase was everywhere a type of gradual manumission and one in which freedom was not always guaranteed. The time it took to raise the money or negotiate manumission could be the thief of freedom. Time was only one of many other possible thieves. This was true no matter where one lived or when they tried to buy their freedom. If, as Dylan Penningroth has described, enslaved people's "independent economies were founded on an economy of time," so too was the economy of freedom.[68]

Because of slavery's unequal balance of power, enslaved people in the process of buying their freedom were susceptible to being cheated and, although they tried to use the law, they could not depend on it. Instead, they had to depend on their ability to influence and judge the word of their enslavers and those they called on for support. Recognizing all the possible pitfalls of freedom, many worked to make sure they had some kind of security by amassing social capital. The enslaved knew much about the intricacies of their enslavers' financial situations and understood slavery's local market. Under conditions that threatened their social lives, enslaved communities were forced to watch for signs of financial instability or the possibility of sale, which they could at times turn into opportunities for freedom. The possibility of failure circled around the enslaved. It awaited a mistake, a miscalculation, misplaced trust, a twist of fate, or a slaveholder trick. It lapped at the heels of those seeking freedom. This is also why the enslaved depended on support from those around them and built connections they called on when needed.

When Elisha Tyson, a Maryland Quaker and founding member of the Maryland Abolition Society, stood at the edge of a Baltimore basin, he readily identified the African American man who had been found drowned. The man, recently cheated, had come to Tyson for help. This man, who remains nameless, had supposedly entered into an agreement to pay $500 for his freedom within six years. Surely he could complete such a deal, he must have thought. Six years was a long time. Lunsford Lane raised $1,000 in the same amount of time. The man had already done so well for himself before the six-year term had even expired. He had already paid half the amount he owed. This was when the weight of time came crashing down. After he had paid some $250 for his freedom, his enslaver threatened to sell him. The domestic slave trade had turned this man's dreams into a nightmare. Terrified, the man came to Tyson to ask what could be done to make his enslaver hold up his end of their contract.

When Tyson found that the man had no receipt for the money that he had already paid and that no one had witnessed these payments except his wife, Tyson told the man that "the law was against thee" and he would have to "submit" to the sale. Learning that Tyson believed there was nothing he could do was a crushing blow. The man reacted with what Tyson claimed to be "desperate resolution." With "clenched fist, his eyes raised to heaven, his whole frame bursting with the purpose of his soul" the man declared that he would be dead before the "Georgia man shall have me." Resigning himself to tears, the man claimed that he simply could not be separated from his wife and children in Maryland.[69]

Despite the payments the man had already made, the verbal agreement he had with his enslaver, and the pleas he made to Tyson, Tyson believed, as the law suggested, that the enslaved man had a virtually nonexistent claim to fight his enslaver's breach of contract. While his claim on the law might not have stopped an activist like Isaac Hopper in Pennsylvania, the man's meeting with Tyson left him hopeless. We cannot be sure why, or even if, Tyson did not present the man with other choices, like helping him raise the rest of the money or running away. Perhaps he died accidentally while attempting to escape, or maybe he thought that running away, which still involved being separated from his family, would be as great a burden as being sold. Or he was true to his word and chose death instead of the Georgia man. This man was not alone in deciding that losing his family was the worst of all his options. In studying Black responses to expulsion and reenslavement legislation across the South, historians have found that many of the very limited number of free people who sought "voluntary" enslavement in the antebellum period did so in the interest of maintaining family ties.[70]

Despite Tyson not being able, or willing, to help, this man knew to seek him out for assistance. African Americans across the South looked to forge bonds within their communities to support their efforts to buy freedom. This support came from friends, family, neighbors, employers, partners, even other slaveholders, and sometimes the abolition movement. Through these connections, enslaved and free African Americans worked to situate themselves in the most advantageous position possible from which to negotiate for their freedom. They negotiated permission to hire their time, borrowed money, asked others to intercede on their behalf in legal proceedings, and requested access to family members whom they wished to eventually purchase.

Local strategies and relationships helped to ensure that the enslaved could successfully buy freedom. Another threat of the slave trade was that it could sever the connections they had, familial or otherwise. These networks, necessary to success, show how the process of self-purchase was fundamentally shaped by the actions of the enslaved. Knowing the dangers presented by their position in slave society, African Americans worked across racial lines and across the space between slavery and freedom. These connections, and the ways that they called on them, are also part of how the enslaved valued themselves and their relationships beyond the limits of enslavement.[71]

Most commonly, African Americans worked together to ensure success. Free African Americans throughout the nation used their freedom and capital to invest in the liberation of others, even those to whom they were not directly related. These Black networks were often an extension of family and friendship. If not, other connections could extend the power of, and expand ideas about, kinship. Together they grew communities of freedom. Those who successfully negotiated this network were liberated through the connections made within the Black communities to which they belonged, or those that they made through their efforts.

As in so many other ways, Black churches could be a source of support.[72] When members of the First African Baptist Church in Richmond, Virginia, met in 1843 to discuss church matters they resolved to fund the efforts of a member named Thomas Allen who was trying to buy his freedom for $600. Allen wanted to be free because he was determined to become a foreign missionary in Africa. He wanted to buy his freedom to join the mission of the American Baptist board in Boston, Massachusetts. The church minutes reveal that the First African Baptist Church would not be solely responsible for freeing Allen. He planned to travel to other cities in Virginia to raise money for his cause. Having the support of his church surely opened many doors to him during his travels.

About a year later, the records reveal that, while Allen was successful in purchasing his freedom, the Baptist board had not accepted him as a missionary.

Given this disappointment, Allen requested to resign as a deacon of the Richmond church to become a pastor in New Bedford, Massachusetts. While Allen might have thought there were better opportunities for him to preach his faith in the North, this move may have also been part of his plan to deal with Virginia's removal requirement. He was "granted a cordial dismissal" from the community that had helped him become a free man.[73]

Other African American organizations also played a role in raising money for freedom. In April 1855, the *National Era* reported recent excitement in Washington, DC, over a "private meeting" of African Americans that had been discovered in the city. In raiding the meeting, the authorities had found "scraps of poetry," the constitution of a benevolent society called the Daughters of Jerusalem, and some "handsome regalia" for officers of the society. In addition, they had found a subscription list of donations made for the freedom of a woman named Eliza Howard, which her enslaver had agreed to sell for $650. The meeting was broken up and its members escorted to the "watch-house," where they were held for unlawful assembly.

Following southern slave codes, Washington, DC, prohibited meetings of free and enslaved African Americans. According to the *Era*, the party consisted of four enslaved men and twenty free people of color. As punishment, four of these men were sent to the "work-house," while Joseph Jones, an enslaved man, received corporal punishment in the form of six lashes. The rest were released upon payment of the fine and jail costs, which amounted to over $100. The wealthy abolitionist Gerrit Smith, the antislavery congressman Joshua Giddings, and several other "respectable citizens" contributed to the "liberating fund." The fines paid were more than three times the amount that had been contributed to fund Howard's purchase by the time the meeting was broken up. No mention is made of what became of Eliza Howard's quest for freedom.[74]

The *Era* used this story to deride the slave code of Washington. Still, it tells how African Americans banded together when buying freedom was possible. While African Americans looked to benevolent institutions like these for daily support, Howard's fundraiser brought them together for this larger project. Perhaps discussion of her freedom was the sole purpose of this meeting or just one of many items on their agenda. One of the enslaved men that joined the meeting may have been the group's connection to Howard. They all met at grave risk to help her raise money.

Black community connections were not immune from problems. In Jefferson County, Kentucky, which surrounds Louisville, around 10 percent of manumissions involving money from the beginning of the nineteenth century to 1854 include the involvement of other African Americans. These include familial manumissions (which act as evidence of previous purchase), the naming of other free African Americans as manumitter with no relationship recorded, and cases where free African Americans put forward the security bonds needed to ensure that the emancipated would not become a charge on the state. Several such bonds were put forward by a free African American man named Washington Spralding. Spralding was a Louisville businessman whose father had purchased his freedom. He was known to help other people buy their freedom. His reasons for doing so may not have been solely altruistic but also matters of business.

In 1840, Spralding purchased a woman named Lucy Lattapie with the intent to free her once she had repaid him $350. For unknown reasons, Spralding freed Lattapie even though she still owed him $50. After her emancipation, Lattapie began to work toward purchasing her husband. He was freed four years later. In 1851, Spralding brought Lattapie to the county circuit court claiming nonpayment of the $50 plus interest. He had sued her twice before without success when the final case was dismissed.[75] While he was willing to loan people money to buy their freedom, he was not willing to overlook their debts. As this case shows, freedom networks were often debt networks. The enslaved like Lattapie faced risks and the forces of capitalism no matter to whom they looked for support.

Just as hiring was useful for making money, it could also lead to connections with white people who had power, money, and connections to help the enslaved buy their freedom. Cecilia Thomas was enslaved on a plantation in Charles County, Maryland, just to the south of Washington, DC. When her enslaver died, she and her daughters came under the control of another family member in Alexandria, Virginia. As was so often the case, this spelled bad luck for Thomas. Her new enslaver's husband was dissolute and sold Thomas's children to maintain his bad habits. Probably to help keep the family solvent, Thomas was hired out to a man named Heath Camp in Washington, DC. Eventually Thomas's enslaver sold her while she was pregnant. She arranged to stay with Camp until she gave birth to her daughter.

For good reason, Thomas was afraid of being separated from her husband and losing another child because of her enslaver's financial woes. Camp and Thomas tried to turn the family's need for money to their advantage, convincing a reluctant trader to let Camp purchase Thomas for $400. The trader complained that this was $200 less than he could get for Thomas in the slave markets of the Deep South. Camp helped Thomas expand her support network by appealing to northern abolitionists to raise the money for her freedom. His letter was published in the *New York Evangelist*, and Lewis Tappan and others responded with loans and donations. In November 1834, Thomas and her three-year-old daughter were emancipated by Camp for $375.[76] Camp hoped to hire Thomas's husband and try to help him buy his freedom as well. Thomas was lucky to find someone who acted when she asked for help.

Even though Lunsford Lane was able to successfully purchase his family, he, too, faced difficulties and depended on support. First, Lane could not be emancipated in North Carolina. Instead, he traveled to New York to be officially manumitted by his wife's enslaver, who technically owned him after he had purchased his freedom. As soon as he became free, Lane planned to purchase his family and was working toward it when his life was interrupted by state law. As a free man Lane was now in North Carolina illegally. Lane tried to use his connections, including those with the state legislators he knew from working there, to petition to remain. His request, like that of Aggai Turner in Virginia, was denied. His "network of associations that conferred status did not amount to legal personhood."[77]

Lane's legal freedom had made his very presence illegal and forced his separation from his family. Luckily for Lane, this separation was not permanent. In 1834, Lane unwillingly left North Carolina to try his hand at life in the North, where he would solicit donations for his family's freedom from "friends of the colored man in the North." When Lane returned to complete the purchase of his family, he faced mob violence and was tarred and feathered for being both free and having been tainted by abolition. Shortly after this traumatic experience, Lane and his family left North Carolina for Boston, Massachusetts.[78]

Even desiring freedom could put one at risk and make networking a dangerous endeavor. Peter Still hired himself out in Tuscumbia, Alabama, in the mid-1840s. While hiring himself, Still felt the spark of independence it provided him, just as enslavers feared. This spark made him begin to imagine purchasing his freedom. Still was afraid to trust anyone with his plan in case it caused his enslaver to sell him off as "unsafe property." Still carefully watched the people he knew, looking for someone he could trust with his plan. Despite his distrust and suspicion, in the ultimate nod to the utility of networks, Still realized that he would have to put his trust in someone or he would "never be free." Eventually, Still overheard a local Jewish man named Joseph Friedman make comments that fostered Still's confidence enough that he soon arranged for Friedman to hire him. Still chose wisely. Friedman helped Still with both negotiations and financing. He was able to buy his freedom for $500 with a loan from Friedman that he eventually paid back.[79]

Using his social knowledge with even broader scope, Still decided that if he could use his newfound freedom to get to his relatives in the North, they might be able to help him purchase his wife and children. When Still arrived in Philadelphia, a chance meeting reunited him with his brother, William, and the rest of his long-lost family. William Still and his abolitionist counterparts suggested all manner of plans to reunite the family, including getting someone to travel to Alabama to help them escape. Still was wary of these plans and wished to free them in a legal manner by buying their freedom as he had done for himself.

The abolitionists' preference for illegal action won the day, and a white abolitionist named Seth Concklin was sent to retrieve Still's family. As Still feared, the escape was unsuccessful and his family was taken back to Alabama while Seth Concklin was murdered. Once news of the failed escape reached Still, he again looked to his new networks to secure the legal freedom of his family. A Philadelphia merchant found a contact in Alabama who agreed to buy the Still family for their emancipation. Through an ever-growing network of support that stretched from New York and Philadelphia to Cincinnati and Alabama, Still raised the enormous sum of $5,000 needed to buy their freedom. This network was carefully crafted by Still and others who worked to radiate word of his cause and helped extend Still's individual power.[80]

For Still to emancipate his family, the long-distance communication that was facilitated by his network was key.[81] Communications with lawyers, abolitionists, more supportive enslavers, friends, and family were crucial to assessing the situation back home, or wherever loved ones had ended up. William Still's *The Underground Railroad* includes numerous records of correspondence from abolitionists, fugitives, free people, and enslavers about buying freedom. The connections served to find family, gauge conditions, open negotiations, and levy power and money. For African Americans who were illiterate, this network was indispensable.[82]

Making connections with abolitionists and northerners, while not completely harmless as Lane's story shows, was almost always useful in helping enslaved people buy their freedom or that of loved ones. Activists were not the only people in the North who could help. Formerly enslaved and free African Americans also lived in the North, because they had to by law or because they thought better opportunities awaited them there. Some moved there precisely because those better opportunities could help them buy their loved ones. Those who made it north left behind friends and family. Many spent much of their free lives dedicated to working toward the emancipation of others, if not longing for divine reunion. Buying freedom could bring together those separated across state lines or the barriers between slavery and freedom.

In 1836, the Ohio Anti-Slavery Society published a *Report on the Condition of the People of Color in the State of Ohio*. The report illuminated the prevalence of buying freedom in the state and the separation of families across borders. In addition to documenting individual cases of self-purchase, the report included statistics about self-purchase in the lives of African Americans from two districts within the city of Cincinnati.

One district report centered around 125 African Americans, 95 of whom were formerly enslaved. Twenty-three of these individuals, or 24 percent, had spent $9,112 to free themselves. The report found that of 18 households headed by Black women who were employed as washwomen, 5 had bought their freedom. In the second district surveyed, 69 heads of households had been enslaved. Of these 69 people, 36 had paid for their own freedom and that of 14 children. They had done so for almost $25,000 combined. In this second district, the property held by these families amounted to around $10,000. This was less than half the amount they had invested in liberation. Between the two districts, some 327 family members remained enslaved. Many of these families were still laboring to save additional kin.[83]

This report gives us a sense of what an immense financial undertaking buying freedom could be. It hindered the economic progress of individual families and their communities. It also impeded on other aspects of their lives. The report tells the story of one family whose daughter, when asked why she did not go to school, said, "I'm staying at home to help buy my father." The father was "going out at day's work" while the mother took in washing. The family was also trying to purchase two sons who were still enslaved. Despite the sacrifices they were making for freedom, the family was described as "bearing up under these accumulated wrongs, and struggling onward with a vigor, truly astonishing."[84] As their southern counterparts, who included their friends and family, would have known, working together with the hope of freedom was better than no hope at all.

This report is an important reminder that while buying freedom was experienced differently across different regions, it was central to the lives of many African Americans in the nineteenth-century United States. These interconnections between people, networks, and place should also shape how we understand the process of buying freedom. People moved and took their ideas about slavery, freedom, and self-purchase with them. The desire to be free could not be confined to, or defined by, one place. What African Americans who left slavery and the South would come to see is that slavery's economy was not only regional but shaped the entire nation and their place in it.[85]

As African Americans shared their stories of self-purchase, they helped expose to the world the fact that freedom could be had for a price in the United States.[86] Many argued that, while necessary, buying freedom was not just a marker of the barbarity of slavery but also of the nation's economy and its attendant legal order, which shaped the lives of African Americans no matter where they lived. Buying freedom or being unable to do so caused some to join abolitionists in fighting for slavery's total demise. As a practical matter, self-purchase was hard to critique. In theory, it was certainly up for discussion, and abolitionists would debate its viability as an antislavery tactic for decades to come.

CHAPTER 3

"Ransomed!"

Second-Wave Abolition and Self-Purchase

At 10 o'clock in the morning on December 4, 1833, delegates representing anti-slavery groups from New Hampshire to Ohio opened their meeting with a prayer. The representatives, among whom were men such as Robert Purvis, William Lloyd Garrison, and Lewis Tappan, came together that day in Philadelphia to organize a national abolition society. Over the next three days, the delegates would create the American Anti-Slavery Society (AASS), which would officially usher the abolition movement into its second wave. As with the PAS in an earlier era, the AASS would come to guide the vast majority of abolitionist activism in the United States after 1833. Its founding principle of no compensation for slaveholders would affect how the movement debated self-purchase until the Civil War.[1]

By the end of the convention's third day, the organization was officially constituted under the *Declaration of Sentiments*. William Lloyd Garrison, a leading white abolitionist and publisher of the nation's most important abolitionist newspaper, the *Liberator*, drafted the document at the home of James McCrummell, an African American abolitionist and dentist who lived in Philadelphia.[2] The *Declaration of Sentiments* inscribed the new tenets of the movement. The delegates were sworn to support the "immediate emancipation of slaves, without expatriation." Along with the immediate abolition of slavery and the refusal of colonization, the AASS called for the uncompensated emancipation of all enslaved people in the United States. In doing so, it put the freedom rights of the enslaved above the property rights of their enslavers. Beyond emancipation, members were determined to fight for the full equality of free African Americans.[3]

As for the issue of compensation, AASS members believed that it was morally wrong and economically unsound to compensate enslavers for something that could not belong to them in the first place. Freedom was not a commodity but instead an inalienable right that belonged to everyone.[4] Thus the AASS declared, in blunt opposition to commonly held notions of slaveholding's legality, that slavery itself was a "crime" and freedom was "not an article to be sold." According to the *Declaration*, to pay enslavers for emancipation was a "surrender of the great fundamental principle that man cannot hold property in man." The members thought that if anyone deserved compensation, it was the enslaved.[5]

As the presence at the meeting of Robert Purvis and Thomas Shipley, both important members of the PAS, suggests, second-wave abolition was built not only against old norms but with the previous generation of activists who were still present. It was also conceived within the larger context of transatlantic abolition. The AASS's ideas about what abolition should mean came from what it understood to be the successes and failures of the longer history of the movement. Second-wave activists learned from emancipation in the British Empire, the activism of groups such as the PAS and the American Colonization Society (ACS), and enslaved and free African Americans. Long-standing issues of compensation, colonization, and gradualism all influenced how manumission was treated by antislavery activists across the nation into the nineteenth century. Divides over compensation were not always clearly defined, as activists across the movement responded differently to national events that shifted the terrain of antislavery.

By calling for immediate and uncompensated emancipation, the AASS responded to how ideas about gradual emancipation, racial uplift, and the law had shaped first-wave activists' ideas about buying freedom, as described in the first chapter. Similar to how African Americans shaped buying freedom's place in the early movement, their responses to the changing political landscape and slavery's place in the nation would also help lead to the radicalism of the AASS. By the 1820s, this radicalism took its shape against the apparent limits of gradualism presented by the previous three decades of work and around the heated issue of colonization after the founding of the ACS in 1816.

The ACS was founded in attempt to solve what many believed to be the fundamental problem of abolition: What would happen to free African Americans? Could they be incorporated as free citizens or was America destined to be a white nation? The ACS's answer to the first question, and in response to varying opinions on the second, was to remove them from the United States. Colonization, it claimed, would also benefit African Americans who, once freed from discrimination in the United States, could live up to their fullest potential and make their own case for their freedom and equality. Once African Americans settled on the west coast of Africa, colonizationists could also argue, like most colonial theorists throughout the history of Western empire, that their presence would help "civilize" and Christianize the continent. In these ways, the ACS could, perhaps, help the nation move past the stagnation of antislavery activism in the nation's first decades by gaining the support of enslavers to hasten the end of slavery.

As the work of Beverly Tomek has shown, the reasons people advocated for colonization ranged from anti-Blackness to a sincere commitment to emancipation and racial uplift.[6] Policies shaped by these varying rationales would prove to be an issue for the ACS across its history. Because of its moderate approach and appeal to a wide array of interests, colonization attracted a mix of northern and southern supporters and quickly gained converts across the nation.[7] As with the antislavery organizations that preceded it, the ACS tackled issues of both compensation and manumission.

Throughout the nineteenth century, the ACS transported some 10,000 African Americans to Liberia. The organization's numbers display its difficult path to convincing enslavers to divest from slavery as it became more profitable. They also show the difficulty the ACS had in convincing enslaved and free African Americans to move to Liberia. Of the 10,000 who left for Liberia, 4,500 were born free while around 6,000 were manumitted with the express requirement of removal. A relatively small number, just under 345, had purchased their own freedom. Following in the footsteps of the PAS, the ACS and Pennsylvania Colonization Society sometimes raised money for the purchase of individuals and families so they could be manumitted to Liberia.[8] Of all those who emigrated to Liberia with the ACS, around 3 percent were purchased by the society.[9]

These expenditures on freedom were deemed too impractical for regular practice, as most antislavery groups would agree.

More radical African Americans and their white abolitionist allies questioned the practicality of the entire colonization plan. They believed it was ludi-
crously expensive and constantly fell far short of its goal of sending away African
Americans at the growth rate of either free or enslaved Black communities.[10] In
addition to the problem of politics, this critique was also a problem of funding.
Antislavery advocates, no matter their stance or organizational allegiance, were
fighting for a finite amount of money coming from both philanthropists and
everyday people who supported their cause. Questions about tactics were often
also questions about how to obtain money and how to spend it. Regardless of
the moral qualms one had regarding the practice, no one questioned the fact
that buying freedom was expensive. The white abolitionist and AASS founder
Lucretia Mott claimed that buying the freedom of individuals was an inadvisable
use of movement funds and that activists should adhere to the "overthrow of the
slave system and the emancipation of every slave."[11]

Questioning its use of money was only one tactic that African Americans
used to discredit the ACS. While some free African Americans, at times partnering with the ACS or its members, supported independent emigration plans
to Africa, Canada, and Haiti, most critiqued the inherent anti-Blackness in the
ACS's plan for removal. They claimed that instead of ending slavery, colonization
would strengthen it.[12] The ACS's insistence on colonization, paired with legal
manumissions, concerned abolitionists. William Lloyd Garrison, who originally
supported colonization, described the ACS's work as "a conspiracy based upon
fear, oppression, and falsehood."[13] Indeed, according to Ousmane Power-Greene,
by the 1830s African Americans were fighting "on two fronts: one against slavery
and the other against colonization."[14] This fight would shape the radical politics
of second-wave abolition and would require the movement to push beyond reli-
ance on legal methods like manumission. This was true even as Black activism
and action continued to keep self-purchase relevant to their activism.

An 1833 article in the *Liberator* critiqued the ACS's efforts to buy the freedom of slaves to send them to Africa. The author claimed that to do so without
the total abolition of slavery would only lead enslavers to replace their human

property with the money they made from "northern citizens."[15] Beyond the
moral issue of purchasing people who were inherently free, this author suggested
that abolitionists who spent money on buying people's freedom were partici-
pants, if unwilling ones, in the slave market. Although the money they invested
secured the release of enslaved people, it went directly into the pockets of enslavers who could spend it however they pleased. This author's framing speaks to the
importance of noncompliance with slavery, which would influence all facets of
second-wave activism. However, while some abolitionists believed this noncompliance should apply to all matters of compensation, others made an important
distinction between compensating slaveholders as a class and ransoming individual slaves. In this regard, the movement would learn from England.

Beyond disagreement with the ACS, AASS opposition to compensation
was partly a response to the British Emancipation Act of 1833. Emancipation in
the British Empire caused much discussion among abolitionists in the United
States. Despite years of imperfect reforms meant to ameliorate the condition
of the enslaved in the British colonies of the Caribbean, the enslaved and abolitionists in England remained unsatisfied with the state of slavery in the empire.
Reforms, of course, could not rid slavery of the horrors that were foundational to
the institution. Rebellion in Jamaica around Christmas of 1831, combined with
the renewed vigor of abolitionists, finally pushed the British government to create legislation to abolish slavery.[16]

In 1833, Parliament voted not only to enact gradual emancipation, which
included a mandatory period of apprenticeship for the newly freed, but also to
further compensate West Indian enslavers with both the additional labor of the
apprenticeships and cash. The bill set aside £20 million to pay for enslavers' capital
losses.[17] The payment of such a large sum of money was the result of a compromise over the length of apprenticeship. In reducing the apprenticeship period by
half to appease abolitionists, Parliament tacked on another £5 million to satisfy
slaveholders and their representatives. The apprenticeship system soon dissolved
because of the resistance of the formerly enslaved.[18] Full emancipation was enacted
in the British West Indies on August 1, 1838.[19] Despite its missteps, the British
government had managed to end slavery within the empire's borders. It did so as
slavery and its influence were rapidly expanding within the United States.

Although the English model was thought to be unworkable in the United States, British abolition was greeted with celebration. A month after the official end of the apprenticeship system, the *Liberator* published "Glorious News from the West Indies!" for its American audience. The edition shared news of emancipation from across Jamaica.[20] African American communities and the abolition movement commemorated Emancipation Day on August 1 along with their English counterparts. One such celebration was held at the Belknap Street Church in Boston, Massachusetts. The speaker, S. R. Alexander, hoped that it would not be long before those in the United States could celebrate their own Emancipation Day.[21]

Despite commemorating emancipation, abolitionists in the United States largely rejected the stipulations with which it came. Writing to the *Liberator*, "Paul" lauded British abolition as "one of the most cheering and important events" since the Declaration of Independence. Despite abolition's importance, the author remained steadfast in refusing to support compensation for enslavers. In the letter, Paul described such activity as payment for the deliverance of "property which the felon audaciously purloined."[22]

This letter exemplified the position of second-wave abolitionists on the issue of compensation in the United States. Emancipation was the goal, but the way it was enacted also mattered. Although early antislavery activists and colonizationists believed the legality of slavery to be a settled issue, the AASS's *Declaration* worked to unsettle their confidence. The *Declaration* laid it out clearly: "Laws which are now in force, admitting the right of slavery, are therefore, before God, utterly null and void." All slave law went against enslaved people's inalienable right to be free. The group posited that since "freeing the slave is not depriving [the slaveholder] of property but restoring it [property in self] to its rightful owner," emancipation would correct the problem by "restoring" the enslaved "to himself." This reasoning led abolitionists to describe self-purchase as redemption or ransom, while every enslaver was understood to be a "man-stealer."[23] To pay these kidnappers was to accept their right to own other human beings as property.

The white abolitionist Lewis C. Gunn of Philadelphia wrote about this problem of compensation in an extensive treatise published in the *Pennsylvania*

Freeman in 1836. Gunn opened the letter, which spanned nearly an entire page
of the paper, by claiming that he would not "give one cent in the extremist case
which your imagination can present" to help buy someone's freedom.[24] While
recognizing that his stance may have been described as "ultraism," or the most
extreme form of Garrisonian principles, Gunn expounded on his reasoning. He
argued against abolitionists who likened buying freedom to turning over one's
money during a robbery because in that case the thief knew what they were
doing was illegal. Supported by law, enslavers need not acknowledge that it was
wrong to sell something that abolitionists believed they could not own.

Gunn next questioned abolitionists' ability to offer adequate resources if
they were to help. Simply put, no one had the capacity to help every enslaved
person, so how was anyone to choose exactly who to help? To reinforce his argument regarding finite resources, Gunn urged abolitionists to imagine themselves
in the South, where, unlike in the northern states, they would be "surrounded
by slaves" with "clasped and uplifted hands." While this was a flight of rather
offensive fantasy, Gunn argued that there would be no end to those who sought
support. Certainly, though, there would be an end to the abolitionist's capacity
to buy slaves' freedom.[25]

Black abolitionists had always demanded a willingness to improvise under
force of circumstance, and the issue of buying freedom was no different. This did
not mean, of course, that all African Americans were willing to ransom themselves. Yet, across both first- and second-wave abolition, the act of buying freedom
remained consistent because legal freedom mattered to those trapped by enslavement. Their firsthand experiences would push the movement and the nation to
grapple more forcefully than ever with the question of American slavery.[26]

African Americans seeking to purchase freedom and their ideas about the
controversial process traveled through abolition circuits as they gave lectures,
sought financial support, and shared their stories within abolitionist print culture.
Abolitionists relied on moral suasion techniques through which they attempted
to sway the hearts and minds of Americans toward their cause. Printed matter was
thus the lifeblood of the movement's cultural work to end slavery.[27] Abolitionist
print culture was also an important vehicle for intra-abolition discourse in which
information was shared and ideas and tactics debated. Black activists used the

abolitionist public sphere not only to become free but also to theorize freedom and its process.[28] As they asked for money and debated with fellow abolitionists, they required the movement to deal more carefully with questions of law, complicity, and compensation. As they explained, slavery was a problem for the law but it complicated freedom too. These conversations added to the depth with which abolitionists understood slavery as a problem for the nation.

Activists across the country were, therefore, asked constantly to examine their inaugural principle of no compensation. From their debates, it is evident that most activists were willing to deviate from doctrine in emergency situations. Yet, for the enslaved, fugitives, or those with enslaved families, every case in which the opportunity presented itself to purchase a loved one was an emergency. For many, the importance of legal freedom and familial reunion outweighed the moral quandary of being complicit with slavery. They set out to convince others of this truth. When abolitionists were forced to "weigh principle against expediency" many sided with those who wanted to buy their liberation. According to the historian Aileen Kraditor, even William Lloyd Garrison, believed to be one of the most radically principled of abolitionists, "distinguished between principles, which must never be compromised, and policy, which to serve principle must be flexible."[29]

From the 1830s onward, the pages of abolitionist newspapers like the *Liberator* and the *NASS* are scattered with stories, advertisements, and appeals of those who had bought or sought to buy their freedom. The proliferation of these items in the most important abolitionist newspapers of the nineteenth century suggests at least a tacit approval of self-purchase within abolitionist communities. It was through these stories and contact with Black communities that most abolitionists came to understand the fragile state of life under slavery and in fugitivity. Additionally, it is of note that the ingenious stories of self-purchase and trickery told in Isaac Hopper's *Tales of Oppression* were being published by the *Standard* in the 1840s, once second-wave abolition was in full bloom. The combination of techniques used in *Tales* was a precursor to the activism to come.

In its first year of publication, the *Liberator* ran an article entitled "A Charitable Appeal" which was representative of the types of individual appeals that were published in abolitionist papers. The *Liberator*'s editor, William Lloyd Garrison, called on familial feeling and focused on the effects of slavery on the stability of Black families to aid John Gustive, who was in Boston to raise money to purchase three of his enslaved children. According to the paper, Gustive had already bought his own freedom and that of his wife and eldest daughter. He needed to raise $300 to secure the emancipation of the rest of his family. The sum, Garrison trusted, would be easily obtained as the case involved the "present and eternal welfare of three poor children, who are as dear to their unfortunate parents as ours are to us and who must be torn from their arms if the money be not speedily raised."[30]

Notably, Gustive's appeal was paged with news of the capture of Nat Turner and the terrifying backlash faced by African Americans in the aftermath of his rebellion in Virginia. Like self-purchase, violence was a matter of debate for abolitionists. While most followers of Garrisonian abolition believed in nonresistance and nonviolence, many also thought that using force against slavery, itself a form of violence, was self-defense. Turner's rebellion, as well as the firsthand experiences like those Gustive shared, were used by abolitionists to expose the truths of slavery against the propaganda of enslavers who claimed that slavery was a paternalist institution and beneficial for African Americans. For their part, enslavers in this period worried about slaves' resistance in all forms and the role of abolitionists in fomenting it.[31] Despite complaints about northern activists, Virginia went so far as to discuss ending slavery altogether in response to Turner's rebellion, with the state legislature debating both gradual emancipation and colonization. Neither was legislated; instead, the state's Black Codes were revised to further restrict the rights and privileges of free African Americans and the enslaved.[32]

While the Virginia legislature considered divesting from slavery, abolitionists in the North discussed the role of compensation in large-scale emancipation plans to put an end to the issue once and for all. In 1832, the *Liberator* reprinted an article from the *Genius of Universal Emancipation*. In the article, the *Genius*'s editor, Benjamin Lundy, defended himself against Garrison's claims that Lundy supported compensated emancipation against abolitionist principles. Lundy's original article referred to an 1825 proposal by New York senator Rufus King in which the proceeds of public land sales by the federal government would be applied to the purchase and emancipation of enslaved people for their colonization outside the limits of the United States. Abolitionists, it seems, were not the only ones to be inspired by world events.[33]

Lundy suggested that King's proposition might be better received by abolitionists if it made stronger stipulations for the immediate end of slavery. Lundy believed that the federal government might pay a "reasonable sum" to compromise on the issue if it meant national emancipation. He did not, however, agree to "sanction the principle that man can be rightfully considered property, by the purchase of a single one." Lundy maintained that the *Genius* "NEVER advocated" the position as Garrison presented. Lundy, like Garrison, believed that emancipation in such a manner would be the "most glaring dereliction of principle."[34]

In response, Garrison declared that he was sorry that Lundy, his mentor, would ascribe to any project of compensated emancipation and any payments to slaveholders as a class. To Garrison, the plan was an "abandonment of justice" "calculated to divert the attention" away from the "guilt of the holders of slaves." The stakes were marked not only by questions of principle but also by law. Garrison claimed that the problem turned on constitutional issues. He argued that compensation was beyond the power of the government. For if enslavers had the right to be paid, then they had a right to property in slaves. If this was true, they "ought not to be required to sacrifice their property." But, if it was not, as Garrison wrote, "we ought not to do evil that good may come."[35]

Garrison estimated that this scheme would cost some $400 million in 1832. By the time enslavers would consent to emancipation, which Garrison projected would not occur before 1870, there would be an exponential growth in the enslaved population and in the cost of emancipation. Here he centered the impracticality of funding to critique the plan. Garrison maintained that enslavers deserved no "remuneration for giving up stolen property." Using language that he would come to repeat in the *Declaration of Sentiments*, he demanded that they end their "robberies" and "liberate NOW—to-morrow is too far distant."[36] Although Garrison recognized the exigency present in the cases of individual African Americans such as John Gustive, he refused to admit that enslavers had the right to hold human property by paying for the total abolition of slavery in the United States.

As both moderates and enslavers in Virginia contemplated a solution to the issue of slavery, the new generation of abolitionists' direct-action tactics and general refusal to compromise were a cause of concern for enslavers who felt themselves to be on the defensive. Enslavers in the South feared the enslaved and decried the role that they imagined free African Americans and abolitionists had in directing the rebellious behavior of the enslaved. Enslavers saw abolitionist interference at play in acts from violent rebellion to running away and resisting fugitive recapture, and they attempted to maintain control through brute force and tightening restrictions. The on-the-ground work of activists in the North organized against these restrictions to protect those who sought to escape slavery by securing state protections for those who made it to the North.[37]

Although always a small minority, abolitionist and free Black communities across the nation found themselves dealing with a seemingly ever more dangerous foe who viewed them with similar alarm. In many instances, enslavers and their political supporters at the national level complicated matters for activists. They succeeded in both silencing abolitionist petitions to the federal government and barring the free transit of abolitionist printed matter into the South.[38] Abolitionist efforts to protect fugitives from enslavers against the terms of the Fugitive Slave Act of 1793 were also impeded by Supreme Court cases such as *Prigg v. Pennsylvania*. This decision effectively outlawed northern legal protections for enslaved fugitives. These state laws were created in response to abolitionists' determination to help those escaping slavery through both legal and extralegal means, as detailed in Chapter 1. These efforts became "more organized" and violent in the late 1830s. Stanley Harrold has shown how a "border war" between enslavers and northerners over these issues led to wider disapproval of "aggressive southern action." This sentiment led, at the very least, to sympathy for African Americans, if not direct action on their behalf. For some northerners, this also led to larger questions over the "political and constitutional" problems presented by the Fugitive Slave Act and the power of slave law to influence the laws of the nation. These sentiments would only increase after the Fugitive Slave Act of 1850, which was passed to appease southerners who deemed lax enforcement by both northern states and the federal government to be a serious national issue.[39]

The increasingly dangerous landscape in which enslaved people escaped slavery shaped ideas about buying freedom. Guided by the enslaved people they sought to assist, abolitionists blended illegal support for fugitives with legal methods like buying freedom when circumstances required. Enslavers, however, also worried about the legal tactics of abolitionists. As this chapter will discuss, they wondered about the precedent that support for buying freedom might set for enslaved people who sought to use abolitionist networks.

Enslavers may have exaggerated the extent to which abolitionists were influencing the enslaved. Enslaved people had their own ideas about freedom. Abolitionists, on the other hand, were certainly influenced by the ideas and actions of the enslaved. The stories of enslaved people became crucial tools for the movement to fight enslavers through propaganda and gain converts to their cause. Narratives written by enslaved people shaped the nation's understanding of slavery in the midcentury, just as they continue to fundamentally shape our historical memory of enslavement today.[40] These narratives contributed equally to understandings of self-purchase.

Self-purchase can be read as a trope within the genre, serving practical and political purposes as authors used their narratives to shape ideas about complicity with slavery and slave law, to discuss African Americans' fitness for freedom, and to raise money to buy freedom.[41] As Black abolitionists authors argued, the necessity of buying one's freedom served to expose a nation where one was subjected to the law of slavery wherever one traveled. Their narratives revealed the limits of resistance to that law and produced questions over whether one could ever truly escape the bonds of enslavement. The impotence of higher, or even state, law in the face of slavery is clearly represented in these portrayals of ransomed freedom, as is the deficient morality of a nation that would acquiesce so completely to it.

Moses Grandy, who was forced to pay for his freedom three times before being manumitted, sought support from abolitionists to purchase family members through the publication of his narrative. His story circulated in the pages of abolitionists' newspapers years before its formal publication as he traveled among them to raise money. In 1838, the *Liberator* reported an update on Grandy for the benefit of those who had helped him purchase his son for $450. According to the paper, despite having purchased this son, his wife, and himself, Grandy still had other children in slavery "of whose fate and location he is ignorant."[42] Grandy hoped to secure enough money to save the rest of his children and his grandchildren, bringing three generations of his family together in freedom.

With such a daunting task at hand, Grandy traveled across the northern states to raise money for his family's emancipation and then set sail for England to further his efforts. With support and introduction from American abolitionists, Grandy journeyed throughout the United Kingdom. In June 1843, he joined a meeting of the Birmingham Anti-Slavery Society where his story was shared with the audience and his narrative, as well as its "noble" purpose, was advertised.[43]

During his travels, Grandy became acquainted with the English abolitionist George Thompson, who would write the introduction to his narrative and connect Grandy's personal history of slavery, self-purchase, and fundraising efforts to the abolitionist cause. Thompson described examining a notebook of all the donations that were made by Grandy's supporters in the United States. According to Thompson, the book included people of the "highest respectability." Included was Ellis Gray Loring, the Boston lawyer who would help arrange the redemption of Frederick Douglass and Samuel Sewall, who would go on to serve as a state senator in Massachusetts. Perhaps Thompson worried that American questions over the practicality of buying freedom would stymie Grandy's efforts across the pond and wanted to assure audiences that Grandy's efforts had already been rewarded to smooth his path.

Regardless, having these men support his cause was enough for Thompson to ensure the publication of Grandy's narrative. These donations acted as financial credit and proof of Grandy's reputation, both of which Grandy depended on. Thompson firmly believed that the narrative's publication would raise the money Grandy needed and that it would foster support for the abolitionist cause to ensure the "breaking of every yoke" that bound enslaved people.[44]

The title page of Moses Grandy's 1843 *Narrative of the Life of Moses Grandy; Late a Slave in the United States of America* made its purpose clear. It declared in all capitals that the volume was "PUBLISHED AND SOLD FOR THE

BENEFIT OF HIS RELATIONS STILL IN SLAVERY." Grandy's narrative detailed how, despite buying himself and some members of his family, his freedom would remain incomplete without that of his entire family. Grandy planned to use "whatever profit may be obtained by the sale of this book, and all donations" to redeem his remaining family members who were caught in that "dreadful condition of slavery."[45] The publication of Grandy's narrative acted not only as a testimony against the slave system but also as a practical fundraising tool in the interest of liberation. In many ways the two could not be separated. The necessity of the fundraising itself was also a condemnation of slavery.

One advertisement for Grandy's narrative published by the *British and Foreign Anti-slavery Reporter* claimed that the "extensive sale" of his narrative would help Grandy and "promote" abolition. It also commented on the physical nature of the text, stating that the book was "beautifully got up" and entitled to a place of honor on the "drawing room table, among the elegancies of the season."[46] Even if just a marketing strategy to sell copies, this comment on the beauty of a book about the horrors of slavery is worth noting. The sale of these narratives exposed the muddied connections between the circulation of paper, credit, and bodies, often in overlapping markets.

Black abolitionist authors were not content to merely narrate their experiences. Self-purchase was used as a narrative device that highlighted the "complicity of slavery and freedom," a complicated relationship that Saidiya Hartman has used to describe general emancipation. The limits of freedom, legal or fugitive, are clearly marked in these discussions of self-purchase and can be traced back even earlier to the individual emancipations described in these narratives.[47] Black abolitionists had long understood that slavery and freedom were not independent systems. In fact, participating in the market of slavery gave many a unique perspective from which to critique not only the laws of slavery but those of the nation that affected their freedom and families and made their participation in slavery's economy necessary.

The *Pennsylvania Freeman* shared the story of a woman living in Massachusetts who was trying to buy her enslaved daughter. Upon hearing that her daughter was being advertised for sale in Baltimore among the property of her bankrupt enslaver, the woman "scraped together her earnings and savings." She returned to Massachusetts with her daughter. The paper described the mother as "poor and sick" and deserving of "charity" because of the sacrifice she had made for her family.[48] This article exposes the difficulty of saving the money needed to buy the freedom of a loved one and the physical and psychological toll it could take without the support of abolitionists. Facing the sale of her daughter by a bankrupt enslaver, this woman's story can also be read as a critique of, and response to, the domestic slave trade.

Additionally, the *Liberator* printed an article about a minister who had bought his own freedom and was attempting to raise money to liberate his wife. The man also had children who were enslaved whom he hoped to save. The author used the man's story to moralize against slavery and its effects on families. Like Garrison with the story of John Gustive, the author asked readers to imagine themselves in the position of the man. The article closed by beseeching readers to at least "pity them, and pray for them" if "you could do no more." The implication of this closing was that many could do more.[49]

Articles such as these can be found in every abolitionist newspaper. Unless written by or about authors we can trace elsewhere, like Grandy, they often leave unanswered many questions about the lives of the people on whose behalf the appeals were printed. Despite any information they fail to reveal, they do show that, throughout the nineteenth century, African Americans used abolitionist networks to raise funds for freedom. Their printed appeals helped normalize the technique for readers of abolitionist print culture and guided readers to understand the urgency of the situation for Black families.

Ethical questions about paying for freedom were not only implied but also openly discussed. Moses Grandy, for instance, closed his narrative by describing the importance of liberation for his family. For Grandy, their freedom was a blessing of which "none can know the value, but he who has been a slave." Grandy's message was clear; despite contentions over self-purchase and how emancipation should be obtained, what mattered most was freedom and unification of families. While he greatly appreciated the assistance that his "many friends in the Northern States" had given him, he worked to center his experience of slavery and freedom and the importance of legal emancipation secured by any means.[50] Buying freedom was deeply personal, but this framing had reverberations for abolitionist thought and action.

In 1845, two years after the publication of Grandy's narrative, another letter in the *Standard* took up the issue of "pecuniary ransom." Coming to a conclusion that opposed that of Lewis Gunn, the author argued that it did not matter how abolitionists viewed the rights of slaveholders. The author argued that the enslaved had a "moral right" to "shun future oppression." That meant that abolitionists had the right to help them buy freedom. Perhaps critiquing the slow progress and limited success of abolitionist tactics, the author claimed that if emancipation could be achieved in ten years by moral suasion or immediately by ransom, then it was their duty to do the latter. The author dissolved any question of complicity by clearly detailing the historical relationship between northerners and slavery, stating that northerners were already "practically, the kidnappers or enslavers of the African race in the South." Northerners participated in and profited from the slave trade under a legal system "voluntarily adopted" by them. One would be a "rogue and a cheat of a high grade" to refuse the opportunity to end slavery even if it meant paying for it, especially since all white Americans were already economically complicit with the system.[51]

The intellectual work of African Americans like Grandy, however, did not necessarily translate into universal acceptance. The Black abolitionist William Still, who helped hundreds of fugitives escape slavery as head of the Pennsylvania Anti-Slavery Society's Vigilant Committee, recorded a story about abolitionist Lewis Tappan's refusal to fund freedom. A mother and father had gone to Tappan's New York office looking for assistance in raising the $2,000 they needed to purchase their sons, who were going to be sold by their enslaver in North Carolina. According to Still, Tappan told them that he had "scruples about putting money into the hands of slave-holders" but he was happy to help them escape instead.[52] When Tappan was asked for financial support for compensated manumission, he guided these parents toward illegal action. Thus, to be reunited, this family was forced to negotiate abolitionist ideals in a time of emergency. Although the sons were able to escape successfully, they were still in danger of being recaptured as fugitives. This predicament had likely already been taken into consideration by the parents who hoped to buy their freedom.

Despite the principles of abolitionists like Tappan, the movement produced others who were well known within the movement and beyond for their support of self-purchase. Like Tappan, Gerrit Smith had money to fund abolitionist projects. In fact, Smith was likely the wealthiest American abolitionist, and he established himself as someone who was willing to use his money to fund freedom. Not only did he support African Americans in their efforts to raise money, but he also used his personal wealth for other projects, including giving away parcels of land to Black and poor white New Yorkers and joining other reform causes like the temperance movement.[53] Although Smith was an early member of the ACS, he eventually split from the organization, like William Lloyd Garrison. Smith's predilection for philanthropy was no secret, for he reportedly responded to twenty-five to thirty-five requests for help every day.[54]

Smith's interest in buying freedom was likely related to his own experience. Smith had personal connections to slavery that he sought to make right through compensated manumission. In 1841, Smith began working to redeem the family of a woman whom Smith's wife had enslaved and given to her brother when she was a young girl. After the Smiths became abolitionists, they made every effort to find the woman to redeem her. When the Smiths found her in Mississippi, they engaged a friend to negotiate with the owner to redeem her family of seven at the cost of some $3,500. The newly free family moved to Peterboro, New York, where the Smiths helped them establish a life for themselves. This restitution on the part of Smith seems to have had general support from abolitionist papers. The "noble and costly act" was lauded by many on both sides of the Atlantic.[55] This emancipation was no small financial feat, even for a man of means like Smith.

Smith continued to provide monetary assistance to abolitionist causes. He helped to fund John Brown's preparations for his raid on Harpers Ferry, which sought to overthrow the institution of slavery through a violent reckoning. Smith also supported William L. Chaplin, another New York abolitionist, when he was arrested for aiding fugitives in an escape attempt. Smith provided some $12,000 toward bonds and lawyer's fees. Chaplin, like Smith, was involved with political abolition and worked in the Washington, DC, area to assist enslaved people in buying their freedom as part of his work with the Underground Railroad. After being exposed to the "agony of black families" in Washington and assisting many in the purchase of loved ones, Chaplin thought there should be a "bureau of humanity" established that could "institutionalize" buying freedom. Like Smith, Chaplin believed that buying freedom was not a poor use of movement funds and could be used seamlessly with other forms of resistance.[56]

In an 1852 letter to the *Standard*, Smith reflected on how, despite being "robbed of a great deal [of money] from time to time," he felt himself "morally compelled to pay in the purchase of the liberty of slaves." Smith protested his expenditure on Chaplin's case because he believed it could have been better purposed toward the "cries of our wronged humanity [which] come from numerous directions." However, Smith was comforted by remembering that he was "better off without this money than they, who got it from me, were with it," and that the "robbed may feel very sore under his losses: but still he is better off than the robber."[57] Here, Smith turned Lewis Gunn's characterization of robbery on its head. Those who handed their money over, no matter the circumstance, were still morally superior to those who took it.

The Smith family's financial activities reflected the fundamentally interrelated nature of the freedom-seeking techniques of African Americans. In 1846, Smith wrote to a friend that "I shall have a heart to reduce myself, if not to a poor man—yet well-nigh to a poor man—by purchasing the liberty of the enslaved poor."[58] The Smiths would spend thousands of dollars buying the freedom of enslaved people and assisting fugitives on their way to Canada. As with many in Black communities throughout the country, Smith's efforts to buy freedom were mixed with those that assisted fugitives and the enslaved in other extralegal ways, including open rebellion. Throughout the century, Smith sought to support the cause of freedom in multiple ways. Through a complex vision of slavery's relation to sin that was both personal and national—an idea common to many abolitionists—it seems as though Smith attempted to work out a moral debt with his capital by investing it in freedom.

The actions of Smith and support for the enslaved in the pages of abolitionist newspapers might suggest there was nothing left to debate about buying freedom and that activists had come to accept it as part of their daily work to end slavery. However, the purchase and manumission in 1846 of Frederick Douglass, the most famous African American abolitionist in the world, would spark the most intense discussion over compensated manumission that the movement would ever see. As always, Douglass did not shy away from standing up for his decision and theorizing the necessity of legal freedom in the pages of abolitionist newspapers as he reframed his purchase as ransom. In doing so, Douglass reminded readers that the money had been paid not so much for his outright purchase as a slave but to obtain his rightful release from the kidnappers of his body. Nor was Douglass alone, as Garrison and others defended the purchase of his second freedom.

In 1838, twenty-year-old Frederick Douglass made a successful escape from slavery by secretly traveling from Maryland, where he was enslaved, to New York City. Soon after arriving in the North, he was married to his wife, a free woman named Anna Murray Douglass. Together, the couple settled in New Bedford, Massachusetts. Despite experiencing continued racism and the difficulties of fugitivity, Douglass made the best of his "new world." He became a subscriber to the *Liberator* and began to study the principles of the movement, of which he already had the "spirit."[59] In 1841, he began his first lecture tour with the AASS. As one of the first African Americans to tell his story before abolitionist audiences, Douglass held a novel position as a lecturer. Despite admonitions from white abolitionists to tell audiences only of his experience, Douglass continued to theorize the politics of abolition in his speeches.[60] His will to be free could be stopped by neither slaveholders nor abolitionists. This determination would be further displayed in his response to the debate over the purchase of his freedom.

In 1845, less than a decade after he had escaped slavery, Douglass published the story of his life. The genre-defining *Narrative of the Life of Frederick Douglass* sold thousands of copies. The success of his narrative and lectures led the AASS to send him on a tour of the United Kingdom.[61] This lecture tour was also deemed necessary to protect Douglass against recapture because of his notoriety, which only increased with the publication of his narrative. Although Douglass did not necessarily fear an "open attempt" on his freedom because he believed his abolitionist friends and supporters would protect him, he was nonetheless concerned with being taken back into slavery. Douglass's enslavers, Thomas and Hugh Auld, were so "bitterly incensed against [Douglass]" that they "openly avowed" to spare nothing to return Douglass to slavery. They claimed that, "cost what it may," they would "place him in the cotton fields of the South."[62] Because he dared to not only run away but to also to expose the "secrets and crimes of slavery and slaveholders," Douglass worried that the motives for his recapture were doubly strong. Douglass contemplated these threats deeply and, after arriving in England, found that the "wisdom of this course [had] been fully confirmed."[63] Still, he thought it more likely that his enslavers would succeed in gaining nothing more from him than the "money value of my bones and sinews." This would be the case in the end.[64]

When Douglass climbed aboard the *Cambria* and set sail for Liverpool in the summer of 1845, he soon found himself transformed by his experiences in England. Writing to Garrison, Douglass claimed that he had some of the "happiest moments" of his life there. He found he had "undergone a transformation" and claimed to "live a new life." Not only did Douglass enjoy his newfound allies and friends, but he also experienced something entirely new—the "entire absence of everything that looked like prejudice against me" because of his race.[65] The experience was, in short, liberating for a man who had spent his entire life in the United States and was still legally enslaved.

Douglass longed for loved ones at home and contemplated moving his family so they could enjoy his newfound freedom. While visiting Quaker abolitionists Ellen, Henry, and Anna Richardson in Newcastle upon Tyne in northern England, Douglass discussed his concerns about returning home. Douglass worried for his safety if he returned to the United States under the watchful eyes of the Aulds. Ellen Richardson decided to raise the funds needed to purchase his freedom so that he could go home as a legally free man.[66] The Richardsons would later raise the money for the freedom of the abolitionist William Wells Brown. Although he would later claim that he was not involved in the arrangements, Douglass wrote to a friend in Boston who arranged for Ellis Gray Loring, the Boston attorney and abolitionist, to proceed with the purchase. Loring hired someone in New York, a city that was no stranger to slaveholders and their business interests, who found a lawyer in Baltimore to contact Hugh Auld.

Douglass's manumission was secured for £150, reported by the *Standard* to be $750 in American currency.[67]

In Talbot County, Maryland, which Douglass had made famous in the opening lines of his narrative, the bill of sale between Hugh and Thomas Auld for Frederick Douglass was registered on November 30, 1846. On December 12, Douglass's manumission papers were registered in Baltimore County. Eight years after taking his own freedom, Douglass was now a free man under the laws of the United States. Copies of these bills of sale and manumission were published in the *Standard* to gratify readers by "showing how they manage things in the model republic."[68]

Abolitionists on both sides of the Atlantic criticized Douglass and his supporters almost immediately upon hearing the news. Their discussions on the topic filled the pages of the *Liberator* and other abolitionist papers for months. Henry C. Wright, who was traveling in Great Britain at the same time as Douglass, took issue with his purchase because it went against the ideals of the AASS. Wright, corresponding with Douglass via a letter published in the paper, claimed that Douglass had abandoned his "appeal to mankind" by commodifying himself. To Wright, the problem was not so much "the grovelling thief, Thomas Auld" but the "more daring, more impudent and potent thief—the Republic of the United States of America." In the process of buying his freedom, Wright believed that Douglass had given up his "truly manly" and "sublime" position of righteousness.[69]

The *Liberator* also published a report from a meeting of the Philadelphia Female Anti-Slavery Society held on March 12, 1847, in which the society passed resolutions stating that the "purchasing of the freedom of a slave is an implied acknowledgment of the masters right of property in human beings." They claimed this was "inconsistent" with the *Declaration of Sentiments*. The women reaffirmed their refusal to support such endeavors and resolved that, although the group appreciated the "kind feelings" of Douglass's supporters, they believed the action to be "impolitic and inexpedient." Although Douglass had been someone who had the "strongest claims to the sympathy of the community," he had weakened the "bond that connects the suffering slave with the freeman." His purchase was a "deviation" from principle, and the organization had no choice but to condemn it.[70]

The *Standard* reprinted an article from the *Hartford Charter Oak* that maintained that Douglass was a human being, not a slave, and that the "act of buying a little ticket with 'Free' written on it, at such an enormous price, is worse than folly; it is mischievous, and virtually an acknowledgment of the traffic." The author asked if Douglass was "fatal to the system of oppression by eloquence of only $750 power?" Turning to issues of value, they questioned if it was truly the "market value" that his enslavers were worried about. Instead, the author claimed that it was not Douglass's monetary value, but "the terror of his great speech, his free words of scathing and scalding rebuke of oppression" that the Auld family was after. Believing that Douglass would be no less vocal or "less manful" now, the author concluded that the South had gained money, while Douglass and his supporters had gained nothing but the "*loss* of it." As Douglass would continue his abolitionist work and represent "hope to the oppressed," the letter framed his purchase as an "idle" "waste" of money. The action had too nearly "implied assent to the master's robber claim, to be good in morals or policy." There was just as much reason to fear for Douglass's safety as before because his former enslavers wanted "food for their revenge," not money.[71]

For these abolitionists, then, Douglass's value was incalculable. He was impossible to commodify. His newfound legal freedom was deemed worthless because it caused him to relinquish his principled position. These arguments ignore that Douglass's very success as an abolitionist had made it necessary for him to accept, at least on paper, the purchase of his freedom. He was both "unpopular" and "notorious," which put him at special risk.[72] Living as a fugitive, Douglass had to constantly consider the legal claim that the Aulds had on him until he was manumitted. Depending on where he was captured, it was quite possible that a judge would have recognized Auld's right to reenslave Douglass. Of course, it seems rather unlikely that Douglass, even if recaptured, would have remained enslaved long before he was rescued. However, even a further minute of enslavement or separation from loved ones would have been unacceptable to any self-emancipated person.

In his 1836 discussion of buying freedom, Lewis Gunn revealed what a principled alternative to purchase might have looked like in Douglass's case, as many of these articles suggested. Gunn declared that instead of purchasing a fugitive named Severn Martin's freedom, abolitionists should have allowed Martin to be taken back into slavery. Gunn claimed that he would have printed an "account of the outrage in handbill form" and appeal to his fellow citizens. With this handbill "thrown into every house," Gunn believed that Martin's neighbors would better recognize the wrongs of slavery than they did by saving him from rendition. Instead of relying on moral suasion, as Gunn argued for, Martin's community arranged to buy his freedom to keep him in New Jersey.

Gunn proceeded to argue against calls on common humanity made by Garrison and others. He denied that he would save even his own sister in this manner; rather, he claimed that he would use her as an example to increase abolitionist sentiment. Like many in Douglass's time, Gunn claimed that it was a mistake to buy Severn Martin because that ended discussions regarding the matter. According to Gunn, those who contributed to Martin's freedom would let their "feelings of unholy indignation" against slavery dissipate because they had saved him from it. Gunn argued that after making their contribution, they would no longer have to concern themselves with the evils of slavery again. Certainly this was untrue for African Americans who lived in Martin's community, and it would not ring true for Douglass either.[73] We do not know whether Gunn would have made the same argument a decade later about Frederick Douglass, but his audacious plan for Martin reveals the gulf between the imagined importance of principle and moral suasion when pitted against the very real threat of reenslavement.

Others recognized Douglass's predicament and lent their support. One such letter written against the ideas of Lindley Coates, who criticized Douglass in similar fashion to those above, asked pointedly if a member of Coates's family was in the "grasp of an unprincipled villain of despotic power, and there was nothing but silver or gold would soften his heart," would that not "convert him into a slave-buyer?"[74] The writer understood the logic of the arguments being made in the context of abolitionist principles, but they could not reconcile that logic with the absolute necessity faced by Douglass. William Lloyd Garrison, always principled but willing to compromise when necessary, came to Douglass's defense in a similar manner. Garrison claimed that individual circumstances must take precedence over abstract principles in Douglass's case. As one letter to the *Liberator*, recognizing the need to consider individual circumstances, eloquently expressed, "man is a finite being, of limited powers; and if he cannot do all he would, he ought to do all that he can."[75]

There were three common arguments against the purchase of Douglass's liberty. First, many believed that relinquishing Douglass's stolen freedom and the end of his fugitive status would deprive him of the full strength of his voice in the antislavery cause. Douglass's detractors believed that his position as a fugitive gave him a unique status. Claims that he relinquished this power were often directly linked to Douglass's manhood. Second, buying freedom went against the AASS *Declaration* in that it rewarded the slaveholder for something they could not in actuality own. Therefore, buying Douglass's freedom could be construed as recognizing the right of enslavers to hold property in human beings. Finally, there were many who thought that, despite his legal freedom, Douglass would still be in danger of being kidnapped and that his purchase did nothing but supply Auld with a "donation of $750" compliments of the movement.[76]

Douglass, for his part, defended his actions by stating that he had agreed to his purchase simply because it was necessary. He turned what was a rhetorical debate for some into a matter of life and death and defended himself and all those in his shoes. Douglass argued that manumission would permit him to move more freely about the United States and allow him to do better work as an abolitionist since he could go anywhere without fearing recapture. Regardless of opinion, Douglass consistently centered the anxiety and lived experience of the fugitive. It was clear that the laws of the United States gave Auld the "full power to arrest me anywhere in that country." Responding to his critics, he said there was "no State in the whole American Union, from Texas to Maine, in which I am not overshadowed with this terrible liability."[77]

Douglass also reversed his detractors' arguments about the law and principle. He claimed that he understood his free papers not as a badge of dishonor to the cause but rather as a place from which to deepen their critique of slavery. In response to claims that it would "shorn him of his strength" as an antislavery activist, Douglass wrote that he would hold his free papers as a "brand of infamy, stamping the nation, in whose name the deed was done." Through his arguments, Douglass juxtaposed his ransom with the opportunity it afforded him to extend his efforts to actualize the final and full abolition of slavery.[78]

In 1847, Douglass insisted that after obtaining his legal freedom, "I shall be Frederick Douglass still, and once a slave still." No matter his technical legal status, he would never "forget nor cease to feel the wrongs of my enslaved fellow-countrymen."[79] Douglass reminded his readers not only of the very precarious position of individual fugitives like himself but also of the specific threats faced by those who politicized their experiences as enslaved people. In these discussions, Douglass quickly shifted from the direct threats against his freedom by the Auld family to remonstrate the "laws of the land, and the Constitution of the United States."[80]

No freedom, however secure, could make him forget his own experience, nor the experiences of the millions of people who had not been so lucky. As he claimed, the business transaction through which he obtained his legal freedom would forever be a blight on the government of the United States and a demonstration of its sanctification of American slavery.

Douglass's defense in the pages of the *Liberator*, as well as his later autobiographies, theorized how to reconcile the necessity of buying freedom with the abolitionist principle of noncomplicity with slaveholders. Douglass deftly laid out the necessity of purchasing freedom under the law by masterfully exposing the legal system that made his ransomed liberty necessary. In discussing his stay in England after the publication of his narrative, Douglass contended that, unlike in the UK, the "institutions of this Country do not know me—do not recognize me as a man." He was "not thought of or spoken of, except as a piece of property" by the "religious institutions and political institutions" of his home country. What kept Douglass connected to the nation, rather than any affiliation to its ideals or institutions, was his family and the "painful consciousness" of the oppression faced by so many other African Americans.[81]

By February 1847, Garrison decided that he no longer felt "disposed to occupy much space on this subject." According to Garrison, Douglass had "so ably argued" his position that further discussion was unnecessary.[82] Douglass's eloquent and deeply political defense of his purchase was one of the most prominent theorizations of compensated manumission and self-purchase that the movement had to reckon with. Not only did Douglass attempt to speak from the position of illegal freedom to those white abolitionists who would never experience that liminal state, but he simultaneously worked to critique the state of American freedom as something that could be paid for.

In addition to fundraising for his freedom, English abolitionists raised money to help Douglass start his own newspaper when he returned to the United States. Not only did Douglass's English supporters afford him an opportunity by purchasing his liberty, but they also helped give him an outlet for the full exploitation of this freedom in the form of an abolitionist newspaper where he would continue to center Black political thought on the questions with which the movement grappled. Douglass saw the value of his purchase in the security it provided him to continue "wielding my pen, as well as my voice" to "send slavery and oppression to the grave." To Douglass, and most African Americans, how one obtained freedom did not matter as much as what one did with it.[83]

When he returned from England, Douglass founded his paper, the *North Star*, from Rochester, New York. Fittingly, he dedicated the paper to his "oppressed countrymen." During this period, Douglass also began to diverge from Garrisonian ideas. He shifted toward political abolition, joining those who believed that the Constitution was an antislavery document and that national political power was necessary for abolition to succeed. Eventually Douglass would argue that the nation's founding document that had defined his fugitive status would "afford slavery no protection when it shall cease to be administered by slaveholders."[84] The discord over constitutional questions within the abolition movement cut across lines of race and legal status. However, one can imagine how Douglass's vision of the nature of American law was influenced by his personal experience of fugitivity and buying freedom. His life experiences led to his concern over the law's administration. First his ransom, then the passage of the Fugitive Slave Law of 1850, and later the *Dred Scott* decision would force Douglass and the movement to rethink tactics once again. Moral suasion, like gradual emancipation before it, was taking too long. Enslavers, it seemed, had the law on their side, and more direct action was needed if abolitionists were going to win the war against slavery.

Shortly after Douglass established the *North Star*, the Black abolitionist Samuel D. Burris was arrested in Delaware for aiding fugitive slaves. Burris was born free in Delaware and moved to Philadelphia with his family. Soon after moving to the abolitionist hub, he joined other activists in rescuing enslaved people from the South. Just as enslavers feared, Burris was interfering with the institution by assisting enslaved people to escape from under the noses of enslavers. After his arrest, Burris was held in a Dover, Maryland, jail for months because he could not pay the bail costs that were in excess of $5,000. When his case went to trial, he was convicted and sentenced to a fine of $500, prison fees, and ten months in prison. After his release, he was to be sold into term slavery for a total of fourteen years. The state had certainly decided to make an example of him—exactly the type of example Douglass had feared being made into himself.

Rather than allowing Burris to suffer such a fate, the Pennsylvania Anti-Slavery Society arranged to secretly purchase his freedom when he went up for sale after serving his time in prison. When Isaac S. Flint, a "strange trader," arrived at the sale, he played the part of a slave buyer. Flint examined Burris from the soles of his feet to the crown of his head, just as any enslaver would have done. After examining Burris as if he were purchasing property instead of freedom, Flint competed with traders in human flesh. Given Flint's convincing performance and violation of his body, Burris believed that his freedom was gone for good as the gavel came down on Flint's offer of $500. This terrible ruse did not last long, however. Once Flint had secured the bill of sale, he whispered to Burris that he had been bought with "abolitionist gold" and would soon return to his family in Philadelphia. The family would then move to California, perhaps wishing to put the ordeal behind them from even farther away than Pennsylvania.[85]

In a letter to his brother written during his imprisonment, Burris claimed to suffer "more than death." Even though he was saved from enslavement by his coconspirators, one can only imagine the lasting trauma of having been imprisoned and then sold as a slave for violating the law he knew to be morally wrong. In 2015, the governor of Delaware granted Burris a posthumous pardon for his antislavery activism.[86] Burris's work was indicative of the activism of abolitionists who took radical action against slavery by working as operators on the

Underground Railroad and helping to get slaves to freedom. Dangers loomed in both running away and assisting with escapes, as another carefully planned escape would soon show. As both abolitionists and the enslaved took bolder action, the technique of buying freedom would continue to come to the rescue of the enslaved and their families who were left to pick up the pieces of failure.

On April 15, 1848, the *Pearl* set sail from Washington, DC, with seventy-seven enslaved people on board. The captain and crew were assisting in a mass escape from slavery. Shortly after it left port, the ship was captured.[87] When the owners of many of the captives proceeded to sell the escapees to slave traders in retaliation, friends, family, and abolitionists stepped in to undertake another kind of rescue mission to purchase the freedom of everyone they could.

Just one year after Douglass returned to the United States a legally free man, abolitionists seem to have taken his lessons to heart. Hardly anyone questioned the usefulness of buying freedom in the cases of the *Pearl* escapees. One meeting at the Broadway Tabernacle in New York City raised $2,000 to purchase two of the fugitives, Emily and Mary Edmonson, who were captured aboard the ship with four of their brothers.[88] Abolitionists led by the girls' father, Paul Edmonson, raced against the clock as traders attempted to sell the Edmonson children in New Orleans.[89] Alongside the recent memory of debates over Douglass's freedom, activists were haunted by the specter of the sale of two young Christian women into the fancy-girl trade in New Orleans. The *National Era* was forward in stating that the choice presented was their "*redemption* by purchase, or their prostitution in the slave market" of the city.[90] In addressing the fundraising meeting at the tabernacle, the abolitionist minister Henry Ward Beecher stated that it was not wise to buy slaves as a "general practice" because there was not enough money "in all the coffers of the North" to do so sufficiently. He claimed, however, that this was an "essential case." Despite their catastrophic recapture, the sisters, along with members of other families on the ship, were saved through purchase.[91]

News of the *Pearl* and these rescue attempts made headlines across the nation, and enslavers seized the opportunity to denounce abolitionist influence. Activists were not the only ones to connect the techniques of escape and buying freedom. Even enslavers recognized the power of purchasing freedom in the context of slave resistance. Rather than call out the hypocrisy of abolitionists acting as slave traders or relish taking their money, some enslavers worried about the kind of precedent selling slaves to abolitionists would set for those who remained enslaved. Enslavers understood that these were not any ordinary slave sales, despite attempts like Isaac Flint's to make them appear so. In 1848, the *National Era* republished an article from Kentucky's *Louisville Journal* that spoke to the unease enslavers felt about the release of the Edmonson sisters. The author believed that it set a bad example for others who dreamed about escaping bondage. The redemption of the Edmonson sisters revealed that if one failed in running away, which was an ever-present threat, it was still possible that one could "expect to be bought and set free by the Abolitionists." The author believed that the Edmonsons' enslavers should have "refuse[d] to part with them to these New Yorkers upon any terms" because of this danger.[92]

During a feud between Frederick Douglass and William Lloyd Garrison, Garrison claimed that "fugitive slaves had no special insight into abolition."[93] Douglass's defense over the purchase of his freedom showed that fugitivity was, in fact, an experience that not all could fully understand. By attempting to reframe questions of principle and necessity, those who bought their freedom helped to refine abolitionist ideology and expand tactics. Found across abolitionist print culture, their stories show that whatever qualms some activists may have had with the practice, those who bought their freedom were in a special position to expose the basest injustices of slavery's law and market, as well as the relation between them. While legal freedom allowed abolitionists like Douglass additional protections for their activism to end slavery in the United States, many other African Americans bought freedom for themselves and their loved ones to end slavery's threat to their familial connections. Carving out space under slave law did not only happen when one broke it, as Douglass argued. Sometimes one also had to engage with it to find another kind of freedom.

As the next decade of activism would show, Douglass's legal freedom did indeed matter beyond the scope of pure abolitionist principles. Reflecting on his manumission in 1855, Douglass claimed that, all things considered, he thought the "very best thing was done." Writing in a world now affected by the Fugitive Slave Act of 1850, which threatened Black freedom as never before, Douglass was grateful to have his legal freedom. It was to this "commercial transaction," as he called it, that he owed his "exemption from the democratic operation of the Fugitive Slave Bill of 1850."[94] As Douglass noted, the necessity of compensated manumission would only increase after 1850. After the passage of the new law, many others would join Douglass in asking what the "laws of morality, or those of economy" were in the face of such an existential threat.[95]

CHAPTER 4

"Purchaser of My Body and Soul"

Buying Freedom and National Politics After 1850

On a winter's day in 1848, the enslaver Enoch Price sat down in St. Louis, Missouri, to write a letter to an abolitionist in Massachusetts. Price wrote to Edmund Quincy because he had received one of the eight thousand copies of William Wells Brown's *Narrative of William W. Brown, An American Slave* printed since its publication in 1847. The author himself had sent Price one in the mail. He likely read the narrative with great interest because, as he told Quincy in his letter, William Wells Brown was his slave. Perhaps unable to locate Brown himself, Price wrote to Quincy, the abolitionist who had written the introductory letter to Brown's book, and offered to let Brown buy his freedom. In what might have been an attempt to appear magnanimous before another white man who hated slavery, or to strike a bargain that would allow him to recoup anything he could from property that he knew he could not successfully reclaim, Price offered Brown's freedom for $325. He claimed that this was half of what he originally purchased Brown for and just a fraction of what he could get if he wished to "speculate on him."

Price thought that Brown or the "friends, who sustain him . . . could afford to pay" this low price. While offering a bargain that he clearly thought the abolitionists should not refuse, Price's letter spoke to the invaluable nature of legal freedom that African American abolitionists had previously described. According to Price, if Brown bought his free papers he could "go wherever he wishes to." By framing the offer so, Price made clear that he understood the importance of freedom and its connection to free movement as he boldly dangled it in Brown's face. His plan backfired. Instead of accepting Price's offer, Brown published the exchange, including his refusal of the offer, in the 1849 edition of his narrative. Brown would never "become a purchaser of my body and soul" because God had made him "as free as he did Enoch Price." Brown assured Price that he would "never receive a dollar" from him or his "friends with my consent."[1]

Brown escaped slavery in St. Louis, Missouri, in 1834. As a self-emancipated but unlawfully free man, he created a new life for himself in both Canada and the northern United States. In 1849, he traveled to Great Britain on an abolitionist lecture tour, where he experienced a new kind of freedom. Unlike Douglass now, though, Brown was still enslaved under American law and at increased risk of recapture if he returned home after the passage of the Fugitive Slave Act of 1850. By 1854, Brown had a change of heart and, like Douglass, allowed a group of British abolitionists, including the Richardson sisters, to buy his body, if not his soul, from Enoch Price.

Reaction to William Wells Brown's manumission made clear that abolitionists had learned from Douglass and his supporters years earlier. Although the editors regretted Brown's decision, the *Pennsylvania Freeman* reprinted an article from the *Liberator* that commended the contributions of Brown's supporters. He could now return to the United States without being "subject to the terrible liability of being seized as a fugitive and scourged to death on a Southern plantation."[2] While many activists understood that buying freedom was a practical method because it could be used to save people when other abolitionist measures failed, the political stakes of successful rescues during this period were higher as they came to take on national significance within the heated sectional divide in the decade before the Civil War. These tensions grew more pronounced and more violent as "cross-border skirmishing" increased as southerners attempted to forcefully return enslaved people and were met with ever more militant self-defense by African Americans and their allies.[3] Even in this era, self-purchase had a role to play for enslaved people and abolitionists alike.

The Compromise of 1850 was meant to quell these growing tensions around slavery. The new Fugitive Slave Act was the part of the bargain meant to pacify enslavers who had long complained that the Fugitive Slave Act of 1793 had never been properly upheld by northern states or the federal government against the interference of abolitionist activists. The compromise also included the end of the slave trade in the District of Columbia and the admission of California to the Union as a free state. The territories of Utah and New Mexico would decide their fate based on popular sovereignty.[4]

Much stronger than its 1793 counterpart, the new legislation facilitated the ease with which enslavers could reclaim enslaved people and kidnap free African Americans. Its most egregious measures included allowing commissioners to deputize any member of the public for capture missions, lowering the bar for sufficient proof needed to claim someone as a slave, and increasing the fine for those caught aiding fugitives. It left no avenue for the claimants to defend themselves before a jury and incentivized judges to return people claimed as fugitives through a fee structure that guaranteed ten dollars for doing so and only five dollars for releasing the captive as a free person. Over three hundred fugitives were reenslaved in the 1850s. While that number may account for only a small percentage of the thousands of people who had escaped slavery over the course of the nineteenth century, these recaptures, many of which became front-page news, spread fear among those who lived like William Wells Brown and in their communities.[5]

At the height of the fugitive slave crisis, knowing that they would now be in an even more vulnerable position, African Americans who escaped slavery continued to turn to self-purchase to protect the freedom they had already taken. In using self-purchase in this new context, they refined movement politics as they simultaneously rejected the necessity of manumission by arguing against the new law as unconstitutional and as immoral as slavery. Still, many also had to accept the necessity of legal freedom in a nation that was now even more unjustly under the institution's sway.

Despite the new level of danger that African Americans faced, they had been here before. They responded by using both the legal and extralegal methods they had long made use of to escape the watchful eyes of enslavers. Indeed, the new Fugitive Slave Act was a direct response to these earlier abolitionist efforts and their successful evasion of the law. Historians estimate that between one thousand and five thousand people a year escaped slavery in the decades before the Civil War.[6] Enslavers who were unsatisfied with earlier enforcement efforts thought the 1850 act would stop not only enslaved people and their abolitionist allies but also northern states from using local personal liberty laws to stop captures that were explicitly protected by federal legislation. One of these state laws, in Massachusetts, was known as the "Latimer Law." It was named after a fugitive named George Latimer who escaped with his pregnant wife from Norfolk, Virginia, in 1842. Shortly after Latimer arrived in Boston he was arrested on charges of larceny by his enslaver, James Gray. After his release, Boston activists negotiated to buy his freedom for $400 with the help of abolitionist lawyers. The law named after him prevented the use of state facilities in the capture of fugitives. After 1850 African Americans and their allies kept personal liberty laws alive, fighting in courts, putting pressure on commissioners, and helping fugitives who were reclaimed escape or buy their freedom.[7]

Even though most fugitives remained free, the new act enraged activists and terrified African Americans. For many white northerners it was evidence that enslavers held dangerous power over the federal government and showed that they could use that power not only to lay claim to enslaved people but to overstep the civil liberties of all American citizens. For many that was a step too far. William Wells Brown claimed that the act "converted the entire country, North and South, into one vast hunting ground."[8] He obviously took that description to heart in his own experience. Harriet Jacobs, who was also at risk of recapture, described the act as "disastrous" for Black families. From New York, she detailed how families who had lived in the city for decades were forced to flee. Centering its effects on the domestic life of African Americans, Jacobs recalled how "many a poor washerwoman" was "obliged to sacrifice her furniture, bid a hurried farewell to friends, and seek her fortune among strangers in Canada." Jacobs was not exaggerating. African Americans moved there in record numbers. By 1860, the country's census recorded 20,000 Black people and 3,500 fugitives.[9]

While many abolitionist responses to the act were about large-scale resistance and big political and constitutional questions, Jacobs focused on its more intimate effects in disrupting people's private lives, forcing them out of their homes, and separating their families just as slavery itself did. Revelations of status could cause the separation of families when a wife or husband found out that their loved one was still enslaved and had to leave to protect themselves from the law. Jacobs herself hid in her employer's home, afraid to go out except when necessity required. She searched the newspapers for arrivals from the South, fearing to see her enslaver's name among them. Jacobs, along with thousands like her, was "condemned" to "incessant fear." Eventually Jacobs left New York for the relative safety of New England.[10]

Response to the Fugitive Slave Act of 1850 pushed questions of law and action even further to the fore of abolitionist discussions over tactics. From their responses, it is clear that African Americans and their abolitionist allies felt themselves to be facing a new phase in their activism against slavery and its political power over the country. E. H. Gray, pastor at a Baptist church in Shelburne Falls, Massachusetts, declared that the "Fugitive Bill is at variance with, contravenes, scorns and overrides the law of God." Gray believed that to obey the act was to "disobey God." William Wells Brown thought that it was an "unconstitutional measure" in every respect.[11] Just as the act changed the legal landscape for African Americans, calls for self-defense as the "first law of nature" and talk of new responsibilities displayed a deepening resistance to slave law. The *Pennsylvania Freeman* asserted that the act would "bring new trials and duties to the friends of justice, freedom and order." Jacobs described how African Americans turned to each other for protection, keeping their "eyes wide open" and forming vigilance committees as needed. This resistance and its role in escalating animosity between northern and southern states would help push the nation toward war.[12]

The culture of danger experienced by Black communities created a new urgency for legal freedom as a matter of survival even as illegal action continued unabated by threats from enslavers and the federal government. Notices of kidnappers, enslavers, and their henchmen recapturing enslaved African Americans, as well as stories of movement efforts to raise money to secure the release of fugitives either before or after they were captured, abounded in abolitionist print culture after 1850. The effects of the Fugitive Slave Act were everywhere, but so, too, were abolitionist responses. The vigilance committees Jacobs described had concentrated their efforts on helping fugitives since the 1840s, as Jesse Olsavsky has shown. By this period, the work of the vigilance committees had homed in on "illegal fugitive aid, not its legal forms," while they still juggled aboveground techniques as needed.[13]

In 1847, not long after the purchase of his freedom, Douglass asked, "What country have I?" Before his manumission, Douglass, like Jacobs, Brown, and others who escaped slavery, lived with the reality that within the boundaries of the United States his freedom was precarious and came with little recourse to the law. Only three years later, enslavers found themselves with increased liberty and federal support to hunt down those who ran away. Enslavers were emboldened and had an axe to grind. As the passage of the Fugitive Slave Act of 1850 made "every citizen of the free States to be a 'slave-catcher,'" Douglass's question was even more pressing than it had been three years earlier. Where could African Americans truly feel safe within the geographical boundaries of the United States?[14] As Jacobs described, many thought there was no satisfactory answer to this question and fled the nation. It is not a coincidence that Black interest in emigration was resurgent in the 1850s and the American Colonization Society saw an increase in activity during this period.[15] Others answered by securing legal release from slavery to remain in the country safely and freely.

I have argued that the way fugitives and Black abolitionist activists engaged with self-purchase is reflective of how those who remained enslaved understood the difficulty and value of buying freedom and worked toward it. While that is certainly true, the context of the fugitive slave crisis in the 1850s overshadowed the role of buying freedom in the everyday lives of enslaved people in the South during the same period. Events at the national level predominated discussions of compensation, which is why they are the focus of this chapter. Whether or not the numbers of people who bought their freedom during the period in response to the Fugitive Slave Act increased at the rate it would appear from abolitionist print culture, the preponderance of stories about buying freedom tells us something about its utility in yet another phase of the restrictive legal landscape in which African Americans and their abolitionist allies maneuvered. They relied on whatever means were necessary to secure freedom.

Abolitionists used these stories to keep the fugitive slave crisis at the forefront of the hearts and minds of white northerners. Cases of self-purchase and compensated manumission offered two advantages for doing so. As it had been for decades, the fundamental outrage of slavery and slave law was inherent in buying freedom. Slavery's extortion provided a critique to which all people who believed in freedom could relate, in a particularly strained political moment. Second, no matter what someone thought of other abolitionist tactics, self-purchase was a legal transaction that even moderates might agree to support in cases that pulled at their heartstrings.

This overrepresentation did not equate with the experiences of enslaved people who remained in the South. Across the region, the enslaved would have found any kind of manumission increasingly difficult as enslavers tried to consolidate their power at the national level and at home. The enslaved also faced questions about what to do with freedom in such a hostile environment.[16] Nor were southerners the only ones who felt the need to deal with the issue of fugitive and legally free African Americans within their borders. In one way or another, anti-Black laws affected all African Americans across status and location from the Midwest to the Deep South.

A small sampling of Maryland manumission records offers us a sense of the difference. The state was, of course, home to so many fugitives from slavery. As for buying freedom, in Anne Arundel County, the county that surrounds Annapolis, 14 manumissions accounting for 21 people out of a total of 112 manumissions included some form of payment from nominal sums to hundreds of dollars in the decade from 1850 to 1860. In the same period, enslaved people in Dorchester County on the state's eastern shore did not exchange any money for freedom. They did, however, exchange time. Out of 35 people manumitted in this period, 4 were delayed manumissions. One woman was to be freed in 1883. Luckily, the war came first.[17]

In Maryland, manumission was outlawed completely in 1860 and cases did appear to cease in some counties. In Queen Anne's County, Maryland, located across from both Baltimore and Washington, DC, around two hundred people were manumitted from 1850 through 1860. From the spring of 1860 until April 1863 there were no manumissions listed. Emancipations started again only during the war. The same is true for Dorchester County, when Lloyd Tubman was manumitted for joining the United States Army in 1864.[18]

The 1850 Kentucky Constitution presents another example of how these restrictions worked to stymie the manumission efforts of African Americans. The constitution allowed the legislature to continue to pass laws relating to emancipation but required that free African Americans leave the state. Those who stayed, or left and returned, were to be declared guilty of a felony and punished according to the law. In Jefferson County, Kentucky, which had the largest population of free African Americans in the state by 1860, this had a drastic and immediate effect on manumissions. There were only three emancipations recorded in the county Court Order books from 1850 to 1854, compared to dozens registered in the previous six years.[19]

In the Deep South, paths to manumission also constricted. Between 1857 and 1860, Mississippi, Arkansas, and Alabama banned manumission. Louisiana banned manumission completely in 1857 after trying several restrictive measures, including requiring enslavers to pay $150 for the obligatory colonization to Liberia of any freed African American in 1852. By 1855 colonization was no longer required, but state courts had to approve all manumissions and to allow the emancipated permission to stay in the state. After 1855 enslavers also had to pay a bond of $1,000 against the formerly enslaved requiring state assistance. These were among the more common restrictions faced by African Americans in southern states. These kinds of payments meant that enslaved people sometimes paid for their freedom by these means as well as for their actual persons. While limitations never fully stopped manumissions, state legislatures played with the fate of African Americans who might otherwise be free. Limited access to manumission might also account for what some abolitionists observed to be an increase in runaways in the 1850s. Given the cost and difficulty of fighting for manumission, some might have felt it not so much harder to make a run for it, even as they faced the bans on the presence of free African Americans in northern states such as Ohio, Illinois, and Indiana.[20] In enacting its own kind of legislation to police Black freedom in the form of the Fugitive Slave Act, the federal government was in step with states across the country.

In the North, the new Fugitive Slave Act worked just as swiftly and dangerously as abolitionists suspected it would. On October 5, 1850, a group of Black New Yorkers gathered in a local park to celebrate the homecoming of James

Hamlet. Hamlet had been arrested just days before under the new Fugitive Slave Act. William P. Powell, the secretary of the meeting, announced to the audience that Hamlet was the first "victim" of the "unconstitutional" act and rejoiced to see him reunited with his wife and children in the city. According to the law, Hamlet was arrested while at work and taken before the local magistrate appointed to deal with fugitive cases. After witness testimony from the son and son-in-law of his enslaver, Mary Brown, the magistrate declared Hamlet to be Brown's property. Hamlet was then delivered to Brown's representatives and taken back to Baltimore, Maryland, where he had escaped from two years earlier. This was supposedly all done so quickly that Hamlet's family did not even know until he was already on his way back to Baltimore. Rumors abounded that his wife died from the shock of the news, but she attended the meeting celebrating his return.[21]

In only a week after his capture, Hamlet returned to New York as a free man. It was not the "genius of universal emancipation" that freed Hamlet but the "irresistible genius of the almighty dollar," as Powell described it. Supporters paid $800 for his freedom. Fundraising was undertaken by the city's *Journal of Commerce*. The New York businessman John H. Woodgate traveled to Baltimore with the money to buy Hamlet's freedom. The paper later complained that abolitionists gave nothing toward his cause. It did point out that Isaac Hollenbeck, an African American man, had contributed money to the fundraiser. The journal claimed to have put abolitionists to further shame by raising almost $4,000 for the manumission and colonization of thirty-nine enslaved people to Liberia. The *NASS* replied to this claim by reminding the *Journal of Commerce* that paying for colonization was not abolitionist business, although it accepted a deed well done in the case of Hamlet. The paper also claimed that the *Journal of Commerce* was decidedly proslavery. It is likely that money for Hamlet's freedom came from supporters of the law who did not want to see its success threatened by any further underground or violent resistance.[22]

In addition to celebrating the release of James Hamlet, Black New Yorkers spoke out against the dangers they faced from "blood-hound commissioners" who cared too little for their freedom. They called on New York's chief magistrate and the mayor to address their precarious position and demanded to know what protections the city would offer them from being kidnapped under the law.

The Black abolitionist Charles B. Ray, who spoke before the October 5 meeting, believed that the unjust legislation should be repealed and declared, "I care not what way freedom comes, provided it does come." His comment merged the problem of buying freedom with all manner of resistance to the Fugitive Slave Act and looked toward the final abolition of slavery. Freedom was what mattered, not how it was achieved. That was true at the individual and state level. African Americans would do whatever it took to secure it for themselves and each other, including paying for it. Hamlet's case was not the only one resolved with the "irresistible genius" of cash. Of the eleven cases brought up under the act in New York City across the decade, three other African Americans were returned by purchase.[23]

Like James Hamlet, Stephen Bennett was also enslaved in Baltimore by a man named Edward B. Gallup. In January 1851 Bennett, whose alias was Bill Baker, was arrested in Columbia, Pennsylvania, some sixty-five miles from Baltimore. Bennett escaped Maryland by boat in 1847 because he feared being sold to Georgia. After his arrival in Pennsylvania, Bennett made a new life for himself. He had a wife and child and some $300 worth of property at the time of his arrest. Bennett was arrested and taken before Commissioner Edward Ingraham, who was assigned to deal with fugitive hearings. His case was moved to Philadelphia, where the PAS, still active in supporting African Americans across the state, wrote out a writ of habeas corpus and petitioned to have Bennett's case removed from Ingraham's command to that of a judge they believed would be more sympathetic to his plight. Ingraham was responsible for returning twelve people to their enslavers in the first four years of the law.[24] These legal techniques ultimately failed and Bennet was declared to be a fugitive and given up to his claimant. Given the political climate, Bennet's supporters were likely prepared for this outcome and immediately raised the funds to purchase his freedom. Most of the $700 was gathered in Columbia, the town Bennett called home. His community came together to ensure he would remain with them.[25]

The cases of Hamlet and Bennett typify the most vulnerable moments for African Americans who escaped slavery. Their ordeals also indicate the new dangers they faced and the way their cases were politicized in resistance to the

Fugitive Slave Act. Many certainly purchased their freedom before they were caught in order to stem the threat they faced. These are cases we may never recover. Historian Richard Blackett found that of 147 fugitive cases tried within the first fifteen months of the act, only 49 resulted in release, either through escape, rescue, or trial. Nine of these releases, or around 18 percent, were secured by purchase.[26]

These early cases quickly rang the alarm to the danger that the law posed to African American communities. Activists responded by organizing. In the third week of August in 1850, Black and white abolitionists such as Frederick Douglass, Mary and Emily Edmonson, Jermain Wesley Loguen, and Gerrit Smith gathered in Cazenovia, New York, near Syracuse, to protest the Fugitive Slave Act. The convention was organized by Smith and Douglass and advertised in abolitionist newspapers by the New York Vigilance Committee. It was described as an event for anyone who had escaped from slavery to find "mutual counsel and encouragement" and to enliven discussions about new kinds of action. Support at both the individual level and planning at the national level were needed. The convention approved a collective response to the new law, which was understood to be just the latest success of the slave power. The convention addressed the enslaved directly. Gerrit Smith drafted an open letter to all enslaved people from those in attendance, giving the meeting's blessing for self-defensive violence against slavery. The time had come to pull out all the stops. Smith described the institution itself as a state of war and so "by all the rules of war, you have the fullest liberty to plunder, burn [and] kill." The laws of slavery were to be held in "perfect contempt" and those present encouraged escape. "Liberty or revolution" was the watchword of the meeting.[27]

The radical nature of the convention's message, paired with its centering of fugitive voices, marked a growing turn toward militancy in abolitionist politics over the course of the 1850s. While dismissing laws meant to protect slavery, many in attendance, including Douglass and the Edmonson sisters, had been forced to acquiesce to purchasing their own freedom. Their participation in the convention highlighted the importance that those who ransomed their freedom played within the larger movement. As Charles B. Ray, who also attended the convention, said after the return of James Hamlet, freedom was the imperative no matter the mechanism.

The problem of how to frame philosophical and ethical questions surrounding buying freedom remained a topic of discussion among abolitionists. In 1851, an article from the *National Era* asked how people could buy freedom while not being "guilty of encouraging slavery." This article answered in the typical way by describing purchase as a ransom. The "tyranny" of the necessity evidenced "brotherly love" not acceptance of an immoral system. The author further compared buying freedom to paying extortionist prices for grain as opposed to starving to death. They closed by putting themselves in the shoes of an enslaved person, stating aptly that they would "pity the *necessity* but hate the *metaphysics* that would deny me aid."[28]

Many agreed with the sentiment. William Still recorded the efforts of an abolitionist named Abigail Goodwin from New Jersey who "denied herself even *necessary apparel*" so that she would have money to support movement work. According to Still, Goodwin not only raised money for the Underground Railroad in Philadelphia but also helped buy people's freedom when needed. In a letter reprinted by Still from the 1850s, Goodwin recorded that she sent more money than she had planned to help purchase a family because she believed that "abolitionists there are all opposed to buying slaves, and will give nothing." The money went toward securing the liberation of a family of ten from North Carolina whose enslaver was willing to manumit them for $1,000. Goodwin described her reasoning, stating that although she did not "like buying them, or giving money to slave-holders either," she thought this was a special case because their freedom could be had for "so cheap." The exigency of the circumstances and possible separation of the family, as well as the low price and fear that others would not contribute, had pushed Goodwin to action. She continued to raise and donate money, clothing, and other items through a local benevolent society to help escaping fugitives.[29] While Goodwin clearly worried about the morality of her methods, her actions reflect the legal and extralegal support systems that abolitionists could provide.

Increased support for buying freedom in this tense political moment can also be measured by the proliferation of warnings about impostor fugitives found throughout movement newspapers across the 1850s. Abolitionists warned each other to be on guard against people who traveled among them and posed as enslaved people raising money for freedom. Abolitionists wanted their money to go to those who they believed truly needed it, but impostors did present a larger problem for the movement. Abolitionists had to prove themselves against the propaganda of enslavers who tried to convince the nation of their delusional view that slavery was a paternalist institution. Every tale that turned out to be false could threaten the veracity of the true stories told by the formerly enslaved and thus undermine the moral fiber of the abolitionist position in the eyes of the public. These cases show that abolitionists were concerned enough about continued support for those who genuinely needed to purchase themselves and loved ones that they attempted to warn each other of false fugitives. In doing so, abolitionists validated compensated manumission as they attempted to invalidate imposters.

Given the popularity of the abolitionist lecture circuit as a space for fundraising, it is unsurprising that some would take advantage of this opportunity to raise money for their own purposes. In fact, this kind of fraud was a rather ingenious way to make a living, as long as one did not get caught. An 1852 news item in *Frederick Douglass' Paper* reported that Mrs. Lee, an African American preacher, was falsely taking up collections for the freedom of a man named Mr. Massey. According to the paper, Massey wanted to assure the public that he was a "free man" and completely capable of caring for himself. In 1855, the Reverend Charles Smith was arrested for falsely presenting himself as a preacher from Washington who was attempting to raise money to redeem some of his family members. While Smith succeeded in collecting money from a number of people, he raised enough suspicions that when accreditations were demanded he was found to be a fake. "A Word of Caution," in the same edition that revealed news of Smith's arrest, warned readers about a "certain class of men, who are, apparently, growing quite numerous" and who were trying to "deceive the unwary" by looking for funds to free family members.[30]

Canada's *Provincial Freeman* told readers about William Carter, who was deemed to be a "dangerous man." Carter alternately traveled to raise money to buy his own freedom or that of his family. His story varied depending on his location. Carter was supposedly a free Black property owner in Canada. Carter admitted to having raised $400 in Detroit and wanted to continue his tour in England to get even more money. Carter seemed to have intimate knowledge of abolitionist sentiments and worked people's political positions against them to get donations. In one instance he had supposedly visited a mayor who donated to him and sent him on to a local abolitionist to see if "those pretended friends would give as much" as he had. Perhaps Carter had read the back and forth between the *Journal of Commerce* and the *NASS* in the aftermath of the James Hamlet rescue for this idea. The abolitionist played into Carter's hand, declaring that while it was against his principles, they would not be "out-done by a slave-ocrat." He gave Carter ten dollars.[31]

As to the warnings published against him, Carter claimed that they were solely a matter of "personal dislike." Reflecting the militancy of the decade, Carter was determined to use his pistols if the editor of the *Provincial Freeman*, or any other paper, continued to dispute his identity and threaten his right to raise money "in any way he please[d]." A year later, in 1856, the *NASS* also warned its readers about Carter, describing his physical appearance and surmising that there were others working with him in Canada on "this imposition." They believed that Carter may have been the face of a collective scheme.[32]

The motives and lived experience of African Americans who attempted to defraud abolitionists out of money remain silenced in these articles. Certainly, the broader racism they faced in the free states made economic stability difficult for all African Americans. Carter's technique shows an understanding of what was at stake in the personal and political self-image of individuals. Carter knew the uses of abolitionist networks and planned to take his scheme across the Atlantic, like others before him, and he threatened violence if his plans were stalled. Yet his tactics may also reflect the economic desperation experienced by many Black people in Canada in the 1850s.[33]

There are also interesting claims made to knowledge of a particular kind of authentic Black experience by both those who used it to get money and those who had the power to decide who was deserving of money and who was lying. For those like Carter, Black fugitivity became not only an endangered state of being but a performance. The abolitionists who they tried to deceive were themselves in the precarious position of legitimating certain aspects of what they imagined Black life to be as they policed potentially false claims. They did so even if they had the best of intentions.

The *Provincial Freeman* believed that growing "sympathy" for those who escaped slavery in the 1850s had caused a proliferation of "unprincipled" people to take advantage of allies who were willing to donate money for freedom. Another issue raised by fake cases of fundraising for freedom was how the technique worked within the Black and abolitionist rhetoric of uplift. Notably, Mary Ann Shadd Cary, editor of the *Provincial Freeman*, ended her letter about William Carter by describing him as a "disgrace to the colored people."[34]

In 1859, the *Anti-slavery Bugle* elaborated on this issue. It directed readers who were interested in giving money to the enslaved to look out for those "too lazy to work, but not too honest to steal." The paper suggested that everyone should "thoroughly investigate" any claims before donating. The editors seem unaware of the ways that this suggestion mirrored the surveillance of African Americans and fugitives by supporters of the Fugitive Slave Act. If a "single link" in the "chain of evidence" was questionable, they should not give any money, the *Bugle* claimed. To do so despite reservations would only serve to encourage impostors and was harmful to those who were "fit objects" for the support of abolitionists. Those with the money were the ones who should decide the fitness of the cause. The warning closed with the story of Mrs. Wright, who claimed to be raising money to buy her children. The *Bugle* described her story as "totally unworthy" of belief. Admitting that even they had once found her worthy of charity, the paper now withdrew anything that was previously said in support of her fundraising efforts.[35]

As these concerns over tricksters show, northern communities felt great pressure to help when it was possible to free people through purchase, especially when the alternative was the separation of families and remaining enslaved. Many African Americans, like William Wells Brown, had cause for concern as they recognized the necessity and utility of the legal freedom afforded by purchase, even if they had steeled themselves against it on moral grounds. Some enslavers, like Enoch Price, seemed to hope to use this to their advantage or at least to taunt abolitionists with the opportunity to put their beliefs into action.

While African Americans and their supporters tried to protect their free lives, slaveholders took advantage of the new benefits afforded them by the law to recapture their human property.

Elizabeth Moore had lived in Baltimore for years with her children. In 1851, Daniel Fossbeuner claimed Moore's children as his slaves and had her son William arrested as a fugitive. Moore herself had been subject to some kind of term slavery. According to Fossbeuner, Moore had failed to pay the $100 which they agreed could be exchanged to buy out the remaining eight years of her enslavement. Moore was allowed to go out on her own to make the money. But because she failed to complete these terms, she was not free and her children were technically his property by law. To protect her son, Moore claimed that her own son had died and that William was adopted. However, Fossbeuner identified him by a mark on his head. Next, Fossbeuner claimed Moore's two daughters. Abolitionists believed that Fossbeuner had known of Moore's location for some sixteen years but had never bothered to reclaim her. Now, though, profit and the law were on his side. The children were supposedly worth $1,800. Fossbeuner stood to pocket that entire amount, minus his expenses in finding them, because he had paid nothing for their upbringing. Moore had been responsible for them throughout the years that they lived as free people. Upon William's arrest, it was reported that Moore fell into convulsions as she pleaded for her child.[36] As Harriet Jacobs described, this heart-wrenching scene shows that no matter how long someone had lived as a free person, or what kind of family life they built for themselves, the possibility of their lives falling apart in an instant was ever present. It was exactly this possibility that led many enslaved people to buy freedom, flee the United States, or defend themselves to the death when this moment arrived.

As the tenor of the Cazenovia Convention revealed, violent resistance from African Americans, abolitionists, as well as enslavers increased as the Fugitive Slave Act gave each party new determination to defy or uphold the law. The infamous Christiana, Pennsylvania, uprising in 1851 was one such example of self-defense in the face of recapture. In September 1851, the Maryland enslaver Edward Gorsuch traveled to Pennsylvania to recapture a group of fugitives, including George and Joshua Hammond, Nelson Ford, and Noah Buley. When Gorsuch's armed posse arrived at the home of William Parker, a local African

American man, they were met by armed fugitives and their accomplices who valiantly fought off the attempts of the Gorsuch party to reenslave them. In the ensuing conflict, Gorsuch was killed and his son seriously wounded. Although many were arrested for their part in the uprising, all were acquitted. Some, like William Parker, escaped to Canada. The case lit up national news as a marker of how the Fugitive Slave Act sparked sectional violence and because of the determination of African Americans and their allies to resist reenslavement.[37] Although the fugitives claimed at Christiana did not have to buy their freedom to escape the far-reaching tentacles of slavery, encounters like these showcased the social, physical, and political violence enacted against African Americans by those attempting to carry out the Fugitive Slave Act and the high-stake terms of the conflict. Resistance required a number of self-defensive techniques.

On May 24, 1852, just about an hour north of Christiana, all those present in the Harrisburg office of Commissioner Richard McAllister listened to the complicated history of James Phillips's enslavement in Virginia. Dennis Hudson, for instance, testified that Phillips was given to his brother by their father. In turn his brother sold Phillips to another man, who hired him out to someone else. Witnesses claimed that no one in Virginia had seen Phillips since 1838. Phillips had lived in Pennsylvania for fourteen years when he was arrested at work as a fugitive. In those fourteen years since his escape from Virginia, he had found work driving horses for merchants and the local railroad, made friends, and had gotten married and started a family. He was kidnapped by violent measures and taken before Commissioner McAllister in what abolitionists described as a "state of insensibility." The trial was declared a sham by local supporters, but that did not matter to McAllister, who was known for his proslavery sentiments. Phillips was given over to his captors and taken to the county jail until he could be sent back to Virginia. Crowds gathered in the street to see Phillips taken into the jail. His wife, who was in attendance, produced the "most agonizing screams" upon seeing her husband imprisoned. The next day Phillips was taken to Baltimore and then on to Virginia.[38]

The case raised much indignation in Harrisburg and, as soon as Phillips was taken from the city, supporters set about redeeming him from slavery. The *Harrisburg Standard* published a moving letter written by Phillips to his wife in which he described his fear that he would soon be sold even farther south. Phillips stated that he would "almost rather die than to go South." With evident urgency, he asked his wife to tell everyone at home that he needed help immediately. Phillips had already been doing his own work to arrange to buy his freedom from Virginia and had details for her. He told her they could buy his freedom for $900 and gave her directions for how to secure help, raise the money, and pay his enslaver. The pain of separation is palpable in the published letter. Phillips's fear of sale and further separation from his family permeates the letter and he insists on the speed needed to save him from an even worse fate. Phillips said he was "almost a dying" to see his wife and children. He encouraged his wife and supporters to think nothing of the price, claiming that he was worth twice as much and would work diligently to repay them for his purchase price. By August, Phillips was redeemed by the citizens of Harrisburg and reunited with his family and friends.[39]

The *Pennsylvania Freeman* celebrated James Phillips's homecoming but still worried about the precedent these cases set. The paper worried that paying "exorbitant prices" to rescue fugitives from slavery encouraged enslavers to come after them in the first place. They knew they could reap the benefits of this "pecuniary stimulus," and it led them to capture people who they might otherwise leave "undisturbed."[40] This was not wholly accurate as the ease with which enslavers could retake escapees under the Fugitive Slave Act alone offered them ample stimulus. Certainly, though, enslavers may have thought it was better to get something than nothing, especially given the costs of recapture, which would likely cost more than the enslaved were worth.[41] This may explain why enslavers did not always demand market or extortionist prices for fugitives.

Phillips offered another vantage point to understanding the problem the *Freeman* warned about. Phillips knew that he was worth much more than $900 and that he could easily repay his supporters. While he does not make his meaning completely clear, it seems that Phillips was referring to both his market value and Daina Ramey Berry's idea of soul value at the same time. He also knew enough about the process of redeeming himself and how to negotiate it against the possible offers of slave traders to immediately put the wheels of his freedom in motion. This had to do with his own knowledge of slavery's market but also because he knew that his liberation was a priceless endeavor. It was the only thing that would bring him back to his Harrisburg home and loved ones. Enticing enslavers, as the *Freeman* feared, mattered much less than the purchase of Phillips's freedom and his return. The necessity and urgency of legal freedom is made clear in the cries of Elizabeth Moore as she was separated from her stolen son and daughters probably forever.

Some enslavers and traders did indeed take advantage of the type of goodwill that saved Phillips by taunting abolitionists and those who sought to protect their loved ones. During James Phillips's crisis, the *NASS* ran a story about one enslaver who supposedly captured an enslaved man in California. While still there, the man advertised that he would sell the slave, who was worth $300, for only $100. He supposedly did this to prove a point. He wanted abolitionists to show that they had "honourable principle about them." The enslaver was willing to sacrifice the additional money to see if activists would rather pay for his slave's release than "play their old game" of stealing enslaved people away. The article claimed that the nameless fugitive, on his part, desired to be sold in California rather than be taken back to Mississippi.[42] This seems more like a moral fable for abolitionists to reflect on than a true story. However, it is easy to see how it was based in actual events. While "pecuniary stimulus" may have convinced some enslavers to let the enslaved buy their freedom, others had their own worries about allowing it.

One case in which the determination of both abolitionists and enslavers was made apparent was that of Anthony Burns. In 1854, Burns was captured in Boston, Massachusetts, and given over to Charles Suttle, who claimed him as a slave. Burns was returned to slavery despite the best efforts of the city's activists to rescue him and general disapproval of the trial across the state. Burns's case made national headlines, too, as federal troops made sure that Burns was successfully returned to Virginia. The militarized response was due partly to earlier fugitive rescue missions like that of Shadrach Minkins in Boston in 1851. Enslavers and their sympathizers wanted to ensure that the law was upheld.

After Suttle won Burns back in the Boston courtroom, he sold him to a North Carolina slave trader for $700. The sale included one interesting condition: the trader was not to sell Burns to anyone in the North under any circumstances. In effect, Burns was not to be purchased for manumission. Like the author who considered the sale of the Edmonson sisters to be a bad example to enslaved people, Suttle thought it would set a bad precedent. It was a "point of Southern honor" to keep Burns enslaved. Given the federal effort and national attention to his recapture, Suttle likely believed that for the law to continue to work, Burns's punishment for escaping needed to be harsh and permanent. While keeping Burns enslaved may have given Suttle satisfaction on an individual level, enslavers found "little comfort" in renditions, and recaptures "did even less to appease those committed to secession," according to Richard Blackett.[43] Even when the law worked according to plan, most Americans, whether they were on the side of Suttle or Burns, understood that the stakes of the slavery issue were already much higher for the entire nation.

Unphased by Suttle's arrangement, Burns's supporters in Boston tried to arrange to buy his freedom. The Black abolitionist Reverend Leonard Grimes and others worked to make a deal with Suttle, negotiating with him in both Boston and Virginia. Time and again they were refused. Suttle seemed determined to make his point.[44] While negotiations continued, Burns remained steadfast and determined to return no matter what his enslaver had planned. Threatening the violence that came to define the 1850s, Burns claimed that he would return to the North even if he had to "wade through blood to my neck" and become captain in a "general uprising of the slaves." Burns did not have to go so far. Eventually supporters found him in the possession of another enslaver who was willing to sell him for $1,300. Suttle himself had even reconsidered selling Burns and had asked to be paid $1,500 for Burns and the costs he had incurred while capturing him.[45] If Suttle was going to surrender his principle, he was at least going to make abolitionists pay for it.

The Burns case brought up questions about personal liberty laws and the role of state and local facilities in fugitive renditions. Blackett estimates that it cost the federal government and the state of Massachusetts some $40,000 to return Burns. The *NASS* reprinted a letter to the editor of a Boston newspaper requesting that the members of law enforcement who served during the Burns rendition reject their pay as "blood money" to send a message to southerners that the "love of freedom and order" was not a "marketable commodity" in the North. Burns was redeemed partly with donations made to the Reverend Grimes by US District Attorney Marshall who sought to "mitigate the public opinion which brand[ed]" his office as "kidnappers."[46] Despite these claims, as many African Americans understood, freedom was indeed a valuable and marketable commodity.

As late as 1858 southerners had not given up on their attempts to make an example out of Anthony Burns. In the summer of that year, the *NASS* reprinted an article from the *Virginia Herald* which claimed that Burns was in a Massachusetts penitentiary for robbery. In reality, Burns was in Oberlin, Ohio. The *Herald's* falsehood was meant to suggest to readers, and likely to enslaved people, that the most "prominent incident" of northern Black freedom was the "perpetration of crime and a home in the Penitentiary." Burns and abolitionists would have understood slavery as the true prison. The ultimate "crime of robbery" had been committed by Charles Suttle and other enslavers like him.[47]

In step with fantastic recoveries and rescues that made national headlines, like that of Anthony Burns, less well-known African Americans continued to use compensated manumission to reunite with family members who were still enslaved. In the fall of 1854, *Frederick Douglass' Paper* reported on a man named Edward Brown who hoped to redeem eight of his children who were still enslaved in Virginia. As was so often the case, the Brown family already had a history of buying freedom. Brown had freed himself, his wife, and two of their children. He needed to raise an additional $2,700 to buy the rest of his family. If he succeeded, he would have spent a total of $5,000 for their freedom. After they were reunited, Brown planned to move to Liberia with his family. If Brown decided to emigrate it is possible that the difficulties he experienced while buying his family had made him wary of remaining with them in the United States. Certainly, the decade offered little hope to free African Americans. Given the resurgence of colonizationist activities in the period, it is also possible that he had made a deal with the enslavers of family members or received the support of the ACS to free his children if Brown would agree to leave the country.[48]

Family considerations remained of paramount importance, forcing African Americans to make all manner of difficult decisions like this. The Black abolitionist and Presbyterian minister James W. C. Pennington, who was a fugitive himself, condemned the "chattel principle" of slavery outright. In his narrative, Pennington stated that this original "SIN of slavery" was present and oppressive, even in the institution's "mildest form." Anyone who was forced to buy freedom would have agreed. As an activist, Pennington personally understood the pressing necessity of buying freedom experienced by Edward Brown and his family. Pennington's church had helped raise money to buy the freedom of the Edmonson sisters after the failed mass escape on the *Pearl*.[49]

Pennington's own familial story of self-purchase spanned the pre- and post-1850 United States and he knew dearly the pain of separation. When he escaped in the 1820s, he was forced to leave his mother, father, and eleven siblings in Maryland. After living in the North for some two decades, Pennington decided to try to purchase himself and family members. Pennington did not believe in the practice as a "general rule" but knew that it was convenient to all those involved. Like Burns's supporters, he faced an obstinate enslaver. Pennington claimed that the man, despite practicing the supposedly mild form of slavery, was a "perpetualist." By this Pennington meant that his enslaver was staunchly opposed to manumission and thought that free African Americans were a "great nuisance."[50]

Pennington's enslaver, Frisby Tilghman, wrote back to the lawyer Pennington had hired to conduct the negotiations with an offer of $550 for his freedom and no mention of his parents, whom he hoped to buy. Tilghman also accused Pennington of the theft of himself. Despite his enslaver's obstinance, Pennington remained hopeful. To raise the money, Pennington sold his library of four hundred volumes and got financial support from as far away as Jamaica. While he balked at having to do so just to be "let alone," Pennington raised enough to offer $500 for himself and his parents. Writing to Tilghman, Pennington responded that any deal had to include them. He further asked that the charge of theft be renounced. He never got a response to either of these requests.

Using what he called another "kind of operation," Pennington's father and two brothers eventually made it to Canada. Two of his sisters married free men who were able to buy their freedom. His family's story reminds us of the importance of free family members, whether in the North or South, in securing the freedom of their loved ones who remained enslaved. With the passage of the

Fugitive Slave Act, Pennington traveled to Scotland for his own protection. Supporters in the UK arranged to buy his freedom for $150 with the help of John Hooker in Connecticut.[51] Tilghman may not have believed in manumission, but once he was dead his heirs likely realized that they would never get another cent out of Pennington while he remained in the UK. But this was not the end of Pennington's family saga.

In the early hours of the morning on May 25, 1851, Pennington's brother and nephews Stephen, Jacob, and Robert Pembroke were arrested in New York City. Like Pennington, they had escaped from Maryland and arrived in New York via Philadelphia with the help of William Still. By late morning of the same day, they appeared in court and were surrendered to their enslavers, David Smith and Jacob Grove. Pennington and others complained of malpractice in the case, including his inability to provide counsel to his family because he was told the wrong time for the hearing. Counsel, of course, was not guaranteed by the law, although many African Americans and activists ensured that fugitives received it.[52] A few days later, however, Grove reached out to Pennington offering his brother's freedom for sale. If Pennington did not purchase him, Grove said he would be sold south. The money Grove could get for his property appeared to matter more than its source. Pennington's nephews, Jacob and Robert, were to be sold to a merchant in North Carolina. Pennington used a "brother's heart" to appeal to the public to raise the money to save his brother. Supporters paid over $1,300 for Pembroke's triumphant return to New York. Grove had included his costs for the recovery in the price of Pembroke's freedom. While grateful to those who helped him get free, Pembroke remained determined to save his sons.[53]

While Pembroke was reunited with his brother, he lost his sons in the process. Some abolitionists believed that the blame for this failure lay at the feet of those who had helped them escape unsuccessfully. This failure was even greater than their return because it necessitated Pembroke's ransom and the final loss of his sons. Pennington, however, argued against the authorities who secured their recapture and the law itself. Writing in *Frederick Douglass' Paper* a year after his brother's arrest, Pennington denounced the involvement of local law enforcement in fugitive cases and called for reform to protect the rights of African Americans. Pennington showed that while he was willing to submit to the practicality of buying freedom to be free and see his family again after sixteen years, he was not willing to be treated like a person without rights and at the whim of slave law.[54]

While people like Pennington and William Wells Brown held out as long as they could before acquiescing to self-purchase, many African Americans refused to allow the act to change their political stance against buying freedom. Rebecca Jones was one such person. Jones, a twenty-eight-year-old woman with three daughters, escaped slavery when her family was threatened with sale after the death of their enslaver even though she believed she was supposed to be freed in the will. In 1856, rather than being purchased by supporters, Jones escaped by hiding in a boat and traveling from Virginia to Philadelphia. Jones supposedly refused to pay as little as "three cents" for her freedom. Jones knew the risks that running away entailed.[55] According to William Still, who recorded her story in his book *The Underground Railroad*, Jones's husband escaped years earlier with Shadrach Minkins, one of the first fugitives caught in Massachusetts under the Fugitive Slave Law. Despite recapture, Minkins was not reenslaved. Activists quickly gathered at the Boston courthouse where Minkins was held, forcefully rescued him, and secured his passage to Montreal.[56]

Following in their footsteps, Jones moved on to Boston with her daughters Sarah Frances, Mary, and Rebecca. Although her husband still lived in the city, Jones had not heard from him for some time. In October 1856, she wrote to William Still from Boston about her plans to move to California. The news she had gotten of her husband was unsatisfactory, and Jones was "firm as ever" that she did not want to be reunited with him. The nature of these unsatisfactory revelations about her husband are not revealed by Still, but Jones told Still that her husband had been "making inquiries" about her and lived nearby. She believed her family would be better off in California, perhaps because they would have a better chance of escaping not only slavecatchers but also her husband for reasons that remained private.[57]

As an enslaved woman and girls, Jones and her daughters certainly risked all manner of violence if recaptured by their enslavers. Whatever fear Jones felt about them remaining subject to enslavement, she refused to compromise by accepting their legal manumission. Her refusal may have been rooted in abolitionist principle alone or may have masked some other trauma that Jones did not wish to share. Being threatened with sale and facing separation from her daughters after the death of their enslaver was certainly a terrifying prospect. As with the Edmonson sisters, Jones may have feared their fate as young women. The financial complications of the probate of her former enslaver's will and how it all affected the people he enslaved may have turned her off to any further compensation for her enslaver's family. She may have believed that their enslaver had made enough of a profit off them and that it was his time to lose. As with why she also wanted to protect her family from her husband, Jones had her reasons despite them remaining hidden from our sight. Her story echoes the precarious position of African American women whether they were enslaved, fugitive, or free.

Steadfast refusal in the context of familial complications like those of the Jones family was not unheard of. While J. W. C. Pennington had a complicated relationship with principle and practicality, the reverend and abolitionist Jermain Wesley Loguen was an outspoken opponent of self-purchase and the Fugitive Slave Act of 1850. He remained so across his career. Loguen escaped slavery in Tennessee and lived in both Canada and upstate New York. Loguen, too, was concerned about his family. He thought often of the "cruel bondage" faced by his relatives while he enjoyed his freedom. These thoughts were the "torments [of] the fugitive." Friends in his community attempted to purchase his mother, Cherry, for $250. Her enslaver refused to sell Cherry because Loguen was incapable of owning his mother until he "owned himself." Offered a reunion with his mother, Loguen still refused to purchase his freedom and instead took aim at the law that separated them. In 1850, he spoke before a convention in Syracuse, New York, and decried the new Fugitive Slave Act and the nature of ransomed liberty. Although grateful for the community he built and its support, Loguen reminded the audience that although their concern over the law was new, he had lived as a fugitive for much longer. In refusing to obey the act, Loguen declared that "it outlaws me, and I outlaw it." Practicing what he preached, Loguen risked his freedom by assisting others in escaping slavery's clutches. In 1851, Loguen helped with the successful Jerry Rescue in Syracuse and was forced to flee to Canada to escape trial for his role in it.[58]

Other activists made strategic use of their status to face the Fugitive Slave Act with righteous indignation and self-defense, proving that they would not be cowed by enslavers or federal law. William and Ellen Craft, who made their infamous escape from Georgia by Ellen passing as a disabled white man traveling with her enslaved servant and who refused to have children who would be enslaved, faced the same dangers as Loguen in Boston. When the Crafts heard that their enslaver had sent agents to the city to arrest them, they determined not to go back to slavery, no matter what the cost. Members of the city's vigilance committee stood fast to help them. An armed William Craft blockaded himself in his home to resist arrest, while Ellen was spirited out of the city.

The slave catchers who had come to Massachusetts for them offered an opportunity for the Crafts to purchase their freedom if William would submit to arrest. Believing that they were either trying to trick him or to make a show of force with him, Craft refused on political grounds. Instead, he remained ready to return the trick with violence if needed. Craft believed that his situation was representative of that of hundreds of other fugitives in the city who did not have his notoriety and security nor capacity to resist. Because of his position, Craft said that even if his freedom could be bought for "two cents" he would refuse to do it. He would "stand his ground and try the strength of the law." To protect their freedom, the Crafts later left the United States and moved to England, where they lived for almost two decades, returning to the United States after the Civil War. Like Lougen, they used their story to speak out against the Fugitive Slave Act in the name of all those who were threatened by it. Fugitives like Jones, Loguen, and the Crafts used their outright refusal to buy freedom to register their outrage against state violence and the violence of slavery, and to highlight the connections between the two.[59] They, too, had perhaps learned something from debates about Douglass's freedom in an ever-changing world. Luckily for them, the arrests that they feared dropped off across the North after 1855.[60]

While abolitionists debated and made use of compensation in a political landscape rife with new and old tensions, a movement calling for national compensated emancipation as a way to abolish slavery in the United States also emerged in the Civil War era. Despite the difficult task of convincing abolitionists to pay for emancipation, there were still antislavery activists, like Gerrit Smith and the peace activist Elihu Burritt, who put forward plans for national compensated emancipation. Smith, of course, was no stranger to paying for freedom.

The movement for compensated emancipation, led by Burritt and supported by Smith, was founded on the premise that compensating southern slaveholders for emancipating their slaves would lead to the peaceful end of slavery in the United States. Burritt, who was an advocate for peace, believed that this might be one way to keep the nation from war, an ending which seemed ever more likely as the decade advanced. Despite having to fight against the outright rejection of compensation by America's most influential abolitionists, schemes for national emancipation did find some support.[61]

In the 1840s, Burritt began his reform work as an advocate for world peace. Through his work Burritt became immersed in the world of reform in both the United States and England. He worked on and edited several newspapers and journals devoted to different issues, including abolition, temperance, and peace. Burritt wrote and traveled extensively as a member of the American Peace Society and was editor of its journal, the *Advocate of Peace and Universal Brotherhood*. While in England, Burritt helped form the League of Universal Brotherhood, an international peace group that called for the "elevation of man . . . irrespective of his country, color, character, or condition." It was also while in England that Burritt became interested in free labor ideologies and workers' rights. Combining his interests, Burritt sought to reach out to the laboring classes to become advocates for peace. Abolition was an important issue for Burritt since universal free labor would improve the conditions of all working-class people.[62]

For Burritt, each of these causes were intricately related. William Wells Brown once wrote of Burritt that "if he opposes Slavery, it is upon the grounds of peace." Brown also recalled that some complained that Burritt was too much of a "cloud-traveller" in his ideas. Perhaps they described Burritt in this way because of his audacity to imagine peace or that either abolitionists or enslavers would agree to compensated emancipation.[63] Using England's example of compensation for enslavers in the West Indies, Burritt claimed that this was the only way to peacefully resolve the problem of American slavery. He believed that the movement could attract a large group of followers and be more inclusive than other wings of American abolitionism. The plan, like colonization, could appeal to moderates and perhaps even some enslavers.[64]

Like Rufus King before him, Burritt thought that the funds needed to compensate enslavers could come from selling off lands in the West. Neither Burritt, nor King, ever mentioned what would become of the Native American nations who inhabited those lands. Even in the cause of emancipation, settler colonialism and the success of the American imperial project were related. By the mid-1850s, Burritt threw himself full force into promoting compensated emancipation. Repeating a familiar routine from his days as a lecturer for peace, Burritt wrote about his plan and traveled across the country hoping to gain supporters. He met with varying success. Burritt recalled that at a meeting of the Rochester Ladies Anti-Slavery Society, his proposal for compensated emancipation was denounced with "great and almost bitter energy" by those present at the lecture. One attendee at the meeting, Frederick Douglass, gave "testimony against" the plan in a "courteous way." At another meeting in Trenton, New Jersey, Burritt addressed the state legislature and gained the support of many, including the governor. Burritt claimed that this was the most important group of people he had ever lectured on the merits of compensated emancipation. He must have been fortified by this success.[65]

With the assistance of Gerrit Smith, Burritt finally convened a national meeting on compensated emancipation in Ohio in 1857. The violence in Kansas between anti- and proslavery forces helped propel national interest in a peaceful method to end slavery. Declaring that the stakes were nothing less than the "glorious consummation" of the Union, the convention led to the creation of the National Compensated Emancipation Society (NCES). The society's goal was to foster cooperation "in a generous and brotherly spirit, with the people of the South, and share with them the expense necessary to the extinction of Slavery." Their plan included an answer to the AASS's claim in the *Declaration of Sentiments* that if anyone was to receive money for abolition it should be the enslaved. The NCES's plan offered $25 paid by the federal government to every formerly enslaved person. Enslavers would be paid no more than $250 for each slave. Additional payments could be subsidized by state governments if they so desired. Mixing moral suasion and political abolition techniques, members of the NCES were called on to do whatever they could to "interest the public mind in its favor" and to sustain the movement in order to bring forward measures in Congress to support this "pacific and generous" plan to abolish slavery.[66] Despite holding a national meeting, hardly any abolitionists were interested. It is hard to imagine how this federal plan would have worked given the financial strain of the Panic of 1857. The economic panic may have influenced the more general apathy toward compensation even among moderates who sought the end of slavery.

In 1859, Burritt regrouped and tried once again to organize a convention in Albany, New York. This convention also suffered from low attendance. With the nation now on the eve of the Civil War, William Lloyd Garrison claimed that Burritt's plan was hopeless from both a moral and practical standpoint. Others agreed with Garrison and wondered how Burritt could assume that abolitionists would "have the hypocrisy thus to stultify and contradict themselves" and to make "league with the imperious advocates of human chattel." Critics said that Burritt might ask abolitionists for money, but that his idea demanded that they renounce their "principles and subscribe to a falsehood." It was a "libel upon God and humanity." Not mincing words, his detractors called for the NCES to give up its "suicidal position" and fight for emancipation on principle, not by payment.[67]

A letter published in the *Provincial Freeman* questioned the practicality of Burritt's emancipation plan. The author thought that national events in the United States had already led to the "abrogation of the Compromise line." While abolitionists refused to accept Burritt's plan, enslavers would no longer accept it either. Many believed that enslavers had no reason to accept the end of their institution willingly, especially given the tenor of American politics after the Supreme Court's *Dred Scott v. Sanford* decision in 1857. The *Freeman's* letter argued that the *Dred Scott* decision had "thrown the aegis of protection around the monster" of slavery. The decision stated that African Americans could not be citizens of the United States and found the Missouri Compromise to be unconstitutional, in effect turning the nation into slave territory. Coming after

the Fugitive Slave Act, this decision was the final blow for many who believed
that it exposed all they needed to know about American law and its relation to
African Americans. In early April, African Americans held a meeting in Philadelphia to express their outrage over the decision. They denounced it as the
final proof that in the Constitution and to United States government African
Americans were "nothing" and could be "nothing but an alien, disfranchised and
degraded class." The meeting resolved that to continue supporting a government
that believed this about them was the "height of folly." Robert Purvis, still active
in abolitionist circles, tried to convince his fellow attendees that the decision
itself was unconstitutional.[68]

The question of whether such a powerful section of the nation would ever
surrender their lucrative way of life when they had such little reason to compromise loomed large in discussions of the NCES. Yet there were other questions
about the details of Burritt's plan. Some objected to Burritt's intention to raise
funds by selling land in the West. From the enslaver's point of view, the sale of
public lands by the federal government meant that southern states were already
entitled to a portion of the profits. It seemed unlikely, then, that they would
accept that money as payment to liberate enslaved people. On the other hand,
there were also many northerners who would not want to hand over their portion of the land sales to enslavers. According to the *Provincial Freeman*, they
had "already filched fortunes from the labor of the lash driven slave" and did not
deserve anything further. Despite the national conventions and Burritt's unceas-
ing dedication to compensated emancipation, it is not surprising that Burritt's
plan failed to gain the support it needed to end slavery, given its critics' pointed
appraisals.[69]

Although Burritt was not able to stop the Civil War with his plan for a peaceful solution to the national problem of slavery, schemes for compensated emancipation did not die with the Confederacy's firing on Fort Sumter in Charleston,
South Carolina, in 1861. As the war continued on longer than most Americans
had imagined possible, the Lincoln administration also considered compensated
emancipation to end slavery and end the war. Not long after the war started,
the Lincoln administration put forward a plan in which the federal government

would pay slaveholders $400 per enslaved person. Writing to Senator James A. McDougall, Lincoln claimed that at that rate all the enslaved in Delaware could be paid for with the money it cost to pay for one half day of war. For the cost of eighty-seven days of war, enslaved people in Delaware, Maryland, the District of Columbia, Kentucky, and Missouri could be freed. Lincoln made the comparison to the cost of the war to suggest that compensated emancipation was cheaper than the war effort. It was cheaper both monetarily and in terms of the continued threat of violence and death. However, as had already been argued in abolitionist circles, there was no guarantee that slaveholders would have accepted such a low price, especially considering that some of the most valuable enslaved people were worth upwards of $1,800 by 1860. One scholar of economic history has considered what terms enslavers may have accepted and believes that compensated emancipation would have cost the federal government from between six to nine billion dollars.[70] Both war and paying for freedom were costly ventures.

Although compensated emancipation was likely impossible on a national level, Lincoln did successfully employ it to end slavery in Washington, DC. Abolitionists had long argued that control over both slavery and its abolition in the District of Columbia was within the power of the federal government and consistently implored the government to use its power. The April 1862 District of Columbia Emancipation Act freed all persons "held to service or labor" in the district "by reason of African descent." Enslavers who were loyal to the United States could petition the government for up to $300 per person freed by the act. It also included an appropriation of $100,000 for voluntary colonization of the newly free. Despite wavering on the question of general emancipation, President Lincoln declared before Congress that he "never doubted" that the Constitution gave the federal government the power to control slavery in the district. With the inclusion of payment and colonization, Lincoln was satisfied enough to make use of that power.[71]

Despite celebrating the freedom of the enslaved in the District of Columbia, the inclusion of payment and colonization measures in the act displeased many activists. On one Sunday evening in April, a crowd gathered at Shiloh Church in New York City to give "thanksgiving" and celebrate the news from the District of Columbia. Taking to a pulpit that was lavishly draped in the American flag, the Black abolitionist Reverend Henry Highland Garnet read scripture, celebrated emancipation, and denounced colonization. Charles Sumner, the radical Republican senator from Massachusetts, reacted to the emancipation act in true abolitionist form. He referred to the act as a "ransom" and declared that the money paid to enslavers "belongs rather to the slaves, who had long been "despoiled of every right and possession." Sumner asked if the nation would be willing to "audit this fearful account" and decide what amount should be paid for "prolonged torments of the lash" and "for children stolen, for knowledge shut out, and for all the fruits of labor wrested from [the enslaved] and his fathers." Sumner concluded that any payment for slavery should have gone to the enslaved.[72] This was the ultimate quandary faced by those who paid for freedom. The debt held by enslavers in what they owed to the enslaved and the value of liberation were both unfathomable. They remain so.

*   *   *

In 1845, "T.E." wrote to the *NASS* in support of compensated emancipation, or "pecuniary ransom" as they called it. They believed that if emancipation on a national scale were undertaken without payment it would "breed deadly feuds" and "assassinations" of those who supported slavery by those who had opposed the institution or suffered by it. The author, contrasting emancipation in Haiti with that of British West Indian colonies, determined that paying for freedom was far safer and more likely to lead to a postslavery society that was invested in seeing freedom, and the formerly enslaved themselves, succeed after liberation.[73] Not everyone would agree.

Seven months into the Civil War, the *Liberator* published an article claiming that the idea of human property was the "end of the chain about our own necks." It was a "bit" in our mouths. Slavery was a national problem, and the "chain" was "so tough that a million of men to-day in the field of red-hot civil war make no impression on it." J. H. Fowler, the author, claimed that the violence of the war resulted from the fact that Americans were "appalled at the idea of destroying this 'property.'" To Fowler, the answer to this predicament could never be payment, however. Such an action would "forever tell against the integrity of the nation." It was better to await the "destruction of all property," to "pour out blood," or for everyone to "go into slavery" than to pay for abolition.[74]

"T.E." had threatened race war as the alternative to compensation. Burritt, too, had feared the war and destruction that eventually ended American slavery. Fowler willingly offered the destruction of all property in its place. The war for freedom cost much, and its losses held deep repercussions for what was to come. Over the course of the war, only enslavers in the District of Columbia received any compensation. Unlike "T.E." supposed, the federal plan for emancipation in Washington, DC, did not make enslavers there any more eager to see African Americans succeed in freedom and secure the rights of full citizenship. The race war T.E. threatened would come anyway.

After the purchase of his freedom, William Wells Brown traveled across the northern United States as an agent for the AASS and, for a time, as a proponent of Black emigration to Haiti. In April 1862, exactly a year to the month from the start of the Civil War and the first shots fired at Fort Sumter, Brown toured upstate New York. Brown gave lectures on the course of the war, speaking on topics from "War and its connection with Slavery" to "What shall we do with the Traitors, and What shall be done with their slaves?" Speaking in Poughkeepsie in front of a crowded audience, Brown declared that "the difficulty in settling our national difficulties was not so much what to do with the slaves as what to do with the masters." He contended that the war would not end until slavery was abolished. He was right.

Both abolitionists like Brown and the enslaved put emancipation on the table over the course of the war and fought to make it a military and moral necessity. On January 5, 1863, Brown, along with Henry Highland Garnet and Lewis Tappan, addressed a crowd at Cooper Union in New York City. The audience gathered together to celebrate the passage of the Emancipation Proclamation. The proclamation, enacted by President Lincoln on January 1, 1863, freed enslaved people in all territories in rebellion against the United States. For formerly enslaved activists like Brown, it must have been a moment for elation and sober reflection. At the end of the war two years later, full abolition was enshrined, albeit imperfectly, in the Thirteenth Amendment to the Constitution, which declared: "Neither slavery nor involuntary servitude, except as a punishment for crime whereof the party shall have been duly convicted, shall exist within the United States, or any place subject to their jurisdiction." Through war, the "outraged and guiltless slaves" were now free, but there were still many battles left to win, and the nation's debt for slavery has yet to be paid.[75]

Epilogue

On January 20, 1937, a formerly enslaved man named Willis Dukes sat down to be interviewed by Pearl Randolph in Madison, Florida. Randolph collected Dukes's memories of slavery for the Negro Writers' Unit of Florida's Federal Writers' Project, part of the WPA's slave narrative project. Randolph was one of the very few African American women to be employed by the WPA nationwide.[1]

Dukes was born in the 1850s on a plantation belonging to John Dukes, a man of "moderate circumstances," in Brooks County, Georgia. In Madison, Dukes lived only thirty to forty miles away from where he had grown up enslaved. He told Randolph that almost everything they needed on the plantation was grown and made there by the forty people John Dukes enslaved. They made cloth from the cotton they grew and homemade shoes from leather they tanned. It is perhaps unsurprising, then, that when Dukes, as a child, pictured freedom, he thought of it as a place where he could go to "earn enough money" to buy his mother a silk dress.[2]

Dukes had other reasons for imagining freedom in this way. During his interview, he recalled to Randolph the whispers shared among the enslaved about a man from the plantation who had escaped and was reported to be "living very high" in the North. It was rumored that he was getting an education and saving up money to buy his family. These whispers, Duke said, inspired "ambitions" of escape and visions of freedom across the plantation. When the Civil War came, these rumors made everyone on the plantation especially interested in what would happen and what form their freedom would take.[3]

We cannot know whether these whispers were well founded or if they were based in the common dreams of liberation held in the hearts and imaginations of the enslaved. However, it is more than possible that this legendary figure who had escaped John Dukes's plantation did seek out the opportunity to redeem his family, like so many others who escaped to the North as fugitives—alone and without their families. We can easily imagine that he, like those on the plantation in southern Georgia that Dukes called home, dreamed of both freedom and reunion.[4] As Dukes's recollection shows, those who sought to buy their freedom and that of their loved ones could disrupt the logic of slavery by making an escape from it. They were then whispered about and revered, and they became the source of others' dreams of freedom.

With this man on his mind, Willis Dukes also dreamed of leaving the plantation and going somewhere he could earn his own money. The first thing he wanted to buy with that money was a silk dress for his mother. Processing this memory as an eighty-three-year-old man, Dukes revealed that he understood freedom to be about family, movement, compensated labor, and access to goods that could be gifted as markers of all these things and their interconnectedness. Even during the war and in its aftermath, this idea of freedom was significant to Dukes, and it offered him an alternative vision of a world in which he could exist.

Dukes did not need to buy his freedom, or even follow this tale to the North. His liberation would come through war. After emancipation, he described the joy he felt when he bought his first pair of patent leather shoes, something he had dreamed of since he had been forced to shine those of his enslavers while wearing his own plantation-made brogans as a child. Next he purchased a horse and buggy, which not only made him more popular with women but also increased his capacity to experience movement. These were the things that Dukes, and millions of others like him, were denied during slavery. These were the things that made him feel free—that *made* him free. Dukes had come to understand what so many had before him experienced: that to own oneself was the most precious kind of property.[5]

Two years before the start of the Civil War which would free Dukes, the abolitionist and Unitarian minister William Henry Furness argued before his Philadelphia church that the basis of all property rights began with "every man's inalienable right to himself." Furness reasoned that the right to hold property in human beings "annihilate[d] the very idea of property" and, thus, "exterminate[d] society." He claimed that the laws of the nation that recognized the rights of enslavers were no less than a "giant treason to the liberties of the human race." Speaking on July 3, he stated that this property order was as false to "our solemn Declaration [of Independence]" as it was to both "man and God." Furness closed by asking God for forgiveness for America's "insensibility" toward this fundamental and irreconcilable problem at the heart of the nation.[6]

In arguing that ownership of self was at the root of all other property regimes, Furness produced a familiar idea in the context of a world that would rapidly alter slavery's relationship to property, just as it would shift the nation's relationship with the almost four million people who would soon be free to own themselves. What Furness did not account for, however, was the way his formulation of the "very idea of property" rested on a history of turning human beings into commodities who could be bought, sold, and traded as chattel. Rather than ending society, this form of property was, instead, a foundation for it. These property rights had also made it possible to turn freedom itself into a form of property, something that could also be bought, sold, and traded. Property was a problem not only for the society in which Furness lived, as he gathered his congregation together to preach against property in man, but also for the freedom that was shaped by it.[7]

What Willis Dukes and others before him had to consider was what it meant to worship freedom in what W. E. B. Du Bois once called "a land of dollars."[8] What kind of freedom was self-ownership, exactly? African Americans undertook self-purchase because they understood themselves to be enslaved to, and oppressed by, a property regime that functioned both theoretically and practically. Freedom, a peculiar kind of property, came at a cost.[9] The problem faced by the enslaved was that under the conditions of slavery, freedom could be measured both in and as value. This did not mean, of course, that freedom had no worth.

Perhaps no one contemplated publicly the complicated nature of what it meant to buy yourself in a land of dollars more deeply than Harriet Jacobs. Jacobs, writing both in and as part of the legal landscape that Furness decried, closed her 1861 narrative with a discussion of the complex nature of not only slavery but freedom, too, as a form of property. To Jacobs, both the opportunity for and necessity of buying freedom spoke to the ways in which owning people as property affected not only the lives of the enslaved but also the shape of their freedom.[10]

In 1852, almost two decades after Jacobs had escaped slavery, her friend and employer Cornelia Willis secured Jacobs's final escape for $300. Buying Jacobs's freedom was deemed necessary because, like so many other fugitives she described in her narrative, she was affected by the passage of the Fugitive Slave Act of 1850 and the continued harassment of the Norcom family, who legally enslaved her. Along with other fugitives, Jacobs understood that she was the property of the Norcom family no matter where she was in the United States. That New York no longer recognized people as such made little difference. Even though it would go toward her liberation, money could be exchanged across state lines for property in woman. When Jacobs described herself as "a slave in New York, as subject to slave laws as I had been in a Slave State," she described a property regime that had power and effect far beyond slavery's physical boundaries.[11] As property herself, Jacobs knew that the rights to people like her, recognized as they were by the Constitution, were not at odds with either property or society. In fact, the belief that an enslaver's right to their property was "as sacred as any right" made slavery a problem for which the whole nation had to answer, just as Furness had suggested.[12]

Although Jacobs initially rejected offers to buy her freedom because she believed it to be an act that was morally incongruous with the ways that she understood her own personal value, Jacobs was soon forced to admit that she could not afford to live without the freedom that the law could provide. After Willis concluded the negotiations, Jacobs described the transaction that brought about the legal end of her enslavement as "too much like slavery." It grated against Jacobs's understanding of freedom to see how closely her value as a slave determined the value of her liberation.[13] For Jacobs, there must have been a particularly unsettling connection between the trade in her person, her constant fear as a girl of the sexual advances of Norcom, and the sexual trafficking of enslaved women that further shadowed this final sale.[14] Buying something as precious as freedom was not exactly liberating, although it certainly came with privileges. After her emancipation, she felt as though a "heavy load" had been "lifted from my weary shoulders."[15]

Still, Jacobs bristled at the way her freedom had been traded. After spending most of her life acting on her dreams of being free, Jacobs reflected on the material nature of her final freedom and its commerce signified by that "bit of paper," as she called her manumission documents. Lest anyone question her understanding of, dedication to, or ability to critique freedom won in this way, she made clear that she knew well the "value of that bit of paper." For Jacobs, that paper held the meaning it did precisely because of slavery, not because of its relation to her freedom. She worked to separate these things out from each other, claiming that while she loved her freedom, she did "not like to look upon it."[16]

Jacobs knew intimately, better than many of her readers could ever comprehend, the value that paper had at a practical level, but she also made clear to them that she understood freedom to be something beyond that which could be looked upon, recorded, or reduced to a business transaction. Freedom was not something that could be put in one's pocket.[17] That bit of paper was hard to swallow. It tethered her liberation to the world that slavery's economy had made, the world that had sanctified and protected Norcom's ownership of her and her children, and the world in which even freedom could be had for a price.[18] Yet Jacobs lived in that world, and she understood that freedom from slavery mattered whether it was obtained by exchange or by birth. All human beings were entitled to be free. In telling her story, she hoped to hasten the coming of a world in which no one would be trafficked as property nor forced to traffic in freedom.

Jacobs looked to that future by proposing that her freedom papers may "hereafter prove a useful document to antiquaries."[19] In doing so, she relegated the proof of her freedom to the archive of the future rather than her present. For Jacobs, the utility of her freedom was not represented by an object. Its representation as such only marred its splendor. Jacobs boldly suggested, instead, that her manumission papers should stand across time as a record of the system that called for freedom to be made tangible through a bill of sale. Frederick Douglass, too, played with the meaning of his freedom papers, calling them a "brand of infamy" on the nation as well as "curious papers" later in life. In these formulations, Douglass also spoke to both their power and their meaninglessness.[20]

For Jacobs and Douglass, these manumission documents were physical manifestations of American freedom's incapacity to extend beyond slave law.

The seemingly unlimited power of this law led many like them not only to buy themselves out of it but also to question the very nature of the systems that made self-purchase necessary. Jacobs used the closing pages of her narrative to reflect on the ties that bound freedom and enslavement together through property, offering an early way for readers to understand the limits of emancipation that would be contemplated on a national scale by future generations of activists and scholars. Jacobs likely would have felt a familiarity with Rinaldo Walcott's claim, made amid a new movement for abolition, that "property sits at the nexus of our liberation."[21]

Decades of abolitionist activism and the imaginative resistance of enslaved African Americans would lead the nation toward a new vision for freedom—one that included both the abolition of slavery and African Americans as full birthright citizens who would be equal before the law.[22] This "new birth of freedom," as Abraham Lincoln called it, came as a product of the deadliest war the United States has ever seen. Given the violence inherent in enslavement, the peaceful abolition envisioned by Elihu Burritt through compensated emancipation would likely have never prevailed. In the aftermath of the war, Reconstruction legislation abolished slavery and defined citizenship, and in 1870 African American men won the right to vote.

Earlier in the century, William Lloyd Garrison had predicted that by 1870 enslavers would relinquish their claim on enslaved people. They did so only by force. Questions remained over how that freedom would proceed in peace. The addition of the postwar constitutional amendments and their imperfect enshrinement of abolition, Black freedom, and citizenship suggests that perhaps the problem with American law was not solely a question of administration, as Frederick Douglass had once formulated.

Even the Thirteenth Amendment did less to abolish slavery in the United States than it could have done. By refusing to locate abolition in the rights of humans, Congress's chosen language suggested that it did not fully understand, or perhaps refused to hear, the way that enslaved people like Harriet Jacobs, who laid bare the myriad violence of slavery, understood the relationship between slavery, law, and commerce and their continued social entanglement in the institution's afterlife.[23] Like Jacobs, others worried about the future of freedom and how those remains of slavery might not only be remembered by antiquaries but deployed against them. As the writer-activist Frances Ellen Watkins Harper formulated in 1867, "slavery, as an institution, has been overthrown, but slavery, as an idea still lives in the American Republic." According to Harper, the nation had a great opportunity to overthrow slavery as an idea, too. But, in so many ways, it would refuse to do so fully.[24]

Plans for reparations and justice for the formerly enslaved faltered. They faltered most often on the very meaning of property, which Furness and Jacobs had contemplated years earlier. The sanctity of private property, even without property in man, remained too strong for the nation to overcome in the interest of Black freedom. Former enslavers kept the idea of slavery alive and set out to rebuild what they believed to be their most sacred right: whiteness and power by any means short of the outright legal ownership of African Americans.[25] That mattered little to them as they used other forms of property and violence to maintain control over the formerly enslaved. Thus land redistribution failed and took along with it the full use of the rights now guaranteed to African Americans by the Constitution. Despite the valiant efforts of the newly free to make both political and economic progress, freedom was not as simple as ownership in the shadow of slavery. As Du Bois wrote in 1903, "there was scarcely a white man in the South who did not honestly regard Emancipation as a crime, and its practical nullification as a duty." Given this, Du Bois claimed that the continued work to make meaning of emancipation was the "heavy heritage" of his generation. It is the heavy heritage of ours, too.[26]

Like Harriet Jacobs supposed, today we regard manumission papers as relics of a time when Americans were forced to pay for themselves. If things had gone differently, we might be even further removed from these relics than we are now. Owning human beings did not exterminate society nor the idea of property, as Furness claimed it must. Instead, it reified the meaning of freedom to be a kind of ownership, or mastery, over oneself.[27] While Willis Dukes understood his freedom to be, in part, related to forms of property ownership, this fell far short of all that freedom had come to mean to the enslaved on the plantation who whispered about the man who escaped north and wanted to buy his family. When the enslaved told each other tales about his "living very high," they were

dreaming about so much more than what that man could simply own. This is
why they also speculated about his education and buying his family's freedom.
Living very high was to live very free, and enslaved people dreamed about it constantly. Dukes would continue to do so across the violent decades to come. It was
no coincidence that he reflected on his earlier dreams of freedom as he did in
1937. As Jacobs lamented in her time, it remains to be seen what living very free
truly looks like outside the confines of property.

NOTES

INTRODUCTION

1. Lionel H. Kennedy and Thomas Parker, *An Official Report of the Trials of Sundry Negroes* (Charleston: James E. Schenck, 1822), https://archive.org/stream/dveseytrial /DV1_djvu.txt 67-68; John Marks, "Manumissions Database, Charleston District, South Carolina (1776–1800)," Magazine of Early American Datasets, https://repository.upenn .edu/mead/34/. For more primary sources involving Vesey's rebellion, see Douglas Egerton and Robert L. Paquette, eds., *The Denmark Vesey Affair: A Documentary History* (Gainesville: University Press of Florida, 2017).

2. Kennedy and Parker, *An Official Report*, 67–68.

3. Kennedy and Parker, *An Official Report*, 22. On the repercussions of Vesey's rebellion and an economic reading of those responses, see Justene Hill Edwards, *Unfree Markets: The Slaves' Economy and the Rise of Capitalism in South Carolina* (New York: Columbia University Press, 2021), chap. 4. On the importance of enslaved people's understanding of "cash power" in rebellion, see Douglas Egerton, "Slaves to the Market-place: Economic Liberty and Black Rebelliousness in the Atlantic World," *Journal of the Early Republic* 26, no. 4 (Winter 2006), 617–639, 618, 622, 634.

4. More than thirty manumissions are recorded for 1799. Ten of these manumissions include sums so small they may not traditionally be considered as self-purchase. However, I include any exchange of money as a reminder that for the enslaved even small sums were significant under slavery, a violent system in which enslavers benefited from their unrequited labor, and because those same enslavers were not required to charge for freedom so these payments held some meaning, even if we cannot know today exactly what led to these arrangements. Marks, "Manumissions Database." Douglas R. Egerton, *He Shall Go Out Free: The Lives of Denmark Vesey* (Lanham, MD: Rowman and Little-field, 2004), 73.

5. On the relationship between dispossession and property, see Robert Nichols, *Theft Is Property! Dispossession and Critical Theory* (Durham, NC: Duke University Press, 2020). K. Sue Park discusses the racialized use of foreclosure in early American settler colonialism in "Race, Innovation, and Financial Growth: The Example of Foreclosure,"

in *Histories of Racial Capitalism*, ed. Destin Jenkins and Justin Leroy (New York: Columbia University Press, 2021). On how slavery and the slave trade shaped the nation and
its economy, see Walter Johnson, *Soul by Soul: Life Inside the Antebellum Slave Market*
(Cambridge, MA: Harvard University Press, 2001), and Johnson, *River of Dark Dreams:
Slavery and Empire in the Cotton Kingdom* (Cambridge, MA: Harvard University Press,
2017). See also Sharon Ann Murphy, *Banking on Slavery: Financing Southern Expansion in the Antebellum United States* (Chicago: University of Chicago Press, 2023). More
broadly, in the introduction to the essay collection *American Capitalism: New Histories*,
Sven Beckert and Christine Desan describe the study of "economic life" as "crucial to
understanding the history of the United States." Beckert and Desan, *American Capitalism: New Histories* (New York: Columbia University Press, 2018), 10.

6. Sumner Eliot Matison, "Manumission by Purchase," *Journal of Negro History* 33,
no. 2 (April 1948), 146–167, 156–157.

7. Cheryl Harris has described the way whiteness became a kind of property whose
privileges and status was protected by law. Cheryl Harris, "Whiteness as Property," *Harvard Law Review* 106, no. 8 (June 1993), 1707–1791.

8. Walter Johnson, "On Agency," *Journal of Social History* 37, no. 1 (Autumn 2003),
113–124. For more on enslaved people's economic activities, see Hill Edwards, *Unfree
Markets*.

9. Historians have often argued that manumission was a management technique
that strengthened the hand of enslavers because the possibility of freedom could be
promised to the enslaved to ensure particular behavior, extended service, and payment
in the case of self-purchase. Eva Sheppard Wolf, *Race and Liberty in the New Nation:
Emancipation in Virginia from the Revolution to Nat Turner's Rebellion* (Baton Rouge:
Louisiana State University Press, 2006), 81; Calvin Schermerhorn, *Money over Mastery,
Family over Freedom* (Baltimore: Johns Hopkins University Press, 2011), 66, 79; T. Ste-
phen Whitman, *The Price of Freedom: Slavery and Manumission in Baltimore and Early
National Maryland* (New York: Routledge, 2000), 5, 161; Seth Rockman, *Scraping By:
Wage Labor, Slavery, and Survival in Early Baltimore* (Baltimore: Johns Hopkins Uni-
versity Press, 2008), 60–61, 114, 167, 184; Loren Schweninger, *Black Property Ownership
in the South, 1790–1915* (Chicago: University of Illinois Press, 1990), 66–67; Stephen
Whitman, "Diverse Good Causes: Manumission and the Transformation of Urban
Slavery," *Social Science History* 19, no. 2 (Autumn 1995), 22–270, 348–349; Orlando
Patterson, *Slavery and Social Death: A Comparative Study* (Cambridge, MA: Harvard
University Press, 2018), 212, 217, 241, 247. In a 2009 collection of essays on manumis-
sion in the Atlantic world, Patterson, as well as many of the other essayists in the col-
lection, suggested that manumission was an "integral and necessary part of the process
of slavery," and that through it the "incentive problem was solved." Orlando Patterson,
"Three Notes of Freedom: The Nature and Consequences of Manumission," in *Paths to*

Freedom: Manumission in the Atlantic World, ed. Rosemary Brana-Shute and Randy J. Sparks (Columbia: University of South Carolina Press, 2009), 18.

10. Kelly Marie Kennington, "Law, Geography, and Mobility: Suing for Freedom in Antebellum St. Louis," *Journal of Southern History* 80, no. 3 (August 2014), 575–604, 596.

11. Walter Johnson, "To Remake the World: Slavery, Racial Capitalism, and Justice," in *Race, Capitalism, Justice*, ed. Walter Johnson and Robin D. G. Kelley (Boston: Boston Critic, 2017), 28–29. This contemporary scholarship rests on the foundational work of Black intellectuals such as W. E. B. Du Bois, Cedric Robinson, and Eric Williams, who took seriously how people of African descent understood and reacted to what Robinson described as racial capitalism. See W. E. B. Du Bois, *Black Reconstruction in America, 1860–1880* (New York: Free Press, 1998); Cedric Robinson, *Black Marxism: The Making of the Black Radical Tradition* (Chapel Hill: University of North Carolina Press, 2000); and Eric Williams, *Capitalism and Slavery* (Chapel Hill: University of North Carolina Press, 1994). For slavery, capitalism, and expansion, see Edward Baptist, *The Half Has Never Been Told: Slavery and the Making of American Capitalism* (New York: Basic Books, 2016); Johnson, *River of Dark Dreams*; Sven Beckert and Seth Rockman, eds., *Slavery's Capitalism: A New History of American Economic Development* (Philadelphia: University of Pennsylvania Press, 2016); Calvin Schermerhorn, *The Business of Slavery and the Rise of American Capitalism, 1815–1860* (New Haven, CT: Yale University Press, 2015); and Ian Baucom, *Specters of the Atlantic: Finance Capital, Slavery, and the Philosophy of History* (Durham, NC: Duke University Press, 2005). See also Ned Sublette and Constance Sublette, *The American Slave Coast: A History of the Slave-Breeding Industry* (Chicago: Chicago Review Press, 2017). For more on the domestic slave trade, see Daina Ramey Berry, *The Price for Their Pound of Flesh: The Value of the Enslaved from Womb to Grave, in the Building of the Nation* (Boston: Beacon Press, 2017); Steven Deyle, *Carry Me Back: The Domestic Slave Trade in American Life* (Oxford: Oxford University Press, 2006); Robert H. Gudmestad, *Troublesome Commerce: The Transformation of the Interstate Slave Trade* (Baton Rouge: Louisiana State University Press, 2003); Michael Tadman, *Speculators and Slaves: Masters, Traders, and Slaves in the Old South* (Madison: University of Wisconsin Press, 1989); Johnson, *Soul by Soul*; Jonathan D. Martin, *Divided Mastery: Slave Hiring in the American South* (Cambridge, MA: Harvard University Press, 2004); Whitman, *The Price of Freedom*; Schweninger, *Black Property Ownership*; Rockman, *Scraping By*; Hill Edwards, *Unfree Markets*; Alexandra J. Finley, *An Intimate Economy: Enslaved Women, Work, and America's Domestic Slave Trade* (Chapel Hill: University of North Carolina Press, 2020); Walter Johnson, ed., *The Chattel Principle: Internal Slave Trades in the Americas* (New Haven, CT: Yale University Press, 2005).

12. James W. C. Pennington, *The Fugitive Blacksmith; or, Events in the History of James W. C. Pennington* (London: Charles Gilpin, 1849), iv, https://docsouth.unc.edu/neh/penning49/penning49.html.

13. As Walter Johnson has claimed, "it is not only nonsensical but also unethical to continue asking whether slavery was capitalist without asking what that meant to enslaved people." Walter Johnson, "To Remake the World: Slavery, Racial Capitalism, and Justice," *Boston Review* (February 1, 2017), https://www.bostonreview.net/forum /walter-johnson-to-remake-the-world/. I join scholars like Daina Ramey Berry in developing an "intellectual history of enslaved people's thoughts, expressions, feelings, and reactions to their commodification" that sheds more light on how the enslaved processed their commodification and understood the forces that acted upon them and what they could do with that information. Berry, *The Price for Their Pound of Flesh*, 2. Ed Baptist also describes importance of the narrative practices of enslaved people around this history. Baptist, *The Half Has Never Been Told*, 171–172.

14. Sven Beckert and Seth Rockman, introduction to *Slavery's Capitalism*, 1–3. Julia Ott, "Slaves: The Capital That Made Capitalism," *Public Seminar* (April 9, 2014), https://publicseminar.org/essays/slavery-the-capital-that-made-capitalism/. On slavery and the industrial revolution, see Williams, *Capitalism and Slavery*.

15. Beckert and Rockman, *Slavery's Capitalism*, 10. For more on the historiography of this field, see Beckert and Rockman, *Slavery's Capitalism*, 1–27.

16. Beckert and Rockman, *Slavery's Capitalism*, 11. See also Stephanie Smallwood, *Saltwater Slavery: A Middle Passage from Africa to American Diaspora* (Cambridge, MA: Harvard University Press, 2008). As Amy Dru Stanley has described, "Even things closest to the heart were for sale." Stanley, "Wages, Sin, and Slavery: Some Thoughts on Free Will and Commodity Relations," *Journal of the Early Republic* 24, no. 2 (Summer 2004), 279–288, 284, 287.

17. *Partus sequitur ventrem* was introduced in the mid-seventeenth century to determine the status of enslaved children in colonial Virginia. It held that the status of the mother determined the status of the child. Thus enslaved mothers gave birth to enslaved children. For more on this long history and the role of gender in slavery, see Jennifer L. Morgan, *Reckoning with Slavery: Gender, Kinship, and Capitalism in the Early Black Atlantic* (Durham, NC: Duke University Press, 2021); Morgan, *Laboring Women: Reproduction and Gender in New World Slavery* (Philadelphia: University of Pennsylvania Press, 2004); and Morgan, "*Partus sequitur ventrem*: Law, Race, and Reproduction in Colonial Slavery," *Small Axe* 22, no. 1 (March 2018), 1–17, 1. This also meant that slavery can be understood as a "sexual economy," as Adrienne Davis has described the place of reproduction and Black women's "work" in the institution. Davis, "'Don't Let Nobody Bother Yo' Principle': The Sexual Economy of American Slavery," in *Black Sexual Economies: Race and Sex in a Culture of Capital*, ed. Adrienne Davis (Champaign: University of Illinois Press, 2019), 17. As Morgan describes, enslaved women tried to exert some control over the lives of their children and their status, maintaining their relationship as one of kinship rather than the commodity relation imagined by enslavers. See examples

in Morgan, "*Partus sequitur ventrem*," 15. For more on how they did this across slave societies, see Kathleen Brown, *Good Wives, Nasty Wenches, and Anxious Patriarchs* (Chapel Hill: University of North Carolina Press, 1996); and Sasha Turner, *Contested Bodies: Pregnancy, Childrearing, and Slavery in Jamaica* (Philadelphia: University of Pennsylvania Press, 2017). Amy Dru Stanley, "Histories of Capitalism and Sex Difference," *Journal of the Early Republic* 36, no. 2 (Summer 2016), 343–350, 348.

18. They describe these key dynamics as "accumulation/dispossession, credit/debt, production/surplus, capitalist/worker, developed/underdeveloped, contract/coercion." Jenkins and Leroy, *Histories of Racial Capitalism*, 2, 11. Saidiya Hartman, *Lose Your Mother: A Journey Along the Atlantic Slave Route* (New York: Macmillan, 2008), 6.

19. For Leroy, racial capitalism helps clarify the way that freedom could be "transformed [into] the primary vehicle for black subjugation from a relationship between capitalism and slavery into one between capitalism and freedom." Leroy, "Racial Capitalism and Black Philosophies of History," in *Histories of Racial Capitalism*, 174. Saidiya Hartman describes the "complicity of slavery and freedom." Hartman, *Scenes of Subjection: Terror, Slavery, and Self-Making in Nineteenth-Century America* (New York: Oxford University Press, 1997), 115. Rinaldo Walcott has described "the long emancipation" that separates emancipation as a "legal process" from true freedom, which "is yet to come." Walcott, *The Long Emancipation: Moving Toward Black Freedom* (Durham, NC: Duke University Press, 2021), 1.

20. For an overview of these discussions, see Walcott, *The Long Emancipation*. For how these conceptions of the human come into being in the modern world, see Sylvia Wynter, "1492: A New World View," in *Race, Discourse, and the Origin of the Americas: A New World View*, ed. Vera Lawrence Hyatt and Rex Nettleford (Washington, DC: Smithsonian Institution Press, 1995).

21. Robinson, *Black Marxism*, 169–171.

22. Robinson describes the "disengagement" and "absolute rejection of American society and the persistent denunciation of racialism as a basis of civilized conduct" on the part of African Americans and the "perturbations of the world system" that "constituted the parameters, the conditions of being of Black resistance." Robinson, *Black Marxism*, 310–311. For a contemporary take on Robinson's ideas about the Black radical tradition, racial capitalism, and the economies of enslaved people, see Shauna J. Sweeney, "Gendering Racial Capitalism and the Black Heretical Tradition," in *Histories of Racial Capitalism*, ed. Destin Jenkins and Justin Leroy (New York: Columbia University Press, 2021), 53–83; and Sweeney, "Market Marronage: Fugitive Women and the Internal Marketing System in Jamaica, 1781–1834," *William and Mary Quarterly* 76, no. 2 (April 2019), 197–222.

23. Hill Edwards claims that "enslaved people acted as capitalists" and that their "capitalist enterprise did not equal freedom." Hill Edwards argues that their "investments in their own economic lives only entrenched them even more deeply within the

institution of slavery." Given the terms of racial capitalism, I am wary of thinking about enslaved people as "capitalists" and all that that implies; however, Hill Edwards and I agree that even when it led to literal freedom, the economic activity of enslaved people was still tied up with that of their enslavers, as was the kind of freedom they could buy. Hill Edwards, *Unfree Markets*, 4.

24. Berry, *The Price for Their Pound of Flesh*, xii, 5–7. Berry also discusses buying freedom, 63–70. The interrelation of these values is linked to Stephanie Camp's idea of the three bodies of the enslaved. Camp, *Closer to Freedom: Enslaved Women and Everyday Resistance in the Plantation South* (Chapel Hill: University of North Carolina Press, 2004), 66–68.

25. Robinson, *Black Marxism*, 125.

26. Walter Johnson has shown how this negotiation worked in the slave market as well. Johnson, *Soul by Soul*, 176–188.

27. On the idea of freedom dreams, see Robin D. G. Kelley, *Freedom Dreams: The Black Radical Imagination* (New York: Penguin, 2003).

28. Kennedy and Parker, *An Official Report*, 32, 96.

29. Wolf, *Race and Liberty*, xiii, 81, 238. For more on the importance of manumission and free African American communities, see Eva Sheppard Wolf, *Almost Free: A Story About Family and Race in Antebellum Virginia* (Athens: University of Georgia Press, 2012), 15. In his comparative work on manumission, Orlando Patterson states that as a "marginal person the freedman continued to be viewed as something of an anomaly, and . . . was regarded as potentially dangerous. The community took an active interest in him not only for economic reasons . . . but also for social and symbolic reasons." Patterson, *Slavery and Social Death: A Comparative Study* (Cambridge, MA: Harvard University Press, 1982), 249, 259; John Brown, *Slave Life in Georgia: A Narrative of the Life, Sufferings, and Escape of John Brown, A Fugitive Slave, Now In England*, ed. L. A. Chamerovzow (London, 1855), https://docsouth.unc.edu/neh/jbrown/jbrown.html. On African Americans and citizenship, see Christopher Bonner, *Remaking the Republic: Black Politics and the Creation of American Citizenship* (Philadelphia, University of Pennsylvania Press, 2020); and Martha Jones, *Birthright Citizens: A History of Race and Rights in Antebellum America* (Cambridge: Cambridge University Press, 2018).

30. Wolf, *Almost Free*, 4, 18–26, 31; Kennington, "Law, Geography, and Mobility," 586.

31. Some white national leaders believed, like Thomas Jefferson, that racial difference was a "powerful obstacle" to the emancipation of the enslaved. Jefferson wrote that free African Americans must be "removed beyond the reach of mixture." The American Colonization Society assisted the enslaved with manumission but followed Jefferson's racist logic on removal by seeking to send freed people to their colony in Liberia on the west coast of Africa. Jefferson, *Notes on the State of Virginia* (Philadelphia: Prichard and Hall, 1787), 154, https://docsouth.unc.edu/southlit/jefferson/jefferson.html. For

more on how African Americans responded to and fought against colonization, see Ous-mane K. Power-Greene, *Against Wind and Tide: The African American Struggle Against the Colonization Movement* (New York: New York University Press, 2014).

32. See Laura Edwards, *The People and Their Peace: Legal Culture and the Transfor-mation of Inequality in the Post-Revolutionary South* (Chapel Hill: University of North Carolina Press, 2009); Kimberly S. Hanger, *Bounded Lives, Bounded Places: Free Black Society in Colonial New Orleans, 1769–1803* (Durham, NC: Duke University Press, 1997); Kennington, "Law, Geography, and Mobility," 576–579; Judith Kelleher Schafer, *Becom-ing Free, Remaining Free: Manumission and Enslavement in New Orleans, 1846–1862* (New Orleans: Louisiana State University Press, 2003); Kelly M. Kennington, *In the Shadow of Dred Scott: St. Louis Freedom Suits and the Legal Culture of Slavery in Ante-bellum America* (Athens: University of Georgia Press, 2017); Kimberly M. Welch, *Black Litigants in the Antebellum American South* (Chapel Hill: University of North Carolina Press, 2018); Emily West, *Family or Freedom: People of Color in the Antebellum South* (Lexington: University of Kentucky Press, 2012); Wolf, *Race and Liberty*, 238; Ariela Gross, *Double Character: Slavery and Mastery in the Antebellum Southern Courtroom* (Princeton, NJ: Princeton University Press, 2001); Ted Maris-Wolf, *Family Bonds: Free Blacks and Re-enslavement Law in Antebellum Virginia* (Chapel Hill: University of North Carolina Press, 2015); and William G. Thomas, *A Question of Freedom: The Fam-ilies Who Challenged Slavery from the Nation's Founding to the Civil War* (New Haven, CT: Yale University Press, 2020). One early example of historical work focusing solely on self-purchase is Matison, "Manumission by Purchase."

33. As Rebecca Scott has shown, "words could protect, and words could enslave." Scott and Jean Hébrard, *Freedom Papers: An Atlantic Odyssey in the Age of Emancipation* (Cambridge, MA: Harvard University Press, 2012), 19. Matison, "Manumission by Pur-chase," 153. Samantha Seeley, *Race, Removal, and the Right to Remain: Migration and the Making of the United States* (Chapel Hill: University of North Carolina Press, 2021), 12.

34. Freedom suits have garnered much attention from historians interested in enslaved legal culture in the antebellum era. The enslaved brought these suits for a variety of reasons, from claims of free ancestry, including having a white or Native American ancestor, to contested manumissions, especially those in which wills were never properly carried out. Compensated manumission was also at the root of some of these suits. In her work on freedom suits in St. Louis, Missouri, Kelly Kennington found that courts did not often rule in favor of enslaved who brought freedom suits relating to self-purchase because the enslaved could not enter legal contracts. Kennington, *In the Shadow of Dred Scott*, 18, 128. The Race and Slavery Petitions Project found that more than 50 percent of freedom suits over compensated manumission were successful across the South. For more on freedom suits, see Loren Schweninger, *Appealing for Liberty: Freedom Suits in the South* (Cambridge: Cambridge University Press, 2018), 175; Anne Twitty, *Before Dred*

Scott: Slavery and Legal Culture in the American Confluence, 1787–1857 (Cambridge: Cambridge University Press, 2016); and Lea VanderVelde, *Redemption Songs: Suing for Freedom Before Dred Scott* (Oxford: Oxford University Press, 2014).

35. For more on African American property ownership in the South, see Dylan Penningroth, *Claims of Kinfolk: African American Property and Community in the Nineteenth-Century South* (Chapel Hill: University of North Carolina Press, 2003); and Ira Berlin and Philip D. Morgan, eds., *The Slaves' Economy: Independent Production by Slaves in the Americas* (New York: Routledge, 1995).

36. Alejandro de la Fuente and Ariela Gross, *Becoming Free, Becoming Black: Race, Freedom, and Law in Cuba, Virginia, and Louisiana* (New York: Cambridge University Press, 2020), 125.

37. Henry Bibb, *Narrative of the Life and Adventures of Henry Bibb* (New York: published by the author, 1849), 17, https://docsouth.unc.edu/neh/bibb/bibb.html. For more on the independent production and the benefits accrued to enslavers, see Hill Edwards, *Unfree Markets.*

38. In the 1820s, Georgia made it illegal for the enslaved to sell cash crops and other goods without permission. In 1831, North Carolina made free African Americans obtain a court issued license to "hawk or peddle" goods. Each license cost eighty cents and lasted for only one year. They were granted depending on the "good character" of the applicant. As for self-hire, South Carolina, North Carolina, and Virginia all enacted laws regarding the practice in the eighteenth century. Mississippi's 1822 statute regarding self-hiring proposed fines of fifty dollars for each offence and the state sale of the enslaved if the fine was not paid. Punishments in other states included seizure of the enslaved, forced labor, and fines. Thomas D. Morris, *Southern Slavery and the Law, 1619–1860* (Chapel Hill: University of North Carolina Press, 1996), 348–352; North Carolina General Assembly, *Slaves and Free Persons of Color: An Act Concerning Slaves and Free Persons of Color* (1831), 9–10, https://docsouth.unc.edu/nc/slavesfree/slavesfree.html. For more on self-hire, see Martin, *Divided Mastery*; and Morris, *Southern Slavery and the Law*, chaps 6, 16. Hiring was a fairly common experience. Anywhere from 5 to 15 percent of the enslaved population may have been hired out every year. Morris, *Southern Slavery and the Law*, 132; "Negroes Hiring Their Own Time," *National Anti-slavery Standard* (October 11, 1849), reprinted from the *Jackson Mississippian* (Jackson, MS).

39. Only enslaved people in Delaware, Louisiana, and Tennessee enjoyed legal recognition for the right to contract for freedom. Given its mixed legal history, Louisiana was the sole state in which the enslaved could enter into formal contracts to buy their freedom. Matison, "Manumission by Purchase," 154–155. Kimberly M. Welch, *Black Litigants in the Antebellum American South* (Chapel Hill: University of North Carolina Press, 2018), 169. For more on contracts and freedom suits, see Schweninger, *Appealing for Liberty*, 176–177.

40. Wolf, *Race and Liberty*, xiii, 29–30.

41. In 1820, just two years before Denmark Vesey's plans were uncovered, the South Carolina legislature changed the state's Black Codes, requiring that all manumissions be granted by lawmakers. Historians suggest that these new laws, as well as an earlier backlash against the city's African Methodist Episcopal Church, may have pushed Vesey and his coconspirators toward action. Egerton, *He Shall Go Out Free*, 121–122, 131–132.

42. From 1782 Virginia slaveholders could manumit by will or deed. In contrast, North Carolina enacted legislation in 1830 that required state involvement. Enslavers there had to petition state superior courts for permission to emancipate, publicize their intention to do so, and pay a $1,000 security bond for each emancipated person. Six other southern states required bonds that the newly free had to post to secure their manumissions. These securities were meant to ensure that the emancipated would not become a burden on the state. For those who had just spent substantial sums to purchase their freedom, these bonds required an additional payment or the ability to negotiate with someone who could provide one. Matison, "Manumission by Purchase," 149–150; West, *Family or Freedom*, 23–26, 34–35; Maris-Wolf, *Family Bonds*, 7, 26; Larry Hudson, "All That Cash: Work and Status in the Slave Quarters," in *Working Towards Freedom: Slave Society and Domestic Economy in the American South*, ed. Larry Hudson (Rochester, NY: University of Rochester Press, 1995), 81; Wolf, *Race and Liberty*, 13, 233; North Carolina General Assembly, *Slaves and Free Persons of Color*, 7; Benjamin Klebaner, "American Manumission Laws and the Responsibility for Supporting Slaves," *Virginia Magazine of History and Biography* 63, no. 4 (1995), 443–453, 445; "Free Blacks in Maryland," *New York Times* (February 15, 1860), https://www.nytimes.com/1860/02/15/archives/free-blacks-in-maryland.html.

43. Klebaner, "American Manumission Laws," 448; Michael Schoeppner, *Moral Contagion: Black Atlantic Sailors, Citizenship, and Diplomacy in Antebellum America* (New York: Cambridge University Press, 2019).

44. In seaboard states, beginning with South Carolina in 1822, legislatures passed laws calling for the quarantine of Black sailors, causing conflict with northern states and Atlantic powers such as Great Britain. This was part of the state's legislative response to Vesey's plans. Free African Americans who attempted to migrate to the state risked punishment of ten years' labor or a fine of $500. Those emancipated in North Carolina were forced to leave the state within ninety days or be liable for arrest and sale. The same applied for those who returned to the state. As in North Carolina, the 1850 Kentucky Constitution retained the capacity of the legislature to pass laws allowing for emancipation but required that free African Americans who were emancipated in or had immigrated to Kentucky leave the state. Those who stayed, or left and returned, were to be declared guilty of a felony and punished according to the law. Klebaner, "American Manumission Laws," 448. While many formerly enslaved people stayed put, with or without permission, these laws did have an effect on manumissions. For examples of negotiating

these laws, see de la Fuente and Gross, *Becoming Free, Becoming Black*, 159–165. For more on slave law in Virginia, see Philip J. Schwarz, *Slave Laws in Virginia* (Athens: University of Georgia Press, 2010), 54–57. After 1806 the number of freedom suits based on Native American ancestry surpassed self-purchase as a path to freedom. De la Fuente and Gross, *Becoming Free, Becoming Black*, 100, 90. Howard Bodenhorn suggests that in Virginia the odds of being manumitted went from one in ten in the late eighteenth century to one in two hundred by the 1850s. Bodenhorn, "'To Set Devils Free': Manumission in Nineteenth-Century Virginia," 4, http://www-personal.umich.edu/~baileymj /Bodenhorn.pdf. For more on reaction to and negotiation of removal laws, see West, *Family or Freedom*; and Maris-Wolf, *Family Bonds*.

45. This partial freedom, which involved its own dangers in an economy where enslaved people were at risk of seizure for debts, has been described as "nominal slavery." Larry Koger, *Black Slaveowners: Free Black Slave Masters in South Carolina, 1790–1860* (Jefferson, NC: McFarland and Company, 2012), 70–71; Mary Beth Corrigan, "It's a Family Affair: Buying Freedom in the District of Columbia, 1850–1860," in *Working Toward Freedom: Slave Society and Domestic Economy in the American South*, ed. Larry Hudson (Rochester, NY: University of Rochester Press, 1994),164–165; Wolf, *Almost Free*, 2; Ira Berlin, *Slaves Without Masters: The Free Negro in the Antebellum South* (New York: New Press, 1992), xxv, xxvi; Schweninger, *Black Property Ownership*, 65–67.

46. In the nineteenth century this legal system, first initiated in the Siete Partidas, was fully implemented in the Reglamento de Esclavos of 1842. This code, which regulated slaves, was frequently attacked by enslavers for limiting their power. As in the United States, slaveholders recognized and feared what this kind of infringement on their rights would do to undermine their individual authority and that of the entire slave system. Despite attempts by enslavers to undermine these legal protections, for many enslaved people in the Spanish Empire, this process worked. In Havana, Cuba, for instance, most manumissions were cases of self-purchase, as high as 80 percent in the eighteenth century. For more on this system and comparative manumissions, see John G. Marks, *Black Freedom in the Age of Slavery: Race, Status, and Identity in the Urban Americas* (Columbia: University of South Carolina Press, 2020); de la Fuente and Gross, *Becoming Free, Becoming Black*, 105–114, 46; Alejandro de la Fuente, "From Slaves to Citizens? Tannenbaum and the Debates on Slavery, Emancipation, and Race Relations in Latin America," *International Labor and Working-Class History*, no. 77 (Spring 2010), 155; Shawn Cole, "Capitalism and Freedom: Manumission and the Slave Market in Louisiana, 1725–1820," *Journal of Economic History* 65, no. 4 (December 2005), 1008–1027, 1021; Rebecca Scott, *Degrees of Freedom: Louisiana and Cuba After Slavery* (Cambridge, MA: Belknap Press of Harvard University Press, 2005), 18, 20, 26, 28, 114; Alejandro de la Fuente, "Slaves and the Creation of Legal Rights in Cuba: Coartación and Papel," *Hispanic American*

Historical Review 87, no. 4 (2007), 665, 669, 684. Michelle McKinley suggests a similar interference with the rights of slaveholders in colonial Lima, where the "overlapping jurisdiction created opportunities for enslaved litigants and other dependents to appeal directly to metropolitan sovereigns to adjudicate their complaints." Here, she argues that enslaved people made use not only of the space made for freedom in the Siete Partidas but also ecclesiastical courts to create "fractional freedoms." McKinley, "Fractional Freedoms: Slavery, Legal Activism, and Ecclesiastical Courts in Colonial Lima, 1593–1689," *Law and History Review* 28, no. 3 (August 2010), 749–790, 754, 756. De la Fuente and Gross, *Becoming Free, Becoming Black*, 173.

47. Jennifer M. Spear, "'Using the Faculties Conceded to Her by Law': Slavery, Law, and Agency in Spanish New Orleans, 1763–1803," in *Signposts: New Directions in Southern Legal History*, ed. Sally E. Hadden and Patricia Hagler Minter (Athens: University of Georgia Press, 2013), 66–71, 77, 82. De la Fuente and Gross, *Becoming Free, Becoming Black*, 116, 125–127. The historian Shawn Cole found that self-purchase accounted for more than 30 percent of all manumissions in Louisiana from 1725 to 1820, despite the fact that it became more difficult to do so under American jurisdiction. Cole, "Capitalism and Freedom," 1014, 1018–1021, 1026. Spanish manumission laws affected the growth of Louisiana's free population. De la Fuente and Gross, *Becoming Free, Becoming Black*, 115–116. Jessica Marie Johnson's work on manumission in New Orleans centers the practices of Black women and what she calls "black femme freedom" to secure freedom and reminds us that changes in the law's administration was only one way women of African descent enacted both freedom and access to it. Johnson, *Wicked Flesh: Black Women, Intimacy, and Freedom in the Atlantic World* (Philadelphia: University of Pennsylvania Press, 2020), 186, 187–218.

48. Alejandro de la Fuente and Ariela Gross claim that enslaved people shaped self-purchase in ways "favorable to them." De la Fuente and Gross, *Becoming Free, Becoming Black*, 48. Manuel Barcia and Claudia Varella's work on self-purchase in nineteenth-century Cuba highlights these difficulties including where one was located and what access one had to legal venues, social capital, and money. They argue that these laws were "not followed in practice, and that as time went by, the process of coartación increasingly turned into a battleground between the enslaved who aspired to be free, and those who owned them." Despite the law, as in the United States enslaved people still had to rely on similar methods to make self-purchase work in a society in which enslavers held the upper hand. It was always and everywhere a contested terrain. Barcia and Varella, *Wage-Earning Slaves: Coartación in Nineteenth-Century Cuba* (Gainesville: University of Florida Press, 2020), 12, 17, 149. Rebecca Scott has shown the role self-purchase played in gradual emancipation in Cuba, a similarity which will be shown for the United States in Chapter 1. Scott argues that even with coartación, high market values made it difficult for the enslaved to buy their freedom. The 1880 law that fixed their price allowed people

to take advantage of the *patronato* system. Scott, "Gradual Abolition and the Dynamics of Slave Emancipation in Cuba, 1868–1886," *Hispanic American Historical Review* 63, no. 3 (August 1983), 449–477, 464, 469–472.

49. For an overview of cliometrics, see Robert Fogel and Stanley Engerman, *Time on the Cross: The Economics of American Slavery* (New York: W. W. Norton, 1995), 6–10. For examples, see Fogel and Engerman, "Philanthropy at Bargain Prices: Notes on the Economics of Gradual Emancipation," *Journal of Legal Studies* 3, no. 2 (June 1974), 377–401; Ronald Finley, "Slavery, Incentives, and Manumission: A Theoretical Model," *Journal of Political Economy* 83, no. 5 (October 1975), 923–934; Bodenhorn, "'To Set Devils Free'"; Theodore Babcock, "Manumission in Virginia, 1782–1806," PhD diss., University of Virginia, 1973; Art Budros, "Social Shocks and Slave Mobility: Manumission in Brunswick County, Virginia, 1782–1862," *American Journal of Sociology* 110, no. 3 (November 2004), 539–579.

50. These are "impossible stories," as Hartman would say. Saidiya Hartman, "Venus in Two Acts," *Small Axe*, 12, no. 2 (June 2008), 1–14, 10.

51. For more on nineteenth-century print culture, see Lara Langer Cohen and Jordan Alexander Stein, *Early African American Print Culture* (Philadelphia: University of Pennsylvania Press, 2012), 7; Manisha Sinha, *The Slave's Cause: A History of Abolition* (New Haven, CT: Yale University Press, 2017), 1; Margaret M. R. Kellow, "Conflicting Imperatives: Black and White American Abolitionists Debate Slave Redemption," in *Buying Freedom: Ethics and Economics of Slave Redemption*, ed. Kwame Anthony Appiah and Martin Bunzl (Princeton, NJ: Princeton University Press, 2007), 206–209.

52. The edited collection *Buying Freedom* takes up historical and contemporary discussions of the ethics of slave redemption. See Kwame Anthony Appiah and Martin Bunzl, eds.

53. I've written about this more extensively on the *Black Perspectives* blog. Julia W. Bernier, "Bail Funds, Buying Freedom, and a History of Abolition," *Black Perspectives* (August 13, 2020), https://www.aaihs.org/bail-funds-buying-freedom-and-a-history-of-abolition/. National Bailout, "The Black Codes of Bail," accessed June 15, 2023, https://www.nationalbailout.org/blackcodes.

54. "Letter from Theodore Weld," *Genius of Universal Emancipation* (May 1834).

CHAPTER 1

1. *The Papers of the Pennsylvania Abolition Society* (Philadelphia: Society and Historical Society of Pennsylvania, 1876; hereafter cited as PAS Papers), microform, Reel 20, Manumission Book B, 1788–1795, 252, Historical Society of Pennsylvania, "Manumissions, Indentures, and Other," Pennsylvania Abolition Society Papers Online Exhibit,

https://hsp.org/history-online/digital-history-projects/pennsylvania-abolition-society
-papers/manumissions-indentures-and-other; "Decree of the National Convention of
4 February 1794, Abolishing Slavery in all the Colonies," Liberty, Equality, Fraternity:
Exploring the French Revolution, https://revolution.chnm.org/d/291.

2. For more on the status of people, like Fanny, brought to other parts of the United
States (and Cuba) and on the dangers of reenslavement, see Rebecca Scott, "Paper Thin:
Freedom and Re-enslavement in the Diaspora of the Haitian Revolution," *Law and History Review* 29, no. 4 (November 2011), 1061–1087.

3. PAS Papers, Reel 20, Manumission Book B, 1788–1795, 252. For more examples
of these manumissions and indentures from French colonials, see PAS Papers, Reel 20,
Manumission Book C, 1795, 2–3, 9–10, 12–13, 28–29. A record from 1793 similar to Fanny's shows a girl from Cape Francois named Irene, who was five years younger than Fanny,
being manumitted and indentured. Her enslaver was paid £50 by another woman from
Cape Francois, Haiti, to indenture Irene for eighteen years. PAS Papers, Reel 22, Acting Committee, unnumbered pages. The language of humanity and benevolence is fairly
standard in these documents. For examples of outright manumissions, see pp. 54 and 68.
Garvey F. Lundy, "Early Saint Domingan Migration to American and the Attraction of
Philadelphia," *Journal of Haitian Studies* 12, no. 1 (Spring 2006), 76–94, 80–81, 85; Erica
Dunbar, *A Fragile Freedom: African American Women and Emancipation in the Antebellum City* (New Haven, CT: Yale University Press, 2008), 40–42; Cory Young, "For
Life or Otherwise: Abolition and Slavery in South Central Pennsylvania, 1780–1847,"
PhD diss., Georgetown University, 2021, 59–60; "Pennsylvania Legislation Relating to
Slavery," *Adams County History* 9, article 8 (2003), https://cupola.gettysburg.edu/cgi
/viewcontent.cgi?article=1074&context=ach.

4. PAS Papers, Reel 22, Indenture Book C, 1758–1795, 93; "Pennsylvania Legislation
Relating to Slavery."

5. For an extensive study of these entanglements, see Cory Young's excellent dissertation, "For Life or Otherwise," esp. chap. 3 on the role of women. On the experiences
of women, see Dunbar, *A Fragile Freedom*, 27–29. On children, see Crystal Webster,
Beyond the Boundaries of Childhood: African American Children in the Antebellum North
(Chapel Hill: University of North Carolina Press, 2021).

6. Young argues that, because of gradual abolition, these borders were not as sectional as we have come to understand them. See Young, "For Life or Otherwise," chap. 4.
For more on geography and political boarders, see Stanley Harrold, *Border War: Fighting
over Slavery Before the Civil War* (Chapel Hill: University of North Carolina Press, 2013);
David G. Smith, *On the Edge of Freedom: The Fugitive Slave Issue in South Central Pennsylvania, 1820–1870* (New York: Fordham University Press, 2012); and Cheryl LaRoche,
Free Black Communities and the Underground Railroad (Champaign: University of Illinois Press, 2014). This line was also blurry in other contexts, including the ambiguous

and confused distinctions between kinds of service, namely the difference between servitude and slavery and a person bound to labor and slave, and how these terms and the understandings of them were debated in the period and written into the Constitution itself. For more on these complications, see Hoang Gia Phan, *Bonds of Citizenship: Law and the Labors of Emancipation* (New York: New York University Press, 2013).

7. "An Act for the Gradual Abolition of Slavery—March 1, 1780," Pennsylvania Historical and Museum Commission, http://www.phmc.state.pa.us/portal/communities /documents/1776-1865/abolition-slavery.html. Gary B. Nash and Jean R. Soderlund, *Freedom by Degrees: Emancipation in Pennsylvania and Its Aftermath* (New York: Oxford University Press, 1991), 111. For a legal and political history of abolition in the state, see Young, "For Life or Otherwise," chap. 1.

8. In their classic study of the economics of gradual emancipation, Robert Fogel and Stanley Engerman argued that "freedom for slaves was a commodity that they were prepared to purchase only if it could be obtained at a very moderate cost." Fogel and Engerman, "Philanthropy at Bargain Prices," 401.

9. Eva Sheppard Wolf, for one, has shown how old tropes about enslavers' revolutionary sentiments must be undone by concentrating on the active role enslaved people played in Virginia manumissions. Sheppard Wolf, *Race and Liberty*, xi, 43–44, 63–64. Stephen Whitman, "Diverse Good Causes: Manumission and the Transformation of Urban Slavery," *Social Science History* 19, no. 3 (Autumn 1995), 333–370, 338.

10. As Karen Cook Bell puts it, "the desire for freedom did not originate with the American Revolution. However, the Revolution certainly amplified the quest for liberty." Karen Cook Bell, *Running from Bondage: Enslaved Women and Their Remarkable Fight for Freedom in Revolutionary America* (Cambridge: Cambridge University Press, 2021), 3.

11. Sheppard Wolf, *Race and Liberty*, 66.

12. Ira Berlin, *Slaves Without Masters: The Free Negro in the Antebellum South* (New York: New Press, 2007), 35.

13. Sheppard Wolf's calculations also reveal that around half of enslaved people manumitted by deed had to wait for their freedom. Many of these were people who could not be emancipated because of age requirements. Sheppard Wolf, *Race and Liberty*, 66–67, 79–80. Sheppard Wolf notes that these calculations do not include nominal payments.

14. Sheppard Wolf, *Race and Liberty*, 79–81. Whitman found that over half of the Baltimore manumissions that were promised for a future date were for ten years or more later. Whitman, "Diverse Good Causes," 338, 347. Ira Berlin, *Slaves Without Masters: The Free Negro in the Antebellum South* (New York: New Press, 2007); De la Fuente and Gross, *Becoming Free, Becoming Black*, 92; James Gigantino, *The Ragged Road to Abolition: Slavery and Freedom in New Jersey, 1775–1865* (Philadelphia: University of Pennsylvania Press, 2016), 133.

15. For stories of self-purchase in the mid-Hudson Valley, see Michael Groth, *Slavery and Freedom in the Mid-Hudson Valley* (Albany: State University of New York Press, 2017), 58–60. For more on New York's gradual abolition law, see David Gellman, *Emancipating New York: The Politics of Slavery and Freedom, 1777–1827* (Baton Rouge: Louisiana State University Press, 2006), chap. 8, 153–186.

16. As of 1786, enslaved people between twenty-one and thirty-five years of age could be manumitted. The requirement of a bond was removed, but they would have to be examined by the overseers of the poor and two justices of the peace to ensure they would not become a burden on the state. After 1798, enslaved people could be manumitted until age forty. Gigantino, *Ragged Road*, 22, 67, 73.

17. Gigantino, *Ragged Road*, 33–34, 66.

18. Gigantino, *Ragged Road*, 33–34, 66.

19. Gigantino, *Ragged Road*, 73–74, 78; for examples of self-purchase, see 126; on manumissions and negotiations, see 117–118. Gigantino states that "owners used manumission to stabilize and extend Jersey slavery" (117). He claims that numbers of self-purchase may be higher than he records because enslavers did not have to report an exchange of funds. This, of course, is true for all attempts at accounting for self-purchase. For examples of self-purchase from New Jersey in the PAS Papers, see Reel 22, Acting Committee: Papers relating to slaves purchased and manumitted by M. C. Cope, Thomas Harrison, and Isaac T. Hopper.

20. The document also states that Temperance had been examined by a justice of the peace "as agreeable to law." PAS Papers, Reel 22, Manumissions and related materials, both parties being black, unnumbered pages. Dorcus's name is spelled differently throughout. "An Act for the gradual abolition of slavery . . . Passed at Trenton Feb. 15, 1804" (Burlington, NJ: S. C. Ustick), https://www.loc.gov/resource/rbpe.0990100b/?sp=1. Geneva Smith, "Legislating Slavery in New Jersey," Princeton and Slavery Project, https://slavery.princeton.edu/stories/legislating-slavery-in-new-jersey.

21. On the growth of free African American communities in the region and cities, see Paul J. Polgar, *Standard-Bearers of Equality: America's First Abolition Movement* (Chapel Hill: University of North Carolina Press, 2019), 71–73.

22. *A Statistical Inquiry into the Condition of the People of Color, of the City and Districts of Philadelphia* (Philadelphia: Kite and Walton, 1849), 12.

23. Whitman says prices for an enslaved adult man at the turn of the century were $300–500, and that would take fifteen to sixteen months of wages for a day laborer. Whitman, *The Price of Freedom*, 104–105. Whitman, "Diverse Good Causes," 336, 340, 347.

24. Harry B. Yoshpe, "Record of Slave Manumissions in New York During the Colonial and Early National Periods," *Journal of Negro History* 26 (January 1941), 78–107; for examples, see 78, 79, 83. New York Manumission Society, "Register of Manumissions of Slaves," vol. 3, 46–47, http://digitalcollections.nyhistory.org/islandora/object/islandora

%3A132477#page/36/mode/1up. Isaac T. Hopper, "A List of the Members of the New York Manumission Society," https://archives.tricolib.brynmawr.edu/resources/sfhl-sc -212. On the strategies of the NYMS, which were similar to those of the PAS, see Gellman, *Emancipating New York*, 57–77.

25. *A Statistical Inquiry into the Condition of the People of Color*, 12.

26. Whitman, "Diverse Good Causes," 348–349; Whitman, *The Price of Freedom*, 123–124; Groth, *Slavery and Freedom*, chap. 4; Rockman, *Scraping By*, 167, 183–185. For a comparison on funding, in 1830–1831, African American mutual aid societies in Philadelphia spent just over $5,800. African American Mutual Aid Societies, "Institutions for Mutual Relief," *National Gazette and Literary Register* (March 1, 1831), https:// nationalhumanitiescenter.org/pds/maai/community/text5/negrosocietiesphil.pdf. Thanks to Cory Young for bringing this to my attention.

27. Whitman, *The Price of Freedom*, 88; Groth, *Slavery and Freedom*, 70; Rockman, *Scraping By*, 185.

28. Whitman, *The Price of Freedom*, 88.

29. PAS Papers, Reel 20, Manumission Book A, 1788–1795, 80, Historical Society of Pennsylvania, "Manumissions, Indentures, and Other," Pennsylvania Abolition Society Papers Online Exhibit, https://hsp.org/history-online/digital-history-projects /pennsylvania-abolition-society-papers/manumissions-indentures-and-other. Simon P. Newman, *Embodied History: The Lives of the Poor in Early Philadelphia* (Philadelphia: University of Pennsylvania Press, 2003), 104, 109.

30. National Archives, "To George Washington from Mathew Irwin, 9 July 1789," https://founders.archives.gov/documents/Washington/05-03-02-0079-0001; "To George Washington from Thomas Irwin, 15 July 1791," https://founders.archives.gov/documents /Washington/05-08-02-0238; "To Thomas Jefferson from Richard O'Bryen, 24 August 1785," https://founders.archives.gov/documents/Jefferson/01-08-02-0339; William Reynolds, "Mismatch off Charleston: The Privateer *Congress* vs. HMS *Savage*," *Journal of the American Revolution*, https://allthingsliberty.com/2022/04/mismatch-off-charleston-the -privateer-congress-vs-hms-savage/. On the antislavery uses of these kidnappings, see Gellman, *Emancipating New York*, 82–85.

31. W. Jeffrey Bolster, *Black Jacks: African American Seamen in the Age of Sail* (Cambridge, MA: Harvard University Press, 1998), 26, 86, 135, 157.

32. PAS Papers, Reel 22, Manumissions and related materials, both parties being black, unnumbered pages; Reel 20, Manumission Book C, 1795, 41; Reel 22, Indenture Book C, 1758–1795, 98.

33. For more on indentures and children, see Webster, *Beyond the Boundaries of Childhood*, chap. 3. Sarah Gronningsater argues that African American communities nurtured special techniques "focused on safety, education, and the well-being of children" in the confines of gradual emancipation. Gronningsater, "Born Free in the Master's

House: Children and Gradual Emancipation in the Early American North," in *Child Slavery Before and After Emancipation*, ed. Anna Mae Duane (New York: Cambridge University Press, 2017), 124–125.

34. Young, "For Life or Otherwise," 7–8. On New York State, see Michael Groth, "Slaveholders and Manumission in Dutchess County, New York," *New York History* 78, no. 1 (January 1997), 35, 39–40, 45, 50. Groth, *Slavery and Freedom*, xvii, 44; Christopher Osborne, "Invisible Hands: Slaves, Bound Laborers, and the Development of Western Pennsylvania, 1780–1820," *Pennsylvania History: A Journal of Mid-Atlantic Studies* 72, no. 1 (Winter 2005), 77–99, 80, 84–85; Gigantino, *Ragged Road*, 65, 74.

35. Osborne, "Invisible Hands," 84–86; Young, "For Life or Otherwise," 7.

36. Gigantino's work on New Jersey shows that the state's abolition organization struggled to maintain itself, let alone help enslaved people. Their incapacity shows the importance of strong activist groups like the PAS. Gigantino, *Ragged Road*, 80, 111, 117, 119.

37. Osborne, "Invisible Hands," 84–86; Young, "For Life or Otherwise," 37, 47, 59; Gigantino, *Ragged Road*, 149–161. New York enslavers did the same in the midst of gradual abolition in their state. Gellman, *Emancipating New*, 162–163, 203–205. For an interesting case of term slaves moving out of Pennsylvania to Mississippi in return for manumission, Cory James Young, "Liberating Penn's Woods," in *The Cambridge History of the American Revolution*, Vol. 2, *Continuities, Changes, and Legacies*, ed. Marjoleine Kars, Michael McDonnell, and Andrew M. Schocket, (New York, NY: Cambridge University Press, forthcoming).

38. For instance, Cory Young found only seven manumissions or manumission indentures recorded in Cumberland County, to the west of Harrisburg, between 1799 and 1825. None appear to include outright self-purchase. Cumberland County Records of Deeds, Bills of Sale, Manumissions, Indentures, vol. 1. Compiled by Cory Young, 2018.

39. Young, "For Life or Otherwise," 136.

40. Jennifer Morgan, *Laboring Women*, 56, 68. Morgan says that "resituating heritability was key in the practice of an enslavement that systematically alienated the enslaved from their kin and their lineage." This practice continued through gradual abolition. Morgan, *"Partus sequitur ventrem,"* 1.

41. Osborne, "Invisible Hands," 79, 81. Gigantino understands this as a new kind of slavery. Gigantino, *Ragged Road*, 96.

42. Osborne, "Invisible Hands," 81–83. Gradual emancipation did not produce the idea of term slavery. It was also common in places like Baltimore, where the shifting economy of slavery in the region opened possibilities for other kinds of unfreedom. Like hiring and the domestic slave trade, term slavery was part of how slavery remained flexible and profitable in the Upper South. The enslaved made use of these conditions to escape slavery. Whitman says that in Baltimore, term slaves were popular. They made up around 20 percent of sales between 1789 and 1830. Term slaves came at a 30–50 percent discount,

which was not much more of an investment than hiring someone yearly. Whitman, *Diverse Good Causes*, 351–355. Seth Rockman describes the "appealing investment" that women term slaves were in Baltimore since they could be purchased at discounted rates, but their children would be born lifetime slaves. This reminds us that gradual emancipation did, in fact, matter. Rockman, *Scraping By*, 113–114.

43. Young, "For Life or Otherwise," 137–138, 159–160, 164–165, 184.

44. Young, "For Life or Otherwise," 137–138, 165, 184. As Young has shown, pregnant women decided to run away to obtain freedom for themselves and their unborn children. Karen Cook Bell has found that one third of runaways in the American Revolution were women. Cook Bell, *Running from Bondage*, 9. Dunbar, *A Fragile Freedom*, 27, 31–32; Gigantino, *Ragged Road*, 133.

45. Osborne, "Invisible Hands," 81. Laurence Glasco claims that "the children of Pennsylvania's slaves, in effect, purchased their own freedom through a long period of uncompensated servitude." "Free at Last," in *Free at Last? Slavery in Pittsburgh in the 18th and 19th Centuries* (Pittsburgh: Heinz History Center, 2008), 5.

46. US Census Bureau, "1790 United States Federal Census," Versailles Township, Allegheny County, Pennsylvania, Series M637, Roll 9, Page 134, Image 80.

47. MSS 494, Deed Book Volume 3-C, Box 1, Folder 7, 24, Detre Library and Archives at the Heinz History Center, digitized as "Peter Cosco," *Free at Last? Slavery in Pittsburgh in the 18th and 19th Centuries*, http://exhibit.library.pitt.edu/freeatlast/papers/fp_petercosco.html; "Explore the Newly Discovered Papers," *Free at Last?*, http://exhibit.library.pitt.edu/freeatlast/papers_listing.html. Thomas Cushing, *History of Allegheny County Pennsylvania* 1 (Chicago: A. Warner and Co, 1889), 724–725. Samuel W. Black, "Allegheny County Freedom Papers, Certificates of Freedom, and Indentures," in *Free at Last?*, 11–12, https://exhibit.library.pitt.edu/freeatlast/pdf/freeatlast.pdf. Roger Applegate, "Who Was John McKee?," *Milestones* 31, no. 4, https://www.bcpahistory.org/beavercounty/BeaverCountyTopical/notablepeople/WhoWasJohnMcKee.html. Chris Potter, "Hey, What's the Origin of the Names of McKeesport and McKees Rocks? Who Was This Mr. McKee?," *Pittsburgh City Paper* (March 18, 2004), https://www.pghcitypaper.com/columns/hey-whats-the-origin-of-the-names-of-mckeesport-and-mckees-rocks-who-was-this-mr-mckee-1336128.

48. MSS 494, Deed Book Volume 3-C, Box 1, Folder 7, 187, digitized as "Negro Suck," *Free at Last?*, http://exhibit.library.pitt.edu/freeatlast/papers/i_negrosuck.html. While these are fairly standard terms, Samuel Black claims that from these stipulations it is apparent that "the surrounding community made a Black girl prey to the vices of society." He also discusses the West African roots of the names Suck and Kut. Black, "Allegheny County Freedom Papers," 14–15. For more on indenture terms and negotiations for African American children, see Webster, *Beyond the Boundaries of Childhood*,

chap. 3. See, for instance, indenture of William Lewis, PAS Papers, Reel 22, Acting Committee, unnumbered pages.

49. Torrons and McKee may have known each other through business. In 1817, a "J. Torrens," perhaps Torrons or his son, signed a letter to the Bank of the United States at Philadelphia requesting that a branch be established in Pittsburgh. Complaining of "a want of some general circulating medium," the signatories believed that a branch in their city would allow them to "discharge their eastern debts" and maintain their businesses with "undiminished capital." Perhaps one of the ways men like Torrons and McKee conducted business and paid debts was with the labor of the people they enslaved and controlled. Cushing, *History of Allegheny County*, 590–591.

50. Dunbar, *A Fragile Freedom*, 27, 31–32.

51. On abolitionist and anti-Black ideas about citizenship and the fitness of African Americans, see Polgar, *Standard-Bearers of Equality*, chap. 3. On how these ideas shaped the colonization movement, pairing freedom with removal, see Beverly C. Tomek, *Colonization and Its Discontents: Emancipation, Emigration, and Antislavery in Antebellum Pennsylvania* (New York: New York University Press, 2011).

52. Included in other early Black narrative texts, such as the slave narratives of Olaudah Equiano and Venture Smith, self-purchase acted as an important representational strategy. Thomas E. Will, "Liberalism, Republicanism, and Philadelphia's Black Elite in the Early Republic: The Social Thought of Absalom Jones and Richard Allen," *Pennsylvania History: A Journal of Mid-Atlantic Studies* 69 (Autumn 2002), 571. For a full discussion of the discursive uses of self-purchase and self-making in early narratives like Equiano's, see Phan, *Bonds of Citizenship*, chap. 1.

53. "Richard Allen Manumission Papers, 1780–1783," Historical Society of Pennsylvania, https://digitallibrary.hsp.org/index.php/Detail/objects/13059#.

54. Ira Berlin, "Slavery, Freedom, and Philadelphia's Struggle for Brotherly Love, 1685–1861," in *Antislavery and Abolition in Philadelphia: Emancipation and the Long Struggle for Racial Justice in the City of Brotherly Love*, ed. Richard Newman and James Mueller (Baton Rouge: Louisiana State University Press, 2011), 29; Richard Allen, *The Life, Experience, and Gospel Labors of the Rt. Rev. Richard Allen* (Philadelphia: Martin and Boden, 1833), 7.

55. As Libra Hilde has claimed, the "ultimate good an enslaved man could provide for his loved ones was freedom." Libra Hilde, *Slavery, Fatherhood, and Paternal Duty in African American Communities over the Long Nineteenth Century* (Chapel Hill: University of North Carolina Press, 2020), 120.

56. William Douglass, *Annals of the First African Church, in the United States of America* (Philadelphia: King and Baird, 1862), 118–122, https://archive.org/details/annalsoffirstafroodoug/page/n5/mode/2up.

57. Henry Banks Papers, 1761–1833, Mss1B2264a, Section 1, 429, Virginia Historical Society, Richmond, Virginia. Jones and Allen also show up in PAS indenture records. While this is representative of both men's relationship with the PAS and Black community strategies, it also means they were able to take advantage of the labor market in bound children. See, for example, PAS Papers, Reel 22, Indenture Book C, 1758–1795, pp. 66, 21, 25, 35. Webster, *Beyond the Boundaries of Childhood*, 82.

58. Richard S. Newman, "'Lucky to Be Born in Pennsylvania': Free Soil, Fugitive Slaves and the Making of Pennsylvania's Anti-slavery Borderland," *Slavery and Abolition* 32, no. 3 (September 2011), 419.

59. W. E. B. Du Bois, *The Philadelphia Negro: A Social Study* (Philadelphia: University of Pennsylvania Press, 1996), 10.

60. Pennsylvania Abolition Society, "Constitution and Act of Incorporation of the Pennsylvania Society," (Philadelphia: Hall and Atkinson, 1820), 3.

61. Patrick Rael, "The Long Death of Slavery," in *Slavery in New York*, ed. Ira Berlin and Leslie M. Harris (New York: New Press, 2005), 121; Sinha, *The Slave's Cause*, 122, 225.

62. Richard S. Newman, *The Transformation of American Abolitionism: Fighting Slavery in the Early Republic* (Chapel Hill: University of North Carolina Press, 2002), 4, 5–6. For an overview of the work of early abolition societies, see Polgar, *Standard-Bearers of Equality*, chap. 2.

63. On why African Americans made use of and partnered with the PAS, see Polgar, *Standard-Bearers of Equality*, 83–90. According to Mary Freeman, "the PAS' formal structure for legal aid existed alongside an informal network of Black families and communities." Freeman, "Seeking Abolition: Black Letter Writers and the Pennsylvania Abolition Society in the Era of Gradual Emancipation," *Journal of the Early Republic* 42, no. 1 (Spring 2023), 15. On how African Americans communicated their needs and ideas with the society see also, 2, 5–6.

64. Sinha, *The Slave's Cause*, 2, 118, 120; Nicholas P. Wood, "A 'Class of Citizens': The Earliest Black Petitioners to Congress and Their Quaker Allies," *William and Mary Quarterly* 74 (January 2017), 143, 112–113; Paul J. Polgar, "'To Raise Them to an Equal Participation': Early National Abolition, Gradual Emancipation, and the Promise of African American Citizenship," *Journal of the Early Republic* 31, no. 2 (Summer 2011), 229–258, 232; Christopher Densmore, "Seeking Freedom in the Courts: The Work of the Pennsylvania Society for Promoting the Abolition of Slavery, and for the Relief of Free Negroes Unlawfully Held in Bondage, and for Improving the Condition of the African Race, 1775–1865," *Pennsylvania Legacies* 5, no. 2 (November 2005), 16–19.

65. For examples of how African Americans contacted the PAS during these negotiations, see Freeman, "Seeking Abolition," 17, 23–24. Schermerhorn, *Money over Mastery*, 4. Dee Andrews's article on the communications of the PAS reminds us of the

"geographical expanse of the first emancipation movement" and also its "activist legacy." Dee Andrews, "Reconsidering the First Emancipation: Evidence from the Pennsylvania Abolition Society Correspondence," in "Empire, Society, and Labor: Essays in Honor of Richard S. Dunn," special issue, *Pennsylvania History* 64 (Summer 1997), 231.

66. Nash, *Forging Freedom: The Formation of Philadelphia's Black Community, 1720–1840* (Cambridge, MA: Harvard University Press, 1991), 43, 93; Kirsten Sword, "Remembering Dinah Nevil: Strategic Deceptions in Eighteenth-Century Antislavery," *Journal of American History* 97, no. 2 (September 2010), 317. Sword suggests that freedom suits like Nevill's are evidence of an "intercolonial and transatlantic network of white and black activists who worked together *before* the American Revolution." On Native American slavery in New Jersey law, see Gigantino, *Ragged Road*, 69–70.

67. Thomas Shipley was another member of the PAS whose name is seen frequently in relation to buying freedom. See the manumissions of the fugitives Solomon Brown and Jonathan Pease, PAS Papers, Reel 21, Book G, 87, 100. For a less successful case of a mother and children, see the story of Hannah Marvel, in *Five Years' Abstract of the Transactions of the Pennsylvania Society for Promoting the Abolition of Slavery, the Relief of Free Negroes Unlawfully Held in Bondage, and for Improving the Condition of the African Race* (Philadelphia: Merrihew and Thompson, 1853), 6.

68. Fogel and Engerman developed a formula for determining the "break-even age" for enslavers. Fogel and Engerman, "Philanthropy at Bargain Prices," 384–394. Gigantino, *Ragged Road*, 97–98.

69. PAS Papers Reel 24, Miscellaneous cases considered by Acting Committee, 1791–1792, unnumbered pages, Historical Society of Pennsylvania, "Miscellaneous Cases," Pennsylvania Abolition Society Papers Online Exhibit, https://hsp.org/history-online/digital-history-projects/pennsylvania-abolition-society-papers/miscellaneous-cases/pero-philadelphia-1791.

70. "Pennsylvania Legislation Relating to Slavery."

71. Ashley Council, "Ringing Liberty's Bell: African American Women, Gender, and the Underground Railroad in Philadelphia," *Pennsylvania History* 87, no. 3 (Summer 2020), 494–531, 500. For more on Pennsylvania as a refuge, see Newman, "'Lucky to Be Born in Pennsylvania.'"

72. Lysander Spooner, *A Defence for Fugitive Slaves, Against the Acts of Congress of February 12, 1793, and September 18, 1850* (Boston: B. Marsh, 1850), https://www.loc.gov/resource/llst.045/?sp=1; Simone Browne, *Dark Matters: On the Surveillance of Blackness* (Durham, NC: Duke University Press, 2015), 21–24, 50–56.

73. Julie Winch, "The Making and Meaning of James Forten's *Letters from A Man of Colour*," *William and Mary Quarterly* 64 (January 2007), 137; Wood, "A 'Class of Citizens,'" 143–144.

74. Newman, "'Lucky to Be Born in Pennsylvania,'" 426–427. On the activism of these groups later in the nineteenth century, see Jesse Olsavsky, *The Most Absolute Abolition: Runaways, Vigilance Committees, and the Rise of Revolutionary Abolitionism, 1835–1861* (Baton Rouge: Louisiana State University Press, 2022).

75. Eric Foner, *Gateway to Freedom: The Hidden History of the Underground Railroad* (New York: W. W. Norton, 2016), 57–59; "Formation of the Manhattan Anti-Slavery Society," *National Anti-slavery Standard* (hereafter cited as *NASS*) (September 24, 1840); William Still, *Underground Rail Road Records*, rev. ed. (Hartford: Betts and Company, 1886), 740.

76. This percentage is similar to the *Statistical Inquiry* produced by the PAS. Daniel E. Meaders, ed., *Kidnappers in Philadelphia: Isaac Hopper's Tales of Oppression, 1780–1843* (Cherry Hill, NJ: African Homestead Legacy Publishers, 2009), xiii–xiv, 3. Meaders also relates that Hopper's *Tales* have been verified through court records, PAS papers, and the minutes of the Acting Committee (6–7).

77. For an earlier example of the PAS's work with fugitives, see the 1825 case of Solomon Brown. PAS Papers, Reel 21, Book G, 87, 100.

78. Enslavers knew to look for their slaves and servants in Philadelphia. Many placed runaway ads in the city's newspapers. For an overview of these ads, see Newman, *Embodied History*, 83.

79. Lydia Maria Child, *Isaac T. Hopper: A True Life* (Cleveland, OH: John P. Jewett, 1853), 116–122.

80. Dunbar, *A Fragile Freedom*, 27, 32, 38–40, 50–52. Gigantino describes how African American women in New Jersey were "more likely to fall under white jurisdiction" after freedom. Gigantino, *Ragged Road*, 194.

81. Child, *Isaac T. Hopper*, 243.

82. Child, *Isaac T. Hopper*, 51–55.

83. Child, *Isaac T. Hopper*, 83.

84. For an example of Hopper working with fugitives from other parts of Pennsylvania, see Young, "For Life or Otherwise," 240–242.

85. Child, *Isaac T. Hopper*, 83.

86. Schermerhorn, *The Business of Slavery*, 12, 17, 25.

87. Child, *Isaac T. Hopper*, 133–135.

88. Newman, *Embodied History*, 88–89.

89. Child, *Isaac T. Hopper*, 133–137.

90. Meaders, *Kidnappers in Philadelphia*, 59.

91. For further exploration of the role of women in these networks, see Council, "Ringing Liberty's Bell."

92. Densmore, "Seeking Freedom in the Courts," 18, 19.

93. Smith, *On the Edge of Freedom*, 89, 1, 73; Polgar, *Standard-Bearers of Equality*, 92–96, 101; Martha Schoolman, *Abolitionist Geographies* (Minneapolis: University of Minnesota Press, 2014), 7. Gigantino argues that the fugitive slave issue also pushed second-wave New Jersey abolitionists to deal with slavery in their own state, where some three thousand enslaved people or people subject to term slavery remained in the 1840s. Gigantino, *Ragged Road*, 213–214.

94. On these attempts, see Young, "For Life or Otherwise," chap. 1, chap. 5; Richard S. Newman, Roy E. Finkenbine, and Douglass Mooney, "Philadelphia Emigrationist Petition, Circa 1792: An Introduction," *William and Mary Quarterly* 64 (January 2007), 161; Wood, "A 'Class of Citizens,'" 111–112, 120–122; Newman, *The Transformation of American Abolitionism*, 19, 45, 76–78; Julie Winch, "Self-Help and Self-Determination: Black Philadelphians and the Dimensions of Freedom," in Newman and Mueller, *Antislavery and Abolition*, 74–75; *Second Report of the Committee to Visit the Colored People* (Philadelphia: Pennsylvania Society for Promoting the Abolition of Slavery, 1838), 26–27.

95. Polgar, *Standard-Bearers of Equality*, 34; Groth, "Slaveholders and Manumission in Dutchess County," 35; Dunbar, *A Fragile Freedom*, 29; Fogel and Engerman, "Philanthropy at Bargain Prices," 377–379.

96. For more on the legislative debates, see Young, "For Life or Otherwise," 65–68.

97. Polgar, "To Raise Them," 235; Nash and Soderlund, *Freedom by Degrees*, 133. How freedom would be paid for, including through outright compensation, was also debated by New York legislators in the run-up to the state's gradual abolition act in 1799. Gellman, *Emancipating New York*, 165–168, 170–172.

98. Nash and Soderlund, *Freedom by Degrees*, 133–134.

99. Nash, *Forging Freedom*, 5; Richard Newman, "The Pennsylvania Abolition Society and the Struggle for Racial Justice," in Newman and Mueller, *Antislavery and Abolition*, 120, 129, 131.

100. Fogel and Engerman, "Philanthropy at Bargain Prices," 401; Dunbar, *A Fragile Freedom*, 29.

CHAPTER 2

1. Craig Friend, "Lunsford Lane and Me: Life-Writings and Public Histories of an Enslaved Other," *Journal of the Early Republic* 39, no. 1 (Spring 2019), 1–26, 18–20.

2. Lunsford Lane, *The Narrative of Lunsford Lane, Formerly of Raleigh, N.C.* (Boston: J. G. Torrey, 1842), 6–9, https://docsouth.unc.edu/neh/lanelunsford/lane.html. Friend warns of using "misinterpretations of [Lane's] freedom and his entrepreneurialism

that obscure his enslavement and how he carried the anxieties, limitations, burdens, traumas, and otherness of enslavement and blackness with him into freedom." Friend, "Lunsford Lane and Me," 23–24.

3. Lane, *Narrative*, 9–10.

4. Friend, "Lunsford Lane and Me," 7, 14.

5. Lane, *Narrative*, 15, 53–54; Friend, "Lunsford Lane and Me," 8.

6. Walter Johnson, "The Pedestal and the Veil: Rethinking the Capitalism/Slavery Question," *Journal of the Early Republic* 24, no. 2 (Summer 2004), 299–308, 302.

7. Johnson, *Soul by Soul*, 79, 216–217; Kennington, "Law, Geography, and Mobility, 576–579, 582.

8. Adam Rothman, "The Domestication of the Slave Trade in the United States," in *The Chattel Principle: Internal Slave Trades in the Americas*, ed. Walter Johnson (New Haven, CT: Yale University Press, 2005), 33–34, 40–44, 42.

9. Hill Edwards, *Unfree Markets*, 101, 127, 135, 138, quotes on 135 and 138. See also Hilliard, *Masters, Slaves, and Exchange: Power's Purchase in the Old South* (New York: Cambridge University Press, 2013), on this dynamic.

10. For an overview of the history of the domestic slave trade and its regulation, see Rothman, "Domestication of the Slave Trade."

11. Berry, *The Price for Their Pound of Flesh*, 33, 91, 61, 68, 95–96, 15, 25, 72, 160, 64; Deyle, *Carry Me Back*, 56–60.

12. The slave trade had deleterious effects on Black families. Over 250,000 of those sold would have been married, and 186,000 were sales of children. Someone was sold every 3.6 minutes, leading to the separation of kin groups, much of which was beyond the control of the enslaved. Johnson, *Soul by Soul*, 7; Tadman, *Speculators and Slaves*, 135, 147, 150–151, 164, 169; Herbert G. Gutman, *Slavery and the Numbers Game: A Critique of Time on the Cross* (Chicago: University of Illinois Press, 1975), 124.

13. Johnson, introduction to *The Chattel Principle*, 5. See also Bonnie Martin, "Neighbor-to-Neighbor Capitalism: Local Credit Networks and the Mortgaging of Slaves," in *The Chattel Principle: Internal Slave Trades in the Americas*, ed. Walter Johnson (New Haven, CT: Yale University Press, 2005).

14. Berry, *The Price for Their Pound of Flesh*, xii, 5–7.

15. Schermerhorn, *Money over Mastery*, 160.

16. Amrita Chakrabarti Myers, *Forging Freedom: Black Women and the Pursuit of Liberty in Antebellum Charleston* (Chapel Hill: University of North Carolina Press, 2011), 39; Berlin, *Slaves Without Masters*, xxv; Juliet Walker, *The History of Black Business in America: Capitalism, Race, Entrepreneurship; Volume 1, to 1865* (Chapel Hill: University of North Carolina Press, 2009), 106; Berlin and Morgan, *The Slaves' Economy*, 46–47; Matison, "Manumission by Purchase," 146–167, 152, 155, 166; Penningroth, *Claims of Kinfolk*, 6–7, 42–43, 46–47, 54–55, 51–52; Whitman, *The Price of Freedom*, 1,

24–25; John T. Schlotterbeck, "The Internal Economy of Slavery in Rural Piedmont Virginia," in *The Slaves' Economy: Independent Production by Slaves in the Americas*, ed. Ira Berlin and Philip D. Morgan (New York: Routledge, 1995), 171, 176; John Campbell, "'As a Kind of Freeman'? Slaves' Market-Related Activities in the South Carolina Upcountry, 1800–1860," in *The Slaves' Economy*, ed. Berlin and Morgan, 143; Jonathan D. Martin, *Divided Mastery: Slave Hiring in the American South* (Cambridge, MA: Harvard University Press, 2004), 161–162, 164–165.

17. Schermerhorn, *Money over Mastery*, 4; Gudmestad, *Troublesome Commerce*, 43–45; Tadman, *Speculators and Slaves*, 17, 31, 135, 147, 150–151; Deyle, *Carry Me Back*, 17, 23, 40–41; Johnson, *Soul by Soul*, 3; Hill Edwards, *Unfree Markets*, 173.

18. Du Bois, *Black Reconstruction*, 5; Williams, *Capitalism and Slavery*, 19, 52, 98; Johnson, *Soul by Soul*, 216–217; Schermerhorn, *The Business of Slavery*, 12, 108, 42–43, 63, quote on page 12; Sublette and Sublette, *The American Slave Coast*, 40; Daina Ramey Berry, "'We'm Fus' Rate Bargain,'" in *The Chattel Principle: Internal Slave Trades in the Americas*, ed. Walter Johnson (New Haven, CT: Yale University Press, 2005), 64, 55; Beckert and Rockman, *Slavery's Capitalism*, 1, 11.

19. Schermerhorn, *Money over Mastery*, 23–24.

20. Penningroth, *Claims of Kinfolk*, 49–51.

21. Matison, "Manumission by Purchase," 155–156; Barbara Jeanne Fields, *Slavery and Freedom on the Middle Ground: Maryland During the Nineteenth Century* (New Haven, CT: Yale University Press, 1985), 27; Penningroth, *Claims of Kinfolk*, 54; Martin, *Divided Mastery*, 8, 45–46.

22. Frederick Douglass discusses the indignity of being compelled to give up the money he had to his enslaver Hugh Auld. Frederick Douglass, *Narrative of the Life of Frederick Douglass* (Boston: Anti-Slavery Office, 1845), 99–100, https://docsouth.unc.edu/neh/douglass/douglass.html.

23. Reprinted from the *Louisville Morning Courier*, Louisville, KY; "Negroes Hiring Their Own Time," *NASS* (October 11, 1849), reprinted from the *Jackson Mississippian*, Jackson, MS.

24. Daina Ramey Berry, "'In Pressing Need of Cash': Gender, Skill, and Family Persistence in the Domestic Slave Trade," *Journal of African American History* 92, no. 1 (2007), 24–25. For more on hiring practices in general, see Martin, *Divided Mastery*, 1–5, 163, 194; Whitman, *The Price of Freedom*, 1, 161, 165; Schermerhorn, *Money over Mastery*, 4, 135, 141–142; Rockman, *Scraping By*, 114; Whitman, "Diverse Good Causes," 340–341, 334; Matison, "Manumission by Purchase," 162–163; Sublette and Sublette, *American Slave Coast*, 55; Fields, *Slavery and Freedom*, 5; Corrigan, "It's a Family Affair, 166.

25. William A. Poe, "Lott Cary: Man of Purchased Freedom," *Church History* 39, no. 1 (March 1970), 49–61, 50.

26. Lane, *Narrative*, 15. For examples of hiring salaries, see William Still, *The Underground Railroad* (Philadelphia: People's Publishing, 1879), 169, 224, 328–329, https://www.loc.gov/item/31024984/; Martin, *Divided Mastery*, 66–67.

27. "The Reverend Lott Cary," *African Repository and Colonial Journal* (October 1, 1825); "Death of the Reverend Lott Cary," *African Repository and Colonial Journal* (March 1, 1829); Poe, *"Lott Cary,"* 51.

28. For more on the fancy-girl trade, see Edward Baptist, "'Cuffy,' 'Fancy Maids,' and 'One-Eyed Men': Rape, Commodification, and the Domestic Slave Trade in the United States," in *The Chattel Principle: Internal Slave Trades in the Americas*, ed. Walter Johnson (New Haven, CT: Yale University Press, 2005).

29. Still, *The Underground Railroad*, 328–329.

30. "Henry Wright," *Federal Writers' Project: Slave Narrative Project*, Vol. 4, Part 4, Georgia, Telfair-Young (with combined interviews of others), 196–197, https://www.loc.gov/resource/mesn.044/?sp=198.

31. Campbell, "'As A Kind of Freeman'?," 131, 135; Schlotterbeck, "The Internal Economy," 174–175, 178; Roderick A. McDonald, "Independent Economic Production by Slaves on Antebellum Louisiana Sugar Plantations," in *The Slaves' Economy: Independent Production by Slaves in the Americas*, ed. Ira Berlin and Philip D. Morgan (New York: Routledge, 1995), 188–190, 205.

32. Penningroth, *Claims of Kinfolk*, 46–47.

33. For more on the *Federal Writers' Project: Slave Narrative Project*, see Catherine A. Stewart, *Long Past Slavery: Representing Race in the Federal Writers' Project* (Chapel Hill: University of North Carolina Press, 2016), 133–142, 178, 180.

34. "Amanda Jackson," *Federal Writers' Project: Slave Narrative Project*, Vol. 4, Part 2, Georgia, Gary-Jones, 1941, 293, https://www.loc.gov/resource/mesn.042/?sp=292; Berry, "'In Pressing Need of Cash,'" 30, 23; Myers, *Forging Freedom*, 41, 50–53.

35. "William Porter," *Federal Writers' Project: Slave Narrative Project*, Vol. 2, Part 5, Arkansas, McClendon-Prayer, 362, https://www.loc.gov/resource/mesn.025/?sp=367&st=text.

36. "Gus Clark," *Federal Writers' Project: Slave Narrative Project*, Vol. 9, Mississippi, Allen-Young, 23, https://www.loc.gov/resource/mesn.090/?sp=26&st=text.

37. "Duncan Gaines," *Federal Writers' Project: Slave Narrative Project*, Vol. 3, Florida, Anderson-Wilson, 133, https://www.loc.gov/resource/mesn.030/?sp=136; Berlin and Morgan, *The Slaves' Economy*, 1; Penningroth, *The Claims of Kinfolk*, 7, 47; Stephanie M. H. Camp, *Closer to Freedom: Enslaved Women and Everyday Resistance in the Plantation South* (Chapel Hill: University of North Carolina Press, 2004), 78–79. For discussion of how enslavers and southern whites benefited from enslaved peoples' economic activity, see Justene Hill Edwards, "Felonious Transactions: Legal Culture and

Business Practices of Slave Economies in South Carolina, 1787–1860," *Enterprise and Society* 18, no. 4 (December 2017), 773.

38. Edmund Jackson, "The Fugitive," *NASS* (December 31, 1846).

39. Edmund Jackson, "The Fugitive," *NASS* (December 31, 1846).

40. Harriet Jacobs, *Incidents in the Life of a Slave Girl* (Boston: published for the author: 1861), 11–13; Penningroth, *Claims of Kinfolk*, 51.

41. Jean Yellin, *Harriet Jacobs, A Life: The Remarkable Adventures of the Woman Who Wrote "Incidents in the Life of a Slave Girl"* (New York: Basic Books, 2004), 30–31; Henry Louis Gates Jr. *The Classic Slave Narratives* (New York: Signet Classics, 2002), 445–447.

42. Gates, *Classic Slave Narratives*, 445–447, 650–652, 663–664.

43. Jessica Millward, *Finding Charity's Folk: Enslaved and Free Black Women in Maryland* (Athens: University of Georgia Press, 2015), 46, 49.

44. For more on Jacobs's father, see Hilde, *Slavery, Fatherhood*, 103.

45. Penningroth, *Claims of Kinfolk*, 42–43. Penningroth is also careful to caution against understanding the economy of the enslaved solely through the lens of the master-slave relationship and warns that this understanding "shifts attention away from viewing black people's lives on their own terms" (7). Corrigan, "It's a Family Affair," 164–165; Berlin and Morgan, *The Slaves' Economy*, 46–47; Matison, "Manumission by Purchase," 152, 166; Penningroth, *Claims of Kinfolk*, 6. Penningroth claims that for "small and modest amounts of property, no single region stands out" (46).

46. Walter Johnson has described how, in producing a "slaveholding legacy from the broken pieces of a slave family and to broaden slavery's hold over space and extend its history through time, the trade was, most of its opponents and many of its defenders would have agreed, the market of slavery's future." Johnson, introduction to *The Chattel Principle*, 2. Whitman describes confusion over the status of children born to mothers who were in the process of self-purchase. Maryland, for example, legislated in 1809 that all children born during the process of manumission would be enslaved for life unless their mother's manumission had set the terms for her children. Whitman, *The Price of Freedom*, 120–122.

47. Ellen Hartigan-O'Connor, "Gender's Value in the History of Capitalism," *Journal of the Early Republic* 36, no. 4 (Winter 2016), 613–635, 618–620. According to Schermerhorn, "property ownership and commercial activity was integral to African American family life." Schermerhorn, *Money over Mastery*, 71. Hilde, *Slavery, Fatherhood*, 93.

48. Myers, *Forging Freedom*, 51; Corrigan, "It's a Family Affair," 179; Juliet E. K. Walker, *Free Frank: A Black Pioneer on the Antebellum Frontier* (Lexington: University of Kentucky Press,1983), 1; "Joseph Leonidas Star," *Federal Writers' Project: Slave Narrative Project*, Vol. 15, Tennessee, Baston-Young, 1936, Manuscript/Mixed Material, 14, https://www.loc.gov/resource/mesn.150/?sp=73.

49. William Craft, *Running a Thousand Miles for Freedom* (London: William Tweedie, 1860), https://docsouth.unc.edu/neh/craft/craft.html, 27.

50. Elizabeth Keckley, *Behind the Scenes: or, Thirty Years a Slave, and Four Years in the White House* (New York: G. W. Carleton and Co, 1868), 43–62, quotes on 46 and 50. https://docsouth.unc.edu/neh/keckley/keckley.html.

51. Keckley, *Behind the Scenes,* 54–55.

52. Keckley, *Behind the Scenes,* 63.

53. Virginia General Assembly, "An Act to Amend the Several Laws Concerning Slaves," January 25, 1806, https://encyclopediavirginia.org/entries/an-act-to-amend-the-several-laws-concerning-slaves-1806/.

54. Race and Slavery Petitions Project, Petition 11681802, Digital Library on American Slavery, https://dlas.uncg.edu/petitions/petition/2499/.

55. Lewis Turner, Will, 1818, Mss2T8552b, Virginia Historical Society, Richmond, VA; de la Fuente and Gross, *Becoming Free, Becoming Black,* 183; North Carolina General Assembly, *Slaves and Free Persons of Color,* 9; Phillip Schwarz, "Emancipators, Protectors, and Anomalies: Free Black Slaveowners in Virginia," *Virginia Magazine of History and Biography* 95, no. 3 (July 1987), 317–388, 330–331.

56. Other emancipations by owner may have included self-purchase, but often, in these less detailed sources, it is impossible to tell what deals may have been worked out to lead to these moments of official freedom. Klebaner, "American Manumission Laws," 5. These manumissions can be found in a research guide produced by the Alabama Department of Archives and History. The guide, "Slave Legislation to 1832," compiles acts of the legislature relating to manumissions that can be traced in the Alabama Legislative Acts, Journals, and Constitutions. For more on Daniel Reed, see *Journal of the Legislative Council of the Alabama Territory* (St. Stephens: Thomas Eastin, 1818), 45, https://archive.org/details/alabama-senate-journal-1818/SJ_1818_01_02/mode/2up?q=daniel+reed; *Journal of the House of Representatives of the State of Alabama* (Cahawba: Allen & Brickell, 1820), 15, 32, https://archive.org/details/alabama-house-journal-1820/HJ_1820/mode/2up; and *Acts Passed at the Eleventh Annual Session of the General Assembly of the State of Alabama* (Tuscaloosa: McGuire, Henry, and Walker, 1830), Section 9, 1829–1830, https://archive.org/details/alabama-acts-1829-1830/Acts_1829_1830/. On Alabama laws and free African Americans, see Robert Reid, "Free Negroes in Alabama During the Ante-Bellum Period," *Negro History Bulletin* 8, no. 6 (March 1945), 134–139, 143.

57. Hilde, *Slavery, Fatherhood,* 93, 120, 126.

58. Berry, "'In Pressing Need of Cash,'" 30, 23; Myers, *Forging Freedom,* 41, 50–53.

59. Hilde, *Slavery, Fatherhood,* 121–123.

60. Myers, *Forging Freedom,* 40; Camp, *Closer to Freedom,* 28, 32.

61. Myers, *Forging Freedom,* 40; Schermerhorn, *Money over Mastery,* 99, 107, 110, 133, 111, 124. See Johnson, *Wicked Flesh,* 133.

62. Schermerhorn, *Money over Mastery*, 122, 107, 143, 108; Schafer, *Becoming Free*, 47–50; Myers, *Forging Freedom*, 2, 8; Jeffory A. Clymer, *Family Money: Property, Race, and Literature in the Nineteenth Century* (Oxford: Oxford University Press, 2014), 42. For more on the role of Black women in making and defining freedom, see Johnson, *Wicked Flesh*.

63. Loren Schweninger, "The Fragile Nature of Freedom: Free Women of Color in the U.S. South," in *Beyond Bondage: Free Women of Color in the Americas*, ed. David Barry Gaspar and Darlene Clark Hine (Chicago: University of Illinois Press, 2004), 107–108; Myers, *Forging Freedom*, 40.

64. Dorothy S. Provine, *District of Columbia Free Negro Registers, 1821–1861* (Berwyn Heights, MD: Heritage Books, 1996), 277, 249, 301, 511.

65. Corrigan, "It's a Family Affair," 176–177; Mary Beth Corrigan, "A Social Union of Heart and Effort: The African-American Family in the District of Columbia on the Eve of Emancipation," PhD diss., University of Maryland, 1996, 80, 137–148; Myers, *Forging Freedom*, 41.

66. Written by a Friend, as related to him by Brother Jones, *The Experience of Thomas H. Jones, Who Was a Slave for Forty-Three Years* (Boston: Bazin and Chandler, 1862), 34–35, https://docsouth.unc.edu/fpn/jones/jones.html. Libra Hilde also discusses Jones's story. Hilde, *Slavery, Fatherhood*, 132–133.

67. Caitlin Rosenthal discusses what happened to the commodification of the enslaved in cases of self-purchase but concludes that enslavers "exploited" even the internal value of the enslaved and "sought to wield it as monopoly power." As I argue, though, the enslaved used whatever power they had to ensure that they were not completely powerless. Rosenthal, "Capitalism When Labor Was Capital: Slavery, Power, and Price in Antebellum America," *Capitalism: A Journal of History and Economics* 1, no. 2 (Spring 2020), 296–337, 328.

68. Penningroth, *Claims of Kinfolk*, 47.

69. Meaders, *Kidnappers in Philadelphia*, 73; Newman, *Transformation of American Abolitionism*, 65; John Shoemaker, *The Life of Elisha Tyson, the Philanthropist* (Baltimore: B. Lundy, 1825), 5.

70. West, *Family or Freedom*, 18, 95.

71. Stephanie Jones-Rogers, *They Were Her Property: White Women as Slave Owners in the American South* (New Haven, CT: Yale University Press, 2019), 97–99.

72. "Buying a Preacher," *NASS* (August 20, 1846); Ira Berlin, *Many Thousands Gone: The First Two Centuries of Slavery in North America* (Cambridge, MA: Belknap Press, 2004), 235. For more on the role of Black churches as freedom networks, see Cheryl Janifer LaRoche, *Free Black Communities and the Underground Railroad: The Geography of Resistance* (Chicago: University of Illinois Press, 2014), 2; Deyle, *Carry Me Back*, 271–272. For more on the economic power of free African Americans, see Kimberly Welch,

"Arteries of Capital: William Johnson and the Practice of Black Moneylending in the Antebellum U.S. South," *Slavery and Abolition* 41, no. 2 (2020), 304–326, https://doi.org /10.1080/0144039X.2019.1633732.

73. Free African Baptist Church, Richmond, VA, Minute Book, 1841–1857, Mss5:8Bxx6440:1, Virginia Historical Society, Richmond, VA, 47, 77.

74. "The Slave Code in Washington," *National Era* (April 19, 1855); Corrigan, "It's a Family Affair," 180.

75. Jefferson County, Kentucky, Jefferson County Order Books, 1780–1901, vols. 2–20, held at Kentucky Division for Libraries and Archives, Frankfort, KY; for Washington Spralding, see vol. 19. J. Blaine Hudson, "'Upon This Rock'—The Free African American Community of Antebellum Louisville, Kentucky," *Register of the Kentucky Historical Society* 109, nos. 3–4 (Summer–Autumn 2011), 13–19, 29; Race and Slavery Petitions Project, Petition 20785118, November 17, 1851, https://library.uncg.edu/slavery /petitions/details.aspx?pid=6492.

76. "An Affecting Appeal," *Emancipator and Journal of Public Morals* (October 28, 1834); "Cecilia at Liberty," *Emancipator* (December 2, 1834); "Copy of the Bill of Sale," *Emancipator* (December 2, 1834).

77. Lane, *Narrative*, 16–17, 23–31, 33–34, 51; Schermerhorn, *Money over Mastery*, 160; Fields, *Slavery and Freedom*, 36–37; Maris-Wolf, *Family Bonds*, 11–12. Edlie Wong discusses Lane's experience of legal freedom as one of exclusion. Wong, *Neither Fugitive Nor Free: Atlantic Slavery, Freedom Suits, and the Legal Culture of Travel* (New York: New York University Press, 2009), 169–172.

78. Lane, *Narrative*, 43, 46–47. Hilde discusses Lane's story as well. Hilde, *Slavery, Fatherhood*, 126–127.

79. Kate E. R. Pickard, *The Kidnapped and the Ransomed: The Narrative of Peter and Vina Still After Forty Years of Slavery* (Lincoln: University of Nebraska Press, 1995), 212, 213–215, 226.

80. Pickard, *The Kidnapped*, 235, 262, 271, 279–281, 319–338; Still, *Underground Railroad*, 31, 35–36.

81. Mary Freeman describes the importance of letter writing as a "weapon used by Black families and their allies to combat the threats of distance and dislocation." Freeman, "Seeking Abolition," 19.

82. Still, *The Underground Railroad*, 318, 323; Christopher Hager, *Word by Word: Emancipation and the Act of Writing* (Cambridge, MA: Harvard University Press, 2015), 54, 57–59, 61; Heather Andrea Williams, *Help Me to Find My People: The African American Search for Family Lost in Slavery* (Chapel Hill: University of North Carolina Press, 2012), 74.

83. Ohio Anti-Slavery Society, *Report on the Condition of the People of Color in the State of Ohio: From the Proceedings of the Ohio Anti-Slavery Convention, held at Putnam,*

on the 22d, 23d, and 24th of April, 1835 (Boston: Isaac Knapp, 1836), 8–9, https://catalog.hathitrust.org/Record/100785622.

84. Ohio Anti-Slavery Society, *Report*, 6.

85. The movement of free African Americans and fugitive slaves and anti-Black responses to that migration caused some midwestern states to ban their presence. Seeley, *Right to Remain*, 329–330.

86. Hill Edwards has shown how the economic activity of the enslaved reinscribed the power of enslavers over their lives and benefited the white societies in which they lived. She claims that they could not "buy themselves out of slavery" and that their "participation in networks of commodity exchange and wage labor could not bring them out of slavery." Even though some could buy themselves out of slavery, this is true overall. However, even under other conditions, capitalism is not a liberatory system. Hill Edwards, *Unfree Markets*, 157.

CHAPTER 3

1. American Anti-Slavery Society, *Proceedings of the Anti-Slavery Convention* (New York: Dorr and Butterfield, 1833), 3.

2. Sinha, *The Slave's Cause*, 225.

3. American Anti-Slavery Society, *Proceedings of the Anti-Slavery Convention*, 3; Tomek, *Colonization and Its Discontents*, 156.

4. Betty L. Fladeland, "Compensated Emancipation: A Rejected Alternative," *Journal of Southern History* 42, no. 2 (May 1976), 169–186; Kellow, "Conflicting Imperatives," 203. For more on Garrison and second-wave abolition, see Sinha, *The Slave's Cause*; Benjamin Quarles, *Black Abolitionists* (London: Oxford University Press, 1969); Aileen Kraditor, *Means and Ends in American Abolitionism: Garrison and His Critics on Strategy and Tactics, 1834–1850* (Chicago: Elephant Paperbacks, 1989). On manumission and the idea of freedom as a commodity, see Eric Burin, *Slavery and the Peculiar Solution: A History of the American Colonization Society* (Gainesville: University Press of Florida, 2008), 131–132.

5. American Anti-Slavery Society, *Declaration of Sentiments of the American Anti-Slavery Society* (New York: William S. Dorr, 1833), 2.

6. See Tomek, *Colonization and Its Discontents*.

7. Tomek shows that different facets of the abolition movement continued to coexist, with politics and membership shifting and overlapping, throughout the nineteenth century. As she shows, this was especially true in Pennsylvania; on policy, see esp. chap. 2. Even those who would become the leaders of second-wave abolition, such as William Lloyd Garrison and Gerrit Smith, flirted with colonization before learning

from African Americans. Tomek, *Colonization and Its Discontents*, xv, 1, 4–8, 18, 50, 55–56, 155.

8. Burin, *Slavery and the Peculiar Solution*, 91, 95.

9. Matison, "Manumission by Purchase," 166; Sinha, *The Slave's Cause*, 34; Nicholas Guyatt, "The American Colonization Society: 200 Years of the 'Colonizing Trick,'" *Black Perspectives* (December 22, 2016), https://www.aaihs.org/the-american-colonization-society-200-years-of-the-colonizing-trick/; Burin, *Slavery and the Peculiar Solution*, 170.

10. Power-Greene, *Against Wind and Tide*, 53, chap. 3.

11. Lucretia Mott, quoted in Carol Faulkner, *Lucretia Mott's Heresy: Abolition and Women's Rights in Nineteenth-Century America* (Philadelphia: University of Pennsylvania Press, 2011), 167.

12. For instance, see Tomek on the connections between Henry Highland Garnet, the African Civilization Society, ACS, and Martin Delany's Niger Valley Exploring Party. Tomek, *Colonization and Its Discontents*, 206–210. On the long history of fighting colonization, see Power-Greene, *Against Wind and Tide*.

13. William Lloyd Garrison, *Thoughts on African Colonization* (Boston: Garrison and Knapp, 1832), 1, 5, 10.

14. Power-Greene, *Against Wind and Tide*, 50.

15. Paul, "Compensation for Slaves," *Liberator* (August 31, 1833).

16. Fladeland, "Compensated Emancipation," 169–170.

17. William A. Green, *British Slave Emancipation: The Sugar Colonies and the Great Experiment, 1830–1865* (Oxford: Clarendon Press, 1976), 111, 112.

18. For more on the postemancipation British West Indies, see Natasha Lightfoot, *Troubling Freedom: Antigua and the Aftermath of British Emancipation* (Durham, NC: Duke University Press, 2015).

19. "Negro Emancipation," *Bristol Mercury* (May 19, 1838); Charles H. Wesley, "The Abolition of Negro Apprenticeship in the British Empire," *Journal of Negro History* 23, no. 2 (April 1938), 155–199.

20. "Glorious News from the West Indies!," *Liberator* (September 7, 1838).

21. "Reported for the Liberator," *Liberator* (August 14, 1840); "The First of August," *New York Evangelist* (August 12, 1837).

22. Paul, "Compensation for Slaves," *Liberator* (August 31, 1833).

23. American Anti-Slavery Society, *Declaration of Sentiments*, 2, 9.

24. Lewis C. Gunn, "Friend Lundy," *Pennsylvania Freeman* (November 12, 1836).

25. Lewis C. Gunn, "Friend Lundy," *Pennsylvania Freeman* (November 12, 1836).

26. Quarles, *Black Abolitionists*, 41, 59; Sinha, *The Slave's Cause*, 253; Eric Foner, *The Fiery Trial: Abraham Lincoln and American Slavery* (New York: Norton, 2010), 325–326; Harrold, *Border War*, 95, 111.

27. American Anti-Slavery Society, *Proceedings of the Anti-Slavery Convention*, 15.

28. Neil Roberts, *Freedom as Marronage* (Chicago: University of Chicago Press, 2015), 9–11.

29. Kraditor, *Means and Ends*, 222. Kellow also sees this as a tension within the movement between "legal and moral" condemnation of enslavement as an institution and an "emotional and humanitarian response to those who were held in bondage." Kellow, "Conflicting Imperatives," 200, 206.

30. "A Charitable Appeal," *Liberator* (October 1, 1831).

31. For more on violence, see Kellie Carter Jackson, *Force and Freedom: Black Abolitionists and the Politics of Freedom* (Philadelphia: University of Pennsylvania Press, 2019); for examples of violent resistance and fugitive protection in the North, see Harrold, *Border War*, chap. 5. On Turner's rebellion and its aftermath, see Vanessa Holden, *Surviving Southampton: African American Women and Resistance in Nat Turner's Community* (Champaign: University of Illinois Press, 2021).

32. John W. Cromwell, "The Aftermath of Nat Turner's Insurrection," *Journal of Negro History* 5, no. 2 (April 1920), 208–234, 223–230; Harrold, *Border War*, 36.

33. It is unsurprising that King's plan, along with commendations of it by none other than Chief Justice of the Supreme Court John Marshall and former president James Madison, circulated among colonizationists as well, appearing in the ACS's journal, the *African Repository*. On Rufus King and antislavery, see Sinha, *The Slave's Cause*, 184–185; "Plan of Colonization," *African Repository* (October 1, 1838).

34. "Purchase of Slaves," *Liberator* (July 14, 1832); "Plan of Colonization," *African Repository* (October 1, 1838).

35. "Purchase of Slaves," *Liberator* (July 14, 1832).

36. "Purchase of Slaves," *Liberator* (July 14, 1832).

37. According to Stanley Harrold, "white border southerners linked instances of physical intervention with a more comprehensive abolitionist campaign." Harrold, *Border War*, 35–37, 39–45.

38. Sinha, *The Slave's Cause*, 250–251; Harrold, *Border War*, 23, 37–38.

39. Sinha, *The Slave's Cause*, 390–392; Harrold, *Border War*, 20–23, 95, 56, 63. For a more extensive historical take on how the federal government protected the interests of enslavers, see William Jay, *A View of the Action of the Federal Government, in Behalf of Slavery* (Utica, NY: Jackson and Chaplin, 1844).

40. See Sinha, *The Slave's Cause*, chap. 13.

41. Throughout these stories, abolitionist audiences meet industrious enslaved people, a vast array of allies, and duplicitous, violent enslavers. The stories also reveal enslaved people meeting the challenges of raising and successfully using funds to become free, which in turn supported abolitionist rhetoric about racial equality and the ability of African Americans to flourish in freedom. Kellow, "Conflicting Imperatives," 209; Matison, "Manumission by Purchase," 167.

42. "A Ransom," *Liberator* (January 12, 1838).

43. "Birmingham Anti-Slavery Society," *British and Foreign Anti-slavery Reporter* (November 30, 1842); "Life of Moses Grandy," *Liberator* (February 23, 1844).

44. Moses Grandy, *Narrative of the Life of Moses Grandy; Late a Slave in the United States of America* (London: C. Gilpin, 1843), 65–66; "Life of Moses Grandy," *Liberator* (February 23, 1844).

45. Grandy, *Narrative*, 72. In June 1845, Frederick Douglass's narrative was listed in the *Pennsylvania Freeman* for sale for fifty cents. Grandy's narrative, published two years before Douglass's and with a less famous author, would have had to sell an enormous amount of copies to enable the purchase of the rest of his family. "Advertisement," *Pennsylvania Freeman* (June 5, 1845).

46. "Literary Notice," *British and Foreign Anti-slavery Reporter* (November 16, 1842).

47. Hartman, *Scenes of Subjection*, 115.

48. "A Mother's Affection," *Pennsylvania Freeman* (March 28, 1839).

49. "A Minister Begging Money to Purchase His Wife!," *Liberator* (March 2, 1833).

50. Grandy, *Narrative*, 72, 65.

51. T.E., "Communications," *NASS* (April 10, 1845).

52. Still, *The Underground Railroad*, 684. For more on the activism of William Still, see Andrew K. Diemer *Vigilance: The Life of William Still, Father of the Underground Railroad* (New York: Penguin Random House, 2022). Still, *The Underground Railroad*.

53. John Stauffer, *The Black Hearts of Men: Radical Abolitionists and the Transformation of Race* (Cambridge, MA: Harvard University Press, 2004), 96–98, 105–107, 102, 138. Smith's quest for perfectionism also included following William Miller's ideas of "heaven on earth," which failed to appear.

54. An article in the *NASS* discussing Smith's role as a "rich philanthropist" imagined his daily life, "assailed by this who solicit his patronage," and asked if one would really desire to switch places with him for his money. "Gerrit Smith," *NASS* (July 7, 1855). Smith's father had also been a slaveholder. Stauffer, *The Black Hearts of Men*, 63, 128; "Samuel and Family," *Pennsylvania Freeman* (November 3, 1841); "Gerrit Smith's Slaves," *NASS* (February 10, 1842).

55. See also "Slaves Manumitted—Remarkable Case," *NASS* (March 14, 1844). Dr. Brisbane, a slaveholder from South Carolina who sold his twenty-seven slaves upon moving to Ohio, decided to "redeem and liberate each slave he sold." Brisbane spent $6,000 more than he had gotten for them when he purchased them back. He wished to allow them to settle on land he had bought in Ohio. The author of the article believed that his "act of benevolence" commended "itself to the hearts of all."

56. Stanley Harrold, *Subversives: Antislavery Community in Washington, D.C., 1828–1865* (Baton Rouge: Louisiana State University Press, 2002), 102–104.

57. Chaplin was no stranger to the connections between underground and legal attempts at freedom. He was also involved in the failed *Pearl* escape and the redemption of the Edmonson sisters. "The Case of Chaplin," *NASS* (July 22, 1852).

58. Quoted in Stauffer, *The Black Hearts of Men*, 127–128.

59. Frederick Douglass, *My Bondage and My Freedom* (New York: Miller, Orton, and Mulligan, 1855), 336–355, https://docsouth.unc.edu/neh/douglass55/douglass55.html#p365.

60. Douglass, *My Bondage and My Freedom*, 357–361. On Douglass's early life and activism, see David Blight, *Frederick Douglass: Prophet of Freedom* (New York: Simon and Schuster, 2020), 104–110.

61. William F. McFeely, *Frederick Douglass* (New York: Norton and Company, 1991), 116; Blight, *Frederick Douglass*, 139.

62. "Frederick Douglass," *Liberator* (March 6, 1846); "Frederick Douglass," *Liberator* (May 15, 1846); Blight, *Frederick Douglass*, 161–162.

63. Douglass, *My Bondage and My Freedom*, 363–364; McFeely, *Frederick Douglass*, 144; John Stauffer, "Frederick Douglass and the Politics of Slave Redemptions," in *Buying Freedom: Ethics and Economics of Slave Redemption*, ed. Kwame Anthony Appiah and Martin Bunzl (Princeton, NJ: Princeton University Press, 2007), 214–215; Sinha, *The Slave's Cause*, 427–428; "Narrative of Frederick Douglass," *Liberator* (February 20, 1846); "Frederick Douglass," *Liberator* (March 6, 1846); "Frederick Douglass," *Liberator* (May 15, 1846).

64. Douglass, *My Bondage and My Freedom*, 363–364.

65. "Douglass in England," *Liberator* (July 10, 1846); Douglass, *My Bondage and My Freedom*, 370.

66. Blight, *Frederick Douglass*, 171–173.

67. McFeely, *Frederick Douglass*, 136–137.

68. "Letter from Frederick Douglass, No V," *Liberator* (January 30, 1846); McFeely, *Frederick Douglass*, 136–137; Sinha, *The Slave's Cause*, 430; "Frederick Douglass," *NASS* (December 3, 1846); "Frederick Douglass," *NASS* (November 11, 1847). Douglass's manumission shows that experience in the world of business and legal matters acted as a crucial means of support that abolitionists could give to fugitives who wished to obtain their legal freedom. Although some abolitionists, such as Gerrit Smith, had enough money to give freely, it is important to note that the vast majority of the abolition movement was working class and did not have access to vast funding. For many, it would seem especially wasteful to spend exorbitant amounts of money for the purchase of one individual when that money, in a movement of limited means, could go to more collective work.

69. "Letter to Douglass with his Reply," *Liberator* (January 29, 1847).

70. "Ransom of Douglass," *Liberator* (March 19, 1847).

71. "Frederick Douglass," *Liberator* (January 15, 1847).

72. Douglass, *My Bondage and My Freedom*, 376.

73. Lewis C. Gunn, "For the National Enquirer" *Pennsylvania Freeman* (November 12, 1836).

74. B. Webb, "Ransom of Frederick Douglass," *Liberator* (March 5, 1847).

75. Webb, "Ransom of Frederick Douglass," *Liberator* (March 5, 1847).

76. "Frederick Douglass," *NASS* (December 3, 1846).

77. "Mr. Douglass and the Boston Traveller," *Liberator* (August 28, 1846).

78. "Letter to Douglass with His Reply," *Liberator* (January 29, 1847).

79. "Letter to Douglass with His Reply," *Liberator* (January 29, 1847).

80. "Mr. Douglass and the Boston Traveller," *Liberator* (August 28, 1846); Douglass, *My Bondage and My Freedom*, 376.

81. "Reported for the 'National Anti-slavery Standard,'" *Pennsylvania Freeman* (May 20, 1847).

82. "The Ransom of Douglass," *Liberator* (February 2, 1847).

83. "The Frederick Douglass Fund," *NASS* (December 9, 1847); "Douglass," *NASS* (August 26, 1847); Frederick Douglass, *My Bondage and My Freedom* (New York: Miller, Orton and Mulligan, 1855), 392.

84. Sinha, *The Slave's Cause*, 492–493, 426, 495; Frederick Douglass, "The Constitution of the United States: Is It Pro-slavery or Anti-slavery?" (speech delivered March 26, 1860, in Glasgow, Scotland), https://www.blackpast.org/global-african-history/1860-frederick-douglass-constitution-united-states-it-pro-slavery-or-anti-slavery/.

85. Still, *The Underground Railroad*, 746–747; Samuel D. Burns, "Letter from Another Martyr in the Cause of Freedom," *Liberator* (June 30, 1848).

86. Haworth Wetherald, "Selections," *NASS* (September 7, 1848); Samuel D. Burns, "Letter from Another Martyr in the Cause of Freedom," *Liberator* (June 30, 1848); Daniel Victor, "Delaware Pardons an Underground Railroad 'Hero,'" *New York Times* (November 2, 2015), https://www.nytimes.com/2015/11/03/us/delaware-pardon-underground-railroad-samuel-burris.html.

87. The escape was organized by local abolitionists and likely financed, at least in part, by Gerrit Smith. Josephine Pacheco, *The Pearl: A Failed Slave Escape on the Potomac* (Chapel Hill: University of North Carolina Press, 2005), 52–57; "Capture of Runaway Slaves," *NASS* (April 27, 1848); "Escape and Recapture of Seventy Seven Slaves," *NASS* (April 20, 1848); Mark K. Ricks, "The 1848 *Pearl* Escape from Washington, DC: A Convergence of Opportunity, Motivation, and Political Action in the Nation's Capital," in *In The Shadow of Freedom: The Politics of Slavery in the National Capital*, ed. Paul Finkelman and Donald R. Kennon (Athens: Ohio University Press, 2011), 205.

88. "Communications," *North Star* (November 10, 1848); "Beauties of the Slave System," *North Star* (October 13, 1848); "Meeting in Behalf of Slaves," *National Era* (November 2, 1848).

89. Pacheco, *The Pearl*, 49, 188; "The Washington Slave Case," *Liberator* (October 13, 1848); Ricks, "The 1848 *Pearl* Escape," 199–201; Hampden, "Beauties of the Slave System," *North Star* (October 13, 1848).

90. "The Sum Subscribed—At the Meeting Held at the Tabernacle," *National Era* (November 16, 1848); "Selections," *North Star* (November 17, 1848); Kellow, "Conflicting Imperatives," 209; "Selections," *North Star* (November 17, 1848); Pennington, *The Fugitive Blacksmith*, x.

91. The Edmonson family were no strangers to buying freedom. At least five Edmonson sisters and one brother had previously bought their freedom. Others on the *Pearl* were purchased, including the wife and youngest child of Daniel Bell. Bell had also bought his own freedom earlier in life. Like the Edmonson family, the Bells looked to abolitionists and traveled the nation in attempts to raise enough money to buy their loved ones. Daniel Bell himself paid $1,000 for his freedom through the endorsement of notes from supporters, when threatened with sale in Maryland. Despite being emancipated by her enslaver's will, Bell's wife, their eight children, and two grandchildren had been illegally reclaimed as property. In response, the Bell family decided to take advantage of the opportunity presented by the *Pearl* to escape. Besides Bell's wife and two youngest children, the rest of the family was sold as punishment for running away. Abolitionists raised $450 to redeem his wife and one child. Ricks, "The 1848 *Pearl* Escape," 202; "The Sum Subscribed—At the Meeting Held at the Tabernacle," *National Era* (November 16, 1848); "Selections," *North Star* (November 17, 1848).

92. "Untitled," *National Era* (November 16, 1848).

93. Quoted in Sinha, *The Slave's Cause*, 494; Blight, *Frederick Douglass*, 226.

94. Douglass, *My Bondage and My Freedom*, 375–376.

95. Douglass, *My Bondage and My Freedom*, 375.

CHAPTER 4

1. William Wells Brown, *Narrative of William W. Brown, An American Slave* (London: Charles Gilpin, 1849), iii–ix, https://docsouth.unc.edu/fpn/brownw/brown.html.

2. Brown, *Narrative of William W. Brown*, ix; Kellow, "Conflicting Imperatives," 205; "William Wells Brown," *Pennsylvania Freeman* (June 1, 1854).

3. Harrold, *Border War*, 111.

4. Quarles, *Black Abolitionists*, 41, 59; Sinha, *The Slave's Cause*, 253; Foner, *The Fiery Trial*, 325–326; Harrold, *Border War*, 95, 111.

5. Foner, *Gateway to Freedom*, 134; "An Act Respecting Fugitives from Justice and Persons Escaping from the Service of Their Masters," 9 Stat. 562, 31st United States Congress (1850), https://avalon.law.yale.edu/19th_century/fugitive.asp.

6. Foner, *Gateway to Freedom*, 4, 134, 136.

7. Samuel E. Sewall, "The Case of George Latimer," *Liberty Standard* (September 9, 1842); "Case of George Latimer," *Liberty Standard* (November 23, 1842); "Untitled," *British and Foreign Anti-slavery Reporter* (December 28, 1842); Sinha, *The Slave's Cause*, 390–393; Cooper Wingert, "Fugitive Slave Renditions and the Proslavery Crisis of Confidence in Federalism, 1850–1860," *Journal of American History* 110, no. 1 (June 2023), 40–57, 41, 46.

8. Foner, *Gateway to Freedom*, 134; William Wells Brown, *Three Years in Europe; or, Places I Have Seen and People I Have Met* (London: Charles Gilpin, 1852), 248, https:// docsouth.unc.edu/neh/brown52/brown52.html.

9. Foner, *Gateway to Freedom*, 4, 134, 136; Quarles, *Black Abolitionists*, 20, 30. A May 1851 article from the *Springfield Republican* reprinted in the *NASS* claimed that "all or nearly all" of the fugitives living there had gone to Canada. "Fugitive Slaves Fleeing to Canada," *NASS* (May 15, 1851). Jacobs, *Incidents*, 285–292, https://docsouth.unc.edu/fpn /jacobs/jacobs.html. It is difficult to track exact numbers about whether self-purchase increased for fugitives after 1850. Manumission records do not necessarily record whether someone was a runaway, and abolitionist sources, for a variety of reasons, are overpopulated with stories about fugitives.

10. Jacobs, *Incidents*, 285–292.

11. E. H. Gray, *Assaults upon Freedom! or, Kidnapping an Outrage upon Humanity and Abhorrent to God: A Discourse, Occasioned by the Rendition of Anthony Burns* (Shelburne Falls, MA: D. B. Gunn, 1854), 25; Brown, *Three Years in Europe*, 243.

12. Jesse Olsavsky shows how the activities of vigilance committees to protect fugitives were "undermining sectional compromise" and that the Fugitive Slave Act "required an intensified response" from activists. Olsavsky, *The Most Absolute Abolition*, 89. Jacobs, *Incidents*, 287; "The Revival of Kidnapping," *Pennsylvania Freeman* (September 12, 1850). For a map showing the extent of organizing meetings held across the North in response to the Fugitive Slave Act, see Richard Blackett, *The Captive's Quest for Freedom: Fugitive Slaves, the 1850 Fugitive Slave Law, and the Politics of Slavery* (New York: Cambridge University Press, 2019), 16–17, 44–45.

13. Olsavsky, *The Most Absolute Abolition*, 51, 64.

14. Philip Foner, ed., *The Life and Writings of Frederick Douglass* (New York: International Publishers, 1950), vol. 1, 236; "At the Tabernacle May 12, 1847," *Pennsylvania Freeman* (May 20, 1847).

15. The ACS remained active in the period as African Americans and enslavers responded to the "nation's worsening racial climate," according to Beverly C. Tomek. Tomek claims that between 1841 and 1860 the ACS doubled their manumission numbers from the two preceding decades. Tomek, *Colonization and Its Discontents*, 175, 200, 219. Power-Greene, *Against Wind and Tide*, 91, 97, 99, 112–113, 132–133.

16. For examples of these difficulties in Virginia, see Kirt von Daacke, *Freedom Has a Face: Race, Identity and Community in Jefferson's Virginia* (Charlottesville: University of Virginia Press, 2012), chaps. 3, 5. According to von Daacke, the first person to be charged in Albemarle County, Virginia, with illegal residency had purchased his freedom. The man, Randolph Jones, faced two arrests between 1843 and 1848, but the cases were dismissed. In 1851 he was indicted again. When he was arrested in 1852 he was found guilty and was sentenced to be sold. No evidence of Jones's sale as a slave was found. On Jones's story, see von Daacke, *Freedom Has a Face*, 81–85.

17. A total of 112 people were manumitted in Anne Arundel County between 1850 and 1860. Anne Arundel County Court Manumission Record 1844–1851, Maryland State Archives, D4 CR 79, https://msa.maryland.gov/megafile/msa/coagserm /cm1/cm48/000000/000004/pdf/mdsa_cm48_4.pdf. Dorchester County Circuit Court (Manumissions) 1852–1864, Maryland State Archives, C3079, http://guide.msa .maryland.gov/pages/series.aspx?ID=C3079-1. Thank you to Morgan Wilbanks for compiling this research.

18. Queen Anne's County Circuit Court (Manumissions, Index) 1787–1864, CE435-1, Maryland State Archives, http://guide.msa.maryland.gov/pages/series.aspx ?id=CE435. Anne Arundel County Court Manumission Record 1844–1851, D4 CR 79, Maryland State Archives, https://msa.maryland.gov/megafile/msa/coagserm/cm1/cm48 /000000/000004/pdf/mdsa_cm48_4.pdf. Dorchester County Circuit Court (Manumissions) 1852–1864, C3079, Maryland State Archives, http://guide.msa.maryland .gov/pages/series.aspx?ID=C3079-1, https://msa.maryland.gov/megafile/msa/coagser /c3000/c3079/000000/000001/000000/000021/pdf/mdsa_c3079_1_21.pdf. Tubman mustered in the Seventh US Colored Infantry on September 29, 1863, three days after he was manumitted. Tubman may have been related to Harriet Tubman's first husband, John Tubman. National Archives at Washington, DC, *Compiled Military Service Records of Volunteer Union Soldiers Who Served with the United States Colored Troops, 2nd Through 7th Colored Infantry Including 3d Tennessee Volunteers (African Descent), 6th Louisiana Infantry (African Descent), and 7th Louisiana Infantry (African Descent)*, Microfilm Serial: M1820, Microfilm Roll: 107.

19. Klebaner, "American Manumission Laws," 443, 448–449; Jefferson County, Kentucky, Jefferson County Order Books, 1780–1901, vols. 2–20, held at Kentucky Division for Libraries and Archives, Frankfort, KY.

20. Judith Kelleher Schafer, "Roman Roots of the Louisiana Law of Slavery: Emancipation in American Louisiana, 1803–1857," *Louisiana Law Review* 56, no. 2 (Winter 1996), 409–422, 421–422; Klebaner, "American Manumission Laws," 443; Blackett, *The Captive's Quest*, 337, 103, 155; Seeley, *Right to Remain*, 329–330.

21. "Great Mass Meeting in the Park," *NASS* (October 10, 1850); "The First Blood," *NASS* (October 3, 1850); "Let Every Colored Man and Woman Attend the Great Mass

Meeting to Be Held in Zion Church, Church Street, Corner of Leonard, on Tuesday Evening, October, 1,1850," *NASS* (October 10, 1850). For more on Hamlet, see Blackett, *The Captive's Quest*, 378–381.

22. "The First Blood," *NASS* (October 3, 1850); "Let Every Colored Man and Woman Attend . . . ," *NASS* (October 10, 1850); *Fugitive Slave Bill: Its History and Unconstitutionality; With an Account of the Seizure and Enslavement of James Hamlet, and His Subsequent Restoration to Liberty* (New York: William Harned, 1850), 36; Foner, *Gateway to Freedom*, 126–127; Blackett, *The Captive's Quest*, 378–380; "Hamlet," *National Era* (October 10, 1850); "We Have Received Two or Three Communications . . . ," *NASS* (October 10, 1850).

23. "The First Victim Under the New Fugitive Slave Bill," *North Star* (October 3, 1850); "Great Mass Meeting in the Park," *NASS* (October 10, 1850); "Let Every Colored Man and Woman Attend . . .," *NASS* (October 10, 1850); Blackett, *The Captive's Quest*, 377–378.

24. Wingert, "Fugitive Slave Renditions," 50.

25. Five Years' Abstract of the Transactions of the Pennsylvania Society for Promoting the Abolition of Slavery, the Relief of Free Negroes Unlawfully Held in Bondage, and for Improving the Condition of the African Race (Philadelphia: Merrihew and Thompson, 1853) 7; David G. Smith, *On the Edge of Freedom: The Fugitive Slave Issue in South Central Pennsylvania, 1820–1870* (New York: Fordham University Press, 2013), 1, 73; Samuel May, *The Fugitive Slave Law and Its Victims* (New York: American Anti-Slavery Society, 1861), 14; "Philadelphia, Sunday, January 26," *Liberator* (February 14, 1851); Blackett, *The Captive's Quest*, 73.

26. Blackett, *The Captive's Quest*, 69–70.

27. Crayon, "Frederick Douglass," *Liberator* (September 27, 1850); Gerrit Smith, "Liberty-Equality-Fraternity!!!," *NASS* (August 1, 1850), quoted in Stauffer, *The Black Hearts of Men*, 163–164; L. P. Paper, "Convention of Slaves at Cazenovia," *North Star* (September 5, 1850); Frederick Douglass, "Cazenovia Convention Again," *North Star* (September 5, 1850).

28. "Questions and Answers," *National Era* (September 18, 1851).

29. Still, *Underground Railroad*, 618–622.

30. "Mrs. Lee," *Frederick Douglass' Paper* (June 10, 1852); "An Impostor Caged" and "A Word of Caution," *Frederick Douglass' Paper* (July 27, 1855).

31. "An Imposter," *NASS* (July 12, 1856); "To The Provincial Freeman," *Provincial Freeman* (December 29, 1855); "Look Out for the Impostor," *NASS* (November 17, 1855); "An Imposter," *NASS* (July 12, 1856).

32. "An Imposter," *NASS* (July 12, 1856); "To The Provincial Freeman," *Provincial Freeman* (December 29, 1855); "Look Out for the Impostor," *NASS* (November 17, 1855).

33. According to Gary Collison, fugitives in Canada West "found themselves in communities that were not self-sustaining." Collison, *Shadrach Minkins: From Fugitive Slave to Citizen* (Cambridge, MA: Harvard University Press, 1997), 185.

34. "Beware of Impostors," *Provincial Freeman* (April 5, 1856). See also "Impostors," *NASS* (July 14, 1855); Kellow, "Conflicting Imperatives," 209.

35. "Take Notice," *Anti-slavery Bugle* (April 9, 1859).

36. "Slave Case in Baltimore," *NASS* (January 9, 1851).

37. William Parker, "The Freedman's Story," *Atlantic* (March 1866), https://www.theatlantic.com/magazine/archive/1866/03/the-freedmans-story-continued/308738/. For more on violence and the Christiana uprising, see Jackson, *Force and Freedom*, chap. 2.

38. "The Man-Hunt in Pennsylvania," *Pennsylvania Freeman* (June 3, 1852); "James Phillips," *NASS* (July 1, 1852); "James Phillips," *NASS* (July 22, 1852); Wingert, "Fugitive Slave Renditions," 50.

39. "James Phillips," *NASS* (July 1, 1852); "James Phillips," *NASS* (July 22, 1852); "The Man-Hunt in Pennsylvania," *Pennsylvania Freeman* (June 3, 1852); "Another Arrest of a Fugitive," *Liberator* (June 11, 1852); "James Phillips," *Pennsylvania Freeman* (July 24, 1852); "Multiple News Items," *Pennsylvania Freeman* (August 7, 1852).

40. "James Phillips," *Pennsylvania Freeman* (July 24, 1852).

41. Wingert, "Fugitive Slave Renditions," 41.

42. "Slavery in California," *NASS* (July 22, 1852).

43. Blackett, *The Captive's Quest*, 41. For enslavers' doubts about the commitment of the federal government's determination in regard to the law, see Wingert "Fugitive Slave Renditions."

44. Blackett, *The Captive's Quest*, 71; "Anthony Burns," *NASS* (December 30, 1854); "Anthony Burns a Free Man," *NASS* (March 10, 1855); "Burns to Be Redeemed," *NASS* (March 3, 1855).

45. As Blackett has described, "The economic calculus of renditions rarely favored the slaveholder, as the cost of recapture and return was usually greater than the market value of the runaway." Blackett, *The Captive's Quest*, 41, 71. "Anthony Burns," *NASS* (December 30, 1854); "Anthony Burns a Free Man," *NASS* (March 10, 1855); "Burns to Be Redeemed," *NASS* (March 3, 1855).

46. "Anthony Burns," *NASS* (December 30, 1854); "Anthony Burns a Free Man," *NASS* (March 10, 1855); "Burns to Be Redeemed," *NASS* (March 3, 1855); Blackett, *The Captive's Quest*, 427.

47. "Anthony Burns," *NASS* (July 10, 1858).

48. "Edward Brown," *Frederick Douglass' Paper* (September 22, 1854).

49. Pacheco, *The Pearl*, 126.

50. Pennington, *The Fugitive Blacksmith*, iv–v, xi, 9, 12, 61–63.

51. Pennington, *The Fugitive Blacksmith*, 61–64. Hooker, writing to the *NASS* about his purchase, claims that he held Pennington as a slave while he took a walk to see what it felt like to be a slaveholder, suggesting that he might still decide to "send him to a sugar

plantation." Certainly a disturbing joke, if it can even be called such. John Hooker, "Successful Purchase of a D.D.," *NASS* (June 19, 1851).

52. Wingert claims that legal challenges to the law remained the "primary means of opposing renditions." Two-thirds of those claimed as fugitives had representation, according to Wingert. Wingert, "Fugitive Slave Renditions," 46, 52.

53. Blackett, *The Captive's Quest*, 274–275; "Three Fugitive Slaves Arrested in New York and Given Up to Their Owners," *Liberator* (June 2, 1854); "The Late Fugitive Slave Case," *Frederick Douglass' Paper* (June 9, 1854); "A Case for Sympathy," *Frederick Douglass' Paper* (June 16, 1854); "Freedom of a Slave Secured," *Anti-slavery Bugle* (July 8, 1854); "Story of Stephen Pembroke," *Frederick Douglass' Paper* (August 4, 1854).

54. Still, *The Underground Railroad*, 173–174; Blackett, *The Captive's Quest*, 274–275; J.W.C.P., "Look out for the Slave-Catchers," *Frederick Douglass' Paper* (March 16, 1855).

55. Still, *The Underground Railroad*, 326–328.

56. Blackett, *The Captive's Quest*, 409–411. On Minkins, see Collison, *Shadrach Minkins*. Collison mentions Rebecca Jones on pp. 56–57.

57. Still, *The Underground Railroad*, 327.

58. Jermain Loguen, *The Reverend J. W. Loguen, as a Slave and as a Freeman: A Narrative of Real Life* (Syracuse, NY: J. G. K. Truair and Co., 1859), 340, 381–394, 428, https://docsouth.unc.edu/neh/loguen/summary.html; J. W. Lougen, "Editors of the Evening Chronicle," *Frederick Douglass' Paper* (March 31, 1854); Angela F. Murphy, "'My Freedom I Derived from God': Jermain Loguen's Rejection of Freedom Purchase," presented at Society for Historians of the Early American Republic virtual conference, July 17, 2021.

59. William Craft, *Running a Thousand Miles for Freedom; or, the Escape of William and Ellen Craft from Slavery* (London: William Tweedie, 1860), 87–92, https://docsouth.unc.edu/neh/craft/craft.html; "Proposal to Buy William and Ellen Craft," *Pennsylvania Freeman* (November 28, 1850).

60. Blackett, *The Captive's Quest*, 337.

61. Kellow, "Conflicting Imperatives," 202–203; Fladeland, "Compensated Emancipation," 169–170; Green, *British Slave Emancipation*, 119; Stauffer, *The Black Hearts of Men*, 218–220.

62. Merle Curti, ed., *The Learned Blacksmith: The Letters and Journals of Elihu Burritt* (New York: Wilson-Erickson Incorporated, 1937), 29, 31, 37.

63. Brown, *Three Years in Europe*, 221, 272–273.

64. Curti, *The Learned Blacksmith*, 119–120.

65. Sinha, *The Slave's Cause*, 549, 190; Curti, *The Learned Blacksmith*, 120, 131, 138.

66. Sinha, *The Slave's Cause*, 549; Elihu Burritt, "National Compensation Emancipation Society" (New York: 1857), 2–4.

67. Sinha, *The Slave's Cause*, 550; "Compensated Emancipation Convention," *NASS* (January 8, 1859); "The Compensated Emancipation Society," *NASS* (February 5, 1859).

68. "Burritt's Compensated Emancipation," *Provincial Freeman* (September 12, 1857); "Spirited Meeting of the Colored Citizens of Philadelphia," *Liberator* (April 10, 1857). For more on African American responses to the *Dred Scott* decision, see Bonner, *Remaking the Republic*, chap. 5.

69. "Burritt's Compensated Emancipation," *Provincial Freeman* (September 12, 1857).

70. Don E. Fehrenbacher, *Abraham Lincoln: Speeches and Writings, 1859–1865* (New York: Literary Classics of the United States, 1989), 310–311, 316; Andrew Weintraub, "The Economics of Lincoln's Proposal for Compensated Emancipation," *American Journal of Economics and Sociology* 32, no. 2 (April 1973), 171, 175.

71. *An Act for the Release of Certain Persons Held to Service or Labor in the District of Columbia* (April 16, 1862), https://www.archives.gov/exhibits/featured-documents/dc -emancipation-act/transcription.html; Fehrenbacher, *Abraham Lincoln*, 310–311, 316; Kate Masur, *An Example for All the Land: Emancipation and the Struggle over Equality in Washington, D.C.* (Chapel Hill: University of North Carolina Press, 2010), 25.

72. "Religious Rejoicing over the Emancipation Act at Shiloh Church," *Weekly Anglo-African* (April 26, 1862); Charles Sumner, *Ransom of Slaves at the National Capital: Speech of Honorable Charles Sumner of Massachusetts* (Washington, DC: Congressional Globe Office, 1862), 3. According to Barbara Fields, by the Civil War, the idea of freedom dues, common under indentured servitude, were "all but forgotten." Because of slavery's long history, the idea of "providing for freedmen [had] receded into the past." Abolitionists, however, had not forgotten. Fields, "Slavery, Race and Ideology in the United States of America," *New Left Review* 1, no. 181 (May/June 1990), 95–118, 105–106.

73. T.E., "Communications," *NASS* (April 10, 1845).

74. J. H. Fowler, "Compensation," *Liberator* (November 15, 1861).

75. National Archives, "13th Amendment to the U.S. Constitution: Abolition of Slavery" (1865), https://www.archives.gov/milestone-documents/13th-amendment; "William Wells Brown," *Anti-slavery Bugle* (March 10, 1855); "Letter from Paterson," *Weekly Anglo-African* (December 7, 1861); M, "Tour of William Wells Brown," *Liberator* (April 4, 1862); "Proclamation Meetings," *Principia* (January 1, 1863). For more on the importance of the Emancipation Proclamation, see Martha S. Jones, Kate Masur, Louis Masur, James Oakes, and Manisha Sinha, "Historians' Forum: The Emancipation Proclamation," *Civil War History* 59, no. 1 (2013), 7–31; AASS, *Declaration*, 2.

EPILOGUE

1. Stewart, *Long Past Slavery*, 133–142, 178, 180; on the Florida Negro Writers' Unit, see chap. 7.

2. "Willis Dukes," in *Federal Writers' Project: Slave Narrative Project*, Vol. 3, *Florida, Anderson-Wilson (with combined interviews of others)*, 120–122, https://www.loc.gov/item/mesn030/.

3. "Willis Dukes," *Slave Narratives*, 121.

4. Familial reunion was of critical importance to enslaved people beyond Dukes's plantation as well. For those efforts during and after slavery, see Williams, *Help Me to Find My People*, esp. chaps. 4 and 5.

5. "Willis Dukes," *Slave Narratives*, 121. For more on the meaning of freedom and things, see Thavolia Glymph, *Out of the House of Bondage: The Transformation of the Plantation Household* (New York: Cambridge University Press, 2008), chap. 7; W. E. B. Du Bois, *The Souls of Black Folk* (New York: Dover, 1994), 5.

6. W. H. Furness, *The Right of Property in Man: A Discourse Delivered in the First Congregational Unitarian Church* (Philadelphia: C. Sherman and Son, 1859), 5, 7, 19, 23, https://fau.digital.flvc.org/islandora/object/fau%3A68428#page/1/mode/2up.

7. As Saidiya Hartman has formulated, "the question persists as to whether it is possible to unleash freedom from the history of property that secured it." Hartman, *Scenes of Subjection*, 119. Rinaldo Walcott argues that property remains a central problem for abolition and, thus, freedom. Walcott, *On Property: Policing, Prisons, and the Call for Abolition* (Windsor, Ontario: Biblioasis, 2021). Harris, "Whiteness as Property," 1735, 1743. See Nicholas Buccola, *The Political Thought of Frederick Douglass: In Pursuit of American Liberty* (New York: New York University Press, 2012), chap. 2.

8. Du Bois, *The Souls of Black Folk*, 3, 5.

9. Katherine McKittrick has argued that "black freedom is embedded in an economy of race and violence." McKittrick, "Mathematics Black Life," *Black Scholar* 44, no. 2 (Summer 2014), 17.

10. Writers such as Jacobs and Douglass have been described as "liminal autobiographers" because they broke with the genre's earlier attempts to create strict boundaries between the experience of slavery and freedom. William L. Andrews, *To Tell a Free Story: The First Century of Afro-American Autobiography, 1760–1865* (Champaign: University of Illinois Press, 1988), 179. Desmond Jagmohan argues that "*Incidents* was Jacobs' intellectual response to the national discourse on slavery and property." He says that Jacobs understood the wrongs of slavery to rest not only on "domination, but also of ownership because the latter is the root to the distinctive, and especially gendered, wrongs of slavery." Slavery, according to Jagmohan, is therefore a "distinct form of oppression." Jagmohan, "Peculiar Property: Harriet Jacobs on the Nature of Slavery," *Journal of Politics* 84, no. 2 (April 2022), 669–681, 669–670.

11. Gates, *Classic Slave Narratives*, 648, 655; Furness, *The Right of Property in Man*, 5,7.

12. Furness, *The Right of Property in Man*, 4.

13. Yellin, *Harriet Jacobs*, 115–116, 118. Ingrid Diran argues that Jacobs was not interested in securing self-ownership or in using a "fugitive financial calculus that uses the bonded character of capital against the category of ownership itself." By escaping slavery, she wished to "cease to both *have* value and to *be* one, to cost *nothing* and therefore, to be *free*." Diran, "Scenes of Speculation: Harriet Jacobs and the Biopolitics of Human Capital," *American Quarterly* 71, no. 3 (September 2019), 697–718, 713.

14. Yellin, *Harriet Jacobs*, 24; Gates, *Classic Slave Narratives*, 470.

15. Gates, *Classic Slave Narratives*, 658–662.

16. Gates, *Classic Slave Narratives*, 663–664.

17. Jacobs refers to enslavers like Norcom putting enslaved people or their value in his pocket. Gates, *Classic Slave Narratives*, 455, 660.

18. Gates, *Classic Slave Narratives*, 663. Disappointing Jacobs even further was the involvement of the American Colonization Society, which facilitated her manumission. She also bore the burden of the additional $150 that remained to be paid back. Yellin, *Harriet Jacobs*, 115–116, 118.

19. Gates, *Classic Slave Narratives*, 663.

20. "Letter to Douglass with his Reply," *Liberator* (January 29, 1847); Frederick Douglass, *Life and Times of Frederick Douglass* (Hartford, CT: Park Publishing Co, 1881), https://docsouth.unc.edu/neh/douglasslife/douglass.html, 260.

21. On the idea of emancipation as a "non-event" and slavery's afterlife, see Hartman, *Scenes of Subjection* and *Lose Your Mother*; Christina Sharpe, *In the Wake: On Blackness and Being* (Durham, NC: Duke University Press, 2016); Walcott, *On Property*, 96; Julia Bernier, "Bail Funds, Buying Freedom, and a History of Abolition," *Black Perspectives* (August 13, 2020), https://www.aaihs.org/bail-funds-buying-freedom-and-a-history-of-abolition/.

22. On Black activism and citizenship, see Bonner, *Remaking the Republic*; and Jones, *Birthright Citizens*.

23. Amy Dru Stanley, "Instead of Waiting for the Thirteenth Amendment: The War Power, Slave Marriage, and Inviolate Human Rights," *American Historical Review* 115, no. 3 (June 2010), 732–765, 735, 737, 740–744. Stanley discusses more contemporary ramifications for the odd relationship between the Thirteenth Amendment and Commerce Clause (as well as their relation to the rights of women) in human rights legislation and jurisprudence in the United States, in Stanley, "The Sovereign Market and Sex Difference: Human Rights in America," in *American Capitalism: New Histories*, ed. Sven Beckert and Christine Desan (New York: Columbia University Press, 2018), 140–169, esp. 145–146.

24. Eric Gardner "Frances Ellen Watkins Harper's 'National Salvation': A Rediscovered Lecture on Reconstruction," *Commonplace* 17, no. 4 (Summer 2017), http://commonplace.online/article/vol-17-no-4-gardner/. On ideas about Black historical time and the meaning of emancipation, see Justin Leroy, "Racial Capitalism and Black

Philosophies of History," in *Histories of Racial Capitalism*, ed. Destin Jenkins and Justin Leroy (New York: Columbia University Press, 2021), 169–184.

25. Harris, "Whiteness as Property," 1745–1791. On control over Black labor and lives after slavery, see Douglas Blackmon on convict leasing in *Slavery by Another Name: The Re-enslavement of Black Americans from the Civil War to World War II* (New York: Penguin, 2009); David M. Oshinsky, *Worse Than Slavery: Parchman Farm and the Ordeal of Jim Crow Justice* (New York: Free Press, 1997); and Talitha LeFlouria, *Chained in Silence: Black Women and Convict Labor in the New South* (Chapel Hill: University of North Carolina Press, 2015). Anti-Black violence was an important tool in the overthrow of Reconstruction and a constant threat to African Americans and Black freedom and property in the postbellum South. On anti-Black violence during Reconstruction and its relation to Black life and property, see Kidada Williams, *I Saw Death Coming: A History of Terror and Survival in the War Against Reconstruction* (New York: Bloomsbury, 2023).

26. Du Bois, *Souls of Black Folk*, 24.

27. As formulated by Fred Moten: "To be a citizen you have to own yourself, buy yourself (everyday), sell yourself, equate yourself with money, figure yourself as/in relation to the commodity." Moten, *Stolen Life: Consent Not to Be a Single Being* (Durham NC: Duke University Press, 2018), 79. Walcott, *On Property*, 17–18, 96; Harris, "Whiteness as Property," 1713–1714, 1720–1721.

INDEX

abolition, 28, 70, 89, 92, 102; compensated, 75, 136, 141; and discourse, 85, 139; and Elihu Burritt, 135, 148; first-wave, 16; and fugitive escapees, 107; and Great Britain, 84; imperial, 19; movement, 16, 35, 45, 47, 71, 79, 82, 84, 96–97, 104, 137, 148; and Pennsylvania, 19, 21, 39, 42, 47, 79, 84; problem of, 81; second-wave, 4, 16, 38, 79–80, 82, 86; success of, 104; total, 89, 118, 141, 148; uncompensated, 47; and violence, 75; and William Lloyd Garrison, 87. *See also* abolitionism

abolitionism: and American Anti–Slavery Society (AASS), 79–84, 136; and American Colonization Society (ACS), 81, 83; and American North, 51, 55, 75, 77, 111; and American South, 49, 71; and Anthony Burns, 127, 129; and Black abolitionists, 6, 15, 17, 35, 38, 40, 45, 78, 85, 89–92, 94, 97, 101, 109, 114, 118–19, 129, 140; and compensation, 134, 139, 141; and critique of slavery, 6, 16; debates, 4; and direct action, 89; and Elihu Burritt, 135–37; and Enoch Price, 109; and enslaved people, 17; and France, 19; and Frederick Douglass, 97–100, 102–4, 107; and fugitives, 107, 115–16; and Fugitive Slave Act, 111–12, 116, 124; and Gerrit Smith, 73, 95–96; and Haiti, 19; and Henry Bibb, 11; and ideology, 122–23, 133, 136, 144; and illegal action, 76, 90; as interracial movement, 35, 106; and James Phillips, 127; and James W.C. Pennington, 5, 129, 131; and Jermain Wesley Loguen, 133; and Leonard Grimes, 128; and lecture circuit, 121; and Lewis Gunn, 100–2; and Lewis Tappan, 17; and *The Liberator*, 91, 103; limits of, 21, 121, 131; and Maryland, 40, 70; and Moses Grandy, 91–92; and networks, 90, 93, 122, 179n72; and New Jersey, 24, 38; and newspapers, 93;

95, 99–100, 119; and New York, 87–88, 117; and Philadelphia, 79; and politics, 16; and print culture, 15, 39, 85–87, 90–93, 113–14; and public sphere, 86; and Quakers, 98; and resistance methods, 112–13, 115, 131, 137, 148; and reverends, 5; and Robert Purvis, 138; and Samuel D. Burris, 104–5; and self-purchase, 16–17, 70, 78, 83, 85, 87, 90, 93–95, 106–7, 110, 120–21, 135; and Theodore Weld, 17; and the United Kingdom, 83–84, 104, 110; and the United States, 28, 84, 89; and violence, 87, 125; and Virginia, 87; and white abolitionists, 21, 34–35, 38, 45, 49, 82, 119; and William Carter, 121–22; and William L. Chaplin, 95–96; and William Lloyd Garrison, 82, 87; and William Still, 58, 76–77, 94, 120; and William Wells Brown, 98, 110; and worldview, 15; and writings, 15, 90–92, 95. *See also* abolition, gradual abolition

African Americans: and abolitionism, 46, 70, 82, 84–85, 95, 119, 122; and abolitionists, 15–16, 21, 45, 97, 109, 148; and American Anti–Slavery Society (AASS), 79–80; and American Colonization Society (ACS), 80–82; and American North, 48; and American South, 12, 48, 71; and the Atlantic world, 7; and Cedric Robinson, 6; and economic activity, 11, 53; and emancipation, 22, 25, 46; and enslavers, 94; and families, 17–18, 62, 66; and freedom, 3, 8, 10, 31, 33–34, 49, 56, 72, 89–90, 96, 104, 129–32, 141; as fugitives, 111–18, 123–24, 131; and law, 20, 53; and manumission, 23–24, 45, 66, 110, 116, 130; and Missouri Compromise, 137; and networks, 54, 74, 77, 93, 101; and Pennsylvania, 28–29, 48; and Pennsylvania Abolition Society (PAS), 24–25, 35, 38–41, 47, 80, 118; and Philadelphia, 24–26, 41–42,

ACKNOWLEDGMENTS

This book started as a paper in one of Manisha Sinha's graduate seminars in the W. E. B. Du Bois Department of Afro-American Studies at the University of Massachusetts Amherst. There have been many lucky things that have happened to me in my academic life, but none has been more fortuitous than having Manisha as my advisor. This book would not be in your hands, nor would I be the scholar I am today, without her, and I cannot adequately express my gratitude for her support with mere words. She has always believed in me, even when I did not always believe in myself. Thank you for everything.

The Du Bois Department served as a great home for my mind and heart. Britt Rusert and Jim Smethurst taught me how to read and have made me wish more than once that I was a literary scholar. Britt has been a wonderful mentor and, more important, a friend. This project also benefited from the brilliant insights of Elizabeth Stordeur Pryor, who joined my dissertation committee at the last minute and gave me advice that I still hold with me in this project and beyond. I have tried to follow so much of what each of my committee members suggested while working on this manuscript, and I hope it will be apparent to them where their influence lies. Trish Loveland, Bill Strickland, and the rest of the Du Bois Department have also made their mark here. Peter Blackmer, Rosa Clemente, Trent Masiki, and Bob Williams are all I could have asked for in a cohort and, now, lifelong friends. My City College of New York advisors, Anne Kornhauser and Adrienne Petty, encouraged the work that got me to UMass, and I am forever grateful to them for that.

My parents tried to help me do almost everything I could imagine. I have been able to imagine so many things because I knew they would do whatever they could to get me where I wanted to go. Their love, support, and all that they taught me about being in the world and about being good in the world are also at the heart of this project. My dad died from a brain tumor while I was in grad school, and, well, that really sucked. I know he keeps up with me because he sends me wild turkeys and cardinals to prove it, but I still wish he was here. I wish he was going to get a copy of this book, open it up, and read every single word of it. He is not here to do that, and neither are a lot of other people, such as my Meme, my friend Krysten, and all the animals that I loved and have lost in the last ten-plus years while I worked on this book, not that Maddie, Hudson, or Max would have read a book, but the sentiment remains the same. I miss you all every day but especially for the important things such as this. My mom and I, however, still must put up with each other. Not a single word of this book would exist without her, and there is nothing I can say that can reflect the depths of that statement's truth. I love you, Mommy. My cat, Chloe, has spent countless hours keeping me company as I wrote my dissertation and now this book. She is the best cat, and I would be lost without her.

Our family and friends have expanded what my mom and I have been able to do without my dad. I am grateful for you all. I first want to thank those who shared this academic journey with me: Crystal Donkor, Armanthia Duncan, Sean Gordon, Mike Jirik, Johanna Ortner, Neelofer Qadir, Nicole Young, and Karla Zelaya. At some point Crystal and Johanna became my honorary cohort. You have both supported me so fiercely but also so kindly through everything. Johanna is my number one fan and unpaid publicist. I hope someday I will be able to repay her in donuts and *Real Housewives* season passes if not with the astronomical fees she deserves. Neelofer and Haathi have brought me joy every-where but especially beside the sea and taught me new ways to be critical. Time and again (and again) Sean helped me find the words for the things I was trying to say and got a song stuck in my head along the way.

To Charlsie Aigotti, Ashley Bilotta, Cecilia Fieldstone, and Emily Kangas, our friendships have spanned across decades and more laughing and crying than it is possible for even a historian to recall. You have all kept me in the present as I research the past. That is no easy task.

My career has taken me to a lot of places, some good, some bad. However, they have all brought me friendship and moved this project along. The book and

I are all the better for each of these connections. The College of Wooster's History Department brought me lasting friendships and a writing group that has lived on virtually. Beatrice Adams, Lucy Barnhouse, Margaret Ng, Jordan Biro Walters, and Christina Welsch have all moved through this process with me. I cannot thank you enough for all your assistance in making my work better and for entrusting me with your work as well. As a Mellon Postdoctoral Fellow for the Study of Slavery at Georgetown University, I was lucky enough to join a faculty publications group, share a version of Chapter 3 through the History Department's US History Workshop, and ask Adam Rothman a million questions, to which I received a million answers. I am grateful that Adam and others asked me to participate in the incredibly important work that they have undertaken. While at Georgetown I also met Cory Young, whose work and comments helped me immensely with Chapter 1 of this book. Crystal Webster and her work helped me revise that chapter as well.

Karla Vanessa Zelaya kept me alive and shared fond memories of the North in Alabama. Hey babes. While there I was also lucky enough to learn with such students as Morgan Wilbanks and Tori Shaw Clemmons. Morgan has been a wonderful help as an editorial and research assistant on this project. I look forward to seeing all you both will do. I also had the support of colleagues in the University of North Alabama's History Department and beyond. I want to thank Matt Schoenbachler especially. On a practical note, course releases brought my 4/4 load down to 3/3 and helped me to get this work done, and I am grateful to have gotten them. I did not get a pretenure leave to work on this book, so these were a lifesaver. At Washington and Jefferson, I have been lucky to have the friendship of Ketaki Jaywant and Joel Kersting. Thanks also to Victoria List and to Dave Kieran for his mentorship and continued support.

I am also grateful for all the conversations I have had over the years with Benin Ford. As an artist and thinker, he never ceases to amaze me. He was the first person to read this book as a book. Justin Simard, another brilliant friend and coconspirator, read so much of my manuscript more than once. At this point I think he has probably read every word I have ever written. My apologies for that, but I could not ask for a better friend or coauthor. Academics can be just okay sometimes, but I am lucky to know some very best ones and call them my friends. I also want to thank my anonymous readers and the entire team at the University of Pennsylvania Press. Walter Biggins was and is a godsend. This was a long and painful process until I started working with Walter at the University of Pennsylvania Press. Thank you for turning things around for me and my book and for the laughs along the way.

The Kentucky Historical Society Scholarly Research Fellowship, the Virginia Historical Society Andrew W. Mellon Research Fellowship, the Library Company of Philadelphia's Program in African American History, the American Antiquarian Society's Legacy Fellowship, the Gilder Lehrman Institute of American History, and UMass Amherst all provided generous support that shaped the research for this project. I want to extend my thanks to all the librarians, archivists, and staff of these institutions. As I always say, because it is so deeply true, we cannot do what we do without the work that you do. I also worked on revisions for this book during the COVID-19 pandemic, which made travel difficult. I want to thank all the researchers, archivists, librarians, designers, and IT workers who created and maintain the digital humanities projects and archives that supported my work during that time, especially Documenting the American South, Slavery and Anti-Slavery: A Transnational Archive, the Race and Slavery Petitions Project, and various collections of the Library of Congress, including the Slave Narrative Collection. Chapter 2 is based on my article "'Never Be Free Without Trustin' Some Person': Networking and Buying Freedom in the Nineteenth-Century United States," in *Slavery and Abolition* 40, no. 2 (2019). It is republished here with the gracious permission of *Slavery and Abolition* and Taylor and Francis Ltd.

This book, like everything else that is good in life, has been a collective effort. Friends, we made this book, and I love us for it. Thank you.

www.ingramcontent.com/pod-product-compliance
Lightning Source LLC
Chambersburg PA
CBHW030940150426
42812CB00064B/3081/J